Women, Jews, and Muslims
in the Texts of Reconquest Castile

STUDIES IN MEDIEVAL AND EARLY MODERN CIVILIZATION
Marvin B. Becker, General Editor

Women, Jews, and Muslims in the Texts of Reconquest Castile

Louise Mirrer

Ann Arbor

THE UNIVERSITY OF MICHIGAN PRESS

Copyright © by the University of Michigan 1996
All rights reserved
Published in the United States of America by
The University of Michigan Press
Manufactured in the United States of America
⊚ Printed on acid-free paper

1999   1998   1997   1996   4   3   2   1

A CIP catalog record for this book is available from the British Library.

Library of Congress Cataloging-in-Publication Data

Mirrer, Louise.
    Women, Jews, and Muslims in the texts of reconquest Castile /
Louise Mirrer.
        p.   cm. — (Studies in Medieval and early modern civilization)
    Includes bibliographical references and index.
    ISBN 0-472-10723-2 (alk. paper)
    1. Spanish literature—To 1500—History and criticism. 2. Women
in literature. 3. Jews in literature. 4. Muslims in literature.
I. Title. II. Series.
PQ6060.M57   1996
860.9'352042'0902—dc20   96-10301
                                                                   CIP

The University of Michigan Press gratefully acknowledges a grant from the Program
for Cultural Cooperation between Spain's Ministry of Culture and United States
Universities, which support helped to make publication of this book possible.

to David

Acknowledgments

During the various stages of this study, I was fortunate to have received invaluable advice and encouragement from scholars, friends, and family. I owe particular debts of gratitude to Samuel G. Armistead, who provided me with important bibliography on the Muslim princess; Alan Deyermond, who commented on my early work on Leonor López de Córdoba; Lía Schwartz Lerner, who generously shared references throughout the course of this project; and Barbara F. Weissberger, whose open-minded and innovative approaches to literary studies I so respect. I would also like to thank James Grabowska, who kindly reviewed some of my translations, and Sarah Beeman, who saw to so many important, but tedious, details. At the University of Michigan Press, Ellen Bauerle and Christina Milton were instrumental in bringing this project to fruition.

A number of the ideas presented in this book have developed as a result of intellectual and informational exchange during academic lectures and conferences. I especially appreciate the opportunities I have had to discuss my work with colleagues at Dartmouth College, the Graduate Center of the City University of New York, Westfield College–University of London, Fordham University, the University of California–Los Angeles, the University of Minnesota–Twin Cities, and Yeshiva University.

As I worked on this book, I was fortunate to have been able to count on the colleagueship and support of my many friends at Fordham University. I would like to thank in particular Bernadette Bucher, Thelma S. Fenster, Frederick J. Harris, Anne G. Hoffman, Fawzia Mustafa, Peter Schneider, and Eva Marie Stadler. As the book neared production, I was equally fortunate to have acquired a new set of colleagues and friends at the University of Minnesota–Twin Cities. I am deeply appreciative of the goodwill and generosity of Fernando Arenas, Barbara Hanawalt, René Jara, Amy Kaminsky, Carol Klee, Francisco Ocampo, Joanna O'Connell, Carla Rahn Phillips, William Phillips, Luis Ramos-García, Antonio

Ramos-Gascón, Nicholas Spadaccini, Constance Sullivan, Hernán Vidal, and Anthony Zahareas.

David Halle, my sharpest critic, has been a source of intellectual and practical direction throughout. For his unfailing support and encouragement, I am eternally grateful. I am grateful, too, to my parents, Mildred and Gerald Mirrer, who have helped me in so many ways, and to my children, Philip, Carla, and Malcolm, who have provided me with the joy that makes everything worthwhile.

Garland Press, the Hispanic Seminary for Medieval Studies, the University of Minnesota Press, *Shofar,* and *Mester* have allowed me to use in this book materials from published articles and essays. Permissions for reprints of maps and figures were obtained from St. Martin's Press (map 1), Orion Publishing Group (map 2), and the Patrimonio Nacional de España (figs. 1–4).

The completion of this study was facilitated by grants from the American Council of Learned Societies, the National Endowment for the Humanities, and the Fordham University Office of Research. For this support, I am truly thankful.

A Note on the Texts

In citing long passages, or texts in their entirety, I have used, when available and reliable, modern collections and editions. In this way I have attempted to facilitate for nonspecialists further study of the works. In cases of citations from other sources, I have on occasion lightly retouched spelling and punctuation, again to make the texts more accessible to nonspecialists. In translating texts, I have tried to stay as close to the Spanish version as possible. Unless otherwise noted, all translations in this book are my own.

Contents

Introduction

Medieval Castile's most tragic legend tells of havoc wrought by a powerful woman. The story, known as the *Siete Infantes de Lara* (Seven royal princes of Lara),[1] describes a sexually attractive but vengeful Christian noblewoman—Doña Lambra—who believes herself to have been insulted by rival kin. Using threats, screams, and tears, she incites her husband to a series of treacherous acts that result in the deaths of nearly all of the rival family's men.

Among the many bloody scenes occasioned by Doña Lambra's demand for vengeance, one stands out for the depth of its pathos: a rival kinsman, betrayed by Doña Lambra's husband and imprisoned by an enemy Muslim king,[2] is asked by the king to identify the severed heads of some Christians—also betrayed by Lambra's husband and slain by Muslims in battle. In a moment of horror, the Christian captive recognizes the dismembered visages of his own sons, the seven *infantes* of Lara.

The story of vengeance and murder set in motion by the powerful Doña Lambra does not end here. To console the Christian in his tragedy, the Muslim king sends him a gift. It is a Muslim princess, the king's own sister.[3] This virginal woman, ordered by her brother to comfort the bereaved captive, later bears him a new son—a Christian who slays Doña Lambra's husband, thereby avenging the deaths of his seven half brothers.

In the *Siete Infantes*' depiction of Doña Lambra is one stock image of woman from the medieval Castilian literary corpus—the sexually attractive matron of the Christian upper classes whose powerful language and

---

1. See, for a detailed discussion of the various fragments, Menéndez Pidal 1971.
2. Ruy Velázquez had sent the nobleman to the Muslim king with a letter, written in Arabic, ordering the Christian's murder. But the Muslim took pity on the betrayed man and imprisoned, rather than murdered, him.
3. In one version of the story, the princess is a Muslim *fija dalgo,* or noblewoman, not the king's sister.

"feminine" wiles instigate men's treason. Imaginarily liberated from the authority of her husband, this woman's access to the discourses of power leads to tragedy and ruin for the men who fail to silence her. A sobering example of the consequences of women's power,[4] her image occurs repeatedly in texts produced within both the oral and the written traditions of reconquest Spain—a period spanning roughly the ninth through the fifteenth centuries. During this period the southward expansion of obscure, northern Christian principalities slowly realized the end of Muslim dominion on the peninsula and the historic contours of the medieval kingdoms of Castile, León, Aragon, Catalonia, and Portugal were established (see map 1).[5]

The *Siete Infantes*' portrayal of the Muslim princess embodies a second stock image of woman from the medieval Castilian literary corpus.[6] Beautiful and pure, but sexually ripe; of regal family and/or demeanor, yet submissive to Christians; this woman (usually Muslim or Jewish) is denied access to the powerful ranges of language—or, indeed, to any language at all. Supposedly liberated from the strict guardianship of the male kin who kept her secluded, she is offered up to Christians for sexual pleasure and procreation of Christians—the metaphorical equivalent of war booty.[7] Possessed by Christian men, she signifies male Muslim and Jewish defeat.

These two images of woman, placed in relief by the legend of the *Siete Infantes,* exemplify a central point about female representation in medieval Castilian literature: depictions of women are bound up in issues of political and military power, religious difference, and language. Indeed, these two images may be a fantasized resolution of Christian-Muslim military conflict, of Christian-Jewish (nonmilitary) hostility, and of the age-old "battle" of the sexes. Imagined, on the one hand, as possessing a range and depth of power never evidenced in legal, historical, or doctrinal works of the period and, on the other hand, as seductive, will-

---

4. The mother of the seven *infantes* of Lara is also a powerful woman whose access to the discourses of power is deadly for men. See Deyermond 1988, 772, for discussion.

5. See, for discussion, Fletcher 1992, 6. The earliest known version of the *Siete Infantes* is found in Alfonso el Sabio's thirteenth-century *Estoria de España,* although the story tells of events that occurred during the tenth century.

6. This type is found, too, in medieval French epic. See also Armistead and Monroe 1984.

7. My analysis here intersects with Alloula's discussion of the portrayal of Muslim women in postcards from colonial Algeria. See Alloula 1986, 122.

ing, consenting, and submissive to Christians, these women are inventions—pseudoidealizations,[8] or ideal constructions, antithetical to actual experience. Lascivious, aristocratic female Muslims, depicted in the literature of a culture where respectable Muslim women were kept veiled from head to ankles and guarded, protected, and distanced from Christian men's view, are clearly fabrications.[9] So, too, are Christian matrons represented as having power over men's life and death. Though a nearly constant state of war in medieval Castile created pockets of authority in which women could act, and though institutional ambivalence about women's status in religion and politics made for a number of strong queens and influential abbesses, examples of women in decision-making positions in medieval Castile are extremely limited. Moreover, even the more powerful wives—such queens as Isabel—publicly supported and insisted on women's subordination to their husbands,[10] and the most powerful woman of them all, Mary, the Holy Mother, was made subordinate—expressly denied, because she was a woman, the power to absolve sinners.[11]

Female images in the medieval literary corpus worked to disqualify women from legitimately holding power in Castile. They demonstrated that women were unfit for leadership, showing either that they were too weak or that they abused authority when they possessed it. Indeed, the texts appealed for women's exclusion from access to the discourses of power, for the good of everyone appeared to depend on it.

At the same time, the very characteristics that the texts deemed undesirable in women—for example, aggression, sexual assertiveness, and powerful language—were exalted in the literature when applied to men. The latter were praised for their military prowess, their sexual dominion, and their capacity to subdue through menacing or threatening language.

Yet Christian Castilian men were far more likely to be credited with aggressive behavior (either military or sexual) than were Muslim or Jewish men. Indeed, the powerful ranges of language were often reserved for Christian Castilian men alone. In texts specifically detailing the events of reconquest (e.g., epic and frontier ballads), the frequency with which

8. I borrow this term from psychoanalysis. For an interesting discussion of the Kleinean concept and its application in analysis, see S. Mitchell 1988, 225.

9. For a fascinating contemporary discussion of this issue, see Alloula 1986, 7–14. See also Daniel 1983, 73; and Bancourt 1982, 2:663.

10. For discussion of Isabel's express support for women's subordination, see Azcona 1964, 473–81; Pita 1986, 312–13.

11. See Alfonso X el Sabio 1872, *Part.* 1, Title 6, Law 26.

"manly" qualities are absent in images of Muslim and Jewish men is striking.[12] Thus issues of masculinity were often mediated by religious distinctions.

Indeed, the commonplace image of the "friendly Moor"—celebrated as *the* paramount symbol of cross-religious sympathy in much modern criticism[13]—appears largely to derive from the praxis of male gender dominance in medieval Castilian culture, not from any true friendship between Muslims and Christians in reconquest Spain. Routinely described as submissive, weak, ineffectual, or defeated; linked to mothers rather than fathers; shown as incapable of making good on threats of rape against Christian women; and, as in the *Siete Infantes*, handing over their sisters as concubines to male Christian enemies; Muslim and Jewish men were effectively excluded from male status and sexual identity. "Feminized" more than "friendly"—a point sometimes reinforced through the symbolic conversion of male Muslims and Jews into women[14] (their cities termed potential "brides" of Christian rulers, their clothing and mannerisms described as womanly, their size reduced through diminutive epithets attached to their names, and so forth)— "other" men were, like women, disqualified from holding power in Castile. Portrayed as defeated, even as they in reality asserted their presence on the battlefield most forcefully (e.g., the Almohad victories and this group's continued strength even after Christian victory at Las Navas de Tolosa in 1212),[15] and as debilitated, even though in reality they continued to strike at Christian targets (e.g., attacks from the Merinids and frontier skirmishes from 1264 to 1480), male Muslims in the texts of the frontier were a metaphor for the dominion of Christianity. Depicted as speakers of powerless language (or as silent), as home-centered, and as engaged in unproductive labor, even though in reality they could be exceptionally eloquent (e.g., the Jew, Ibn Salib, employed by Alfonso VI in the second half of the eleventh century to persuade the *ta'ifa* kings to pay him tribute), publicly significant (e.g., Alfonso VIII's Jewish ambassador, Ibrahim al-Fajjar, who effected a truce with the Muslim caliph in

---

12. Non-Castilian men might also be treated this way, as the epic *Cantar de Mio Cid* demonstrates in its characterization of the *infantes* of Carrión and the count of Barcelona.

13. There is a long bibliography on this subject. For a different view, see Burshatin 1984 and 1985. For a general discussion of "dominant" western Christian discourse on Arabs, see Said 1978, 1–28; Menocal 1987, 1–25.

14. Brandes 1980, develops this notion of "conversion" in the context of modern Andalusia.

15. Duggan (1989, 146) develops this point.

1214), and extraordinarily productive (e.g., the many Judeo-Spanish poets whose works, written in Hebrew, flourished throughout the period), Jewish men's images in the texts formulated their future exclusion from Spain.

In this book I argue that a dominant-"other" struggle, waged on the terrains of gender, religion, and war, is the most appropriate paradigm for discussing literary texts produced during the last centuries of reconquest. During this period, the presence of women, Muslims, and Jews within the dominant male Christian Castilian culture produced a fascinating, characteristic patterning of literary images. Key here is the notion of struggle. Real women and "others" strained against the boundaries that delineated their participation in the dominant culture.

During the first decades of the eleventh century, disintegration of the powerful Muslim Caliphate of Córdoba into small states (*ta'ifas*) made a Christian-dominant Spain seem possible for the first time in some three hundred years.[16] In the centuries that followed, Muslim invaders from North Africa fought with Muslim groups long-resident in Spain, allowing Christians to conquer nearly all but a narrow band of Muslim territory. But the danger to Christians of a Muslim comeback from North Africa lasted well into the fourteenth century.[17] While Muslim prisoners of war worked on the Cathedral of Santiago de Compostela, Christian ones worked on the Kutubiyya Mosque in Marrakesh.[18] Even after the battle of Las Navas de Tolosa (1212), when the combined forces of León, Castile, Aragon, and Catalonia, along with crusaders from France and Italy, defeated the Almohads,[19] internal conflicts between Christian rulers and their involvement in the Hundred Years' War helped to prevent the end of Muslim dominion in the kingdom of Granada until the last decade of the fifteenth century.[20]

---

16. Strong Muslim rulers, such as Al-Mansur (978–1002), had managed to prevail against Christians in lands as far north as Barcelona and Santiago de Compostela, but the end of unified Muslim rule that followed the death of Al-Mansur's son in 1008 allowed Christians to advance from the Duero to the Tagus and, in 1085, to capture Toledo. See Mackay 1977, 15.

17. See Fletcher 1992, 144.

18. See Fletcher 1992, 136.

19. The fundamentalist Almohads had come from North Africa in the late twelfth century.

20. In 1264, for example, more than half a century after the "definitive" Muslim defeat at Las Navas de Tolosa, the Mudejars of Andalusia and Murcia rebelled against the Christians. At the same time, the armies of Granada, in an offensive against the Christians,

Cultural, intellectual, and economic developments between Christians and Jews reflect a related dynamic, although the military dimension was not a factor in any challenge Jews might present to Christian dominion.[21] While as a religious group Jews were clearly despised and firmly excluded from church and political offices in Christian-dominated Castile, avenues for cultural exchange were opened up in the marketplace because Christians wanted to isolate Jews (and also Muslims) religiously but not economically.[22] Indeed, Jews' economic and intellectual strengths often made them powerful players in the newly dominant Christian states. The best-known example of Jewish participation in the dominant culture is of course the Toledan court of the thirteenth-century Castilian king Alfonso X. Here Jews' interactions with Muslims and Christians were critical to the transmission of scientific learning and culture. Jewish collaboration in the translation of scientific treatises from Arabic to Spanish may even have affected the development of the Spanish language.[23]

There are also examples of Jews who held important positions in the medieval Castilian court, including Samuel Halevi, treasurer to King Pedro I of Castile. Halevi built a synagogue in Toledo in 1357 (now known as El Tránsito) and dedicated its chapel to the Christian king.[24] Even as late as the fifteenth century, high-ranking Jewish officials, such as the Jewish scholar and financier Isaac Abravanel and the *rab de la corte* (court rabbi) Abraham Seneor, were able to occupy positions in the Castilian court.[25]

As regards gender, medieval Castilian women's subordination is well known. Those women who were in decision-making positions were closely scrutinized and subject to intense criticism and control (unlike in the literary depictions) from male politicians and writers. Cases in point are the scathing criticisms writers of the day directed toward Urraca, queen of León-Castile (1109–26), and Catalina de Lancaster, queen of

---

almost succeeded in recovering the kingdom of Murcia. In 1275, the Merinid sultan, Abu Yusef Ya 'qub, crossed over with his army into Spain, securing control of the straits by occupying Algeciras. In 1333, armies from Granada and Morocco retook Gibraltar, while the Merinid sultan, Abu 'l Hassan, began preparations for invading Castile. In 1340, the Christians, attempting to prevent Muslim occupation of the straits, were defeated. For a broad discussion of the continued Muslim threat, see MacKay 1977, 65.

21. See Fletcher 1992; Glick 1992a and 1992b.
22. This point is made by Glick (1992a, 5).
23. See Roth 1990.
24. See Gampel 1992, 26.
25. See Gampel 1992, 31.

Castile (1390–1406).[26] Still, at the highest levels of society, women were not simply passive subordinates. Noblewomen could, for example, play a role in determining men's opportunities for social mobility within the rigid medieval hierarchy. Besides figuring crucially in men's matrimonial strategies, landowning women could affect the social and economic status of their offspring, leaving their patrimony, in the form of *mayorazgo* (perpetual trusts), to second-born sons. This meant that second-born sons, often denied the high social and economic status of older siblings (they commonly went into the military or the church), might, through their mothers, also become wealthy landowners.

As queens, and as concubines of kings, noblewomen also wielded some authority in medieval Castile. Chroniclers of the period took note of this, paying special attention, in their works, to women like Leonor de Guzmán, Alfonso X's mistress and the mother of the bastard Trastamaran dynasty, and María de Molina, the wife of Sancho IV (1284–95) and twice queen regent (during the minorities of her son, Fernando IV, and her grandson, Alfonso XI). Indeed, Castilian history from the eleventh through the fifteenth centuries provides a number of instances of female rulers and of women whose family alliances afforded them positions of at least limited power, including Urraca, María, Leonor, and Catalina; Berenguela, daughter of Alfonso VII of Castile (1158–1214); Constanza, daughter of Pedro I of Castile (1350–69); Leonor, wife of Juan I of Castile (1379–90) and daughter of Pedro IV of Aragon; Juana la Beltraneja, daughter of Enrique IV of Castile (1454–74); and Isabel the Catholic (1474–1504).

In addition to occupying positions of some power in government, medieval Castilian women could inherit and transmit property, manage households, and play key roles in charitable and religious institutions. They also participated, to a degree, in reconquest military ideals, for they were important to the settlement and reproduction of Christians in the newly conquered frontier towns.[27]

The spaces within which Muslims, Jews, and women could assert themselves within the dominant culture show that subordinate groups in medieval Castile were neither passive nor monolithic. The dominant group, moreover, was itself marked by a diversity of belief. Christian Castilians split, for example, over such crucial questions as the type of

---

26. Both these women were accused of ambition and high-handedness. For an interesting study of Urraca, see Reilly 1982.

27. For discussion, see Dillard 1984, 12.

power the monarchy should exercise and the degree of latitude that should be allowed to religious minorities. These kinds of splits permeated the dominant culture from the eleventh through the fifteenth centuries—just before Christian hegemony was achieved with the obliteration of Jews and Muslims. The competing theories proposed by two schools of Castilian intellectuals—the "caballeros" (those who believed in the compatibility of arms and letters) and the "letrados" (those who believed that letters were the domain of those fluent in Latin and should remain separate from arms)—are illustrative.

The "caballeros," as Nader points out (1979, 25), saw the state somewhat pluralistically as

> made up of mutually dependent and yet precariously balanced and competing political groups. If the monarch [was] the ultimate authority in the state, he [was] the first among equals, and his duty [was] to maintain a balance among all parties so that no one group [could] tyrannize over the others.

Subordinate cultures were looked at by the "caballeros" with some degree of empathy. Muslims, for example, though seen as enemies of the Christian faith, were also seen as believers in God and as chivalrous, "willing to die in order to defend their honor and property and liberty."[28] One important "caballero" chronicler, Mosén Diego de Valera, wrote also in support of women, advising King Fernando to accept Isabel's intervention in war councils, for example, since "she was not fighting less with her donations and prayers than he was with his lance."[29]

The "letrados" saw the monarchy, and subordinates, in a different light. As Tate puts it, Castile was for them "a unified realm under a single monarch responsible to God alone, the protector of the common weal, and defender of the faith."[30] Muslims, according to a principal "letrado" theorist, Andrés Bernáldez, were no more than "enemies of God, murderers who kill without piety."[31]

Such views as these, especially since they touched on the fundamental question of how to treat subordinate groups, made the cultural and

---

28. Valera 1927, 86, 119, 141. See also Nader 1979, 29.
29. Valera 1978, 87. See also Nader 1979, 28.
30. Tate 1961. See also Nader 1979, 23.
31. Bernáldez 1962, 22. See also Nader 1979, 27.

actual relations between dominant and subordinate groups markedly unmonolithic. There was room for striking variation in the extent to which subordinate groups could assert themselves in relation to the dominant culture, as well as in relation to each other.

But throughout the period, a push to strictly limit the spaces that subordinate groups could occupy within the dominant culture denied Castile a truly pluralistic character. This push—stepped up in the writings of "letrados" and in the popular anti-Semitic movements of the fourteenth century (see map 2)— shows up at the most intimate levels of social life, for instance, in the rigorous separation of Christians from Muslims and Jews. In 1258, for example, the Cortes of Valladolid prohibited Christian families in medieval Castile from employing Jewish or Muslim women to care for their children and prohibited Christian women from nursing minority children.[32] A Muslim or Jewish man who had sexual relations with a Christian woman was punished severely—either put to death by stoning or publicly whipped—even if the woman was a prostitute. The Ordinance on the Enclosure of the Jews and Moors, promulgated by Catalina de Lancaster at Valladolid in 1412, was designed specifically to restrict Jews' and Muslims' relationships with Christians. Among other things, the ordinance required Jews to wear a distinctive yellow garb and to live in ghettos that were locked at night. Restrictions placed on Muslims similarly took personal appearance and dress into account. Mid-thirteenth-century legislation required Muslim men to cut their hair short and to wear long beards. Muslims, moreover, were not permitted to dress in bright-colored clothing or to have white or gold shoes, nor could they live in a Christian's house or employ Christians.[33]

In the public sphere, Jews' and Muslims' prominence often brought disastrous consequences. Samuel Halevi, Pedro I's treasurer, is a case in point. After many years of service to the king, Halevi was tortured and put to death on suspicion of harboring a store of riches.

A wide range of antifeminist cultural practices, shared by Christians, Muslims, and Jews alike,[34] collaborated with religious and legal doctrine to inhibit women's rights and opportunities. Even women who did man-

---

32. See Dillard 1984, 207.
33. See O'Callaghan 1975, 462.
34. These include such misogynist "games" as courtly love (see Lacarra 1988a) and the taming of the shrew (see the discussion of Juan Manuel's "humourous" tale of a fierce and truculent bride transformed by her aggressive husband into an obedient wife in chap. 3 of this book).

age to wield limited power, such as those mentioned earlier in this introduction, did so on a temporary basis and/or along with male advisors,
husbands, and sons. There were no such modulations as regards Jewish
and Muslim women. These women were kept subordinate both by their
own male kin and by the dominant Christian culture.

With the reign of Fernando and Isabel, who took possession of the
royal government in 1474, the limitation of spaces within which Jews
and Muslims could assert themselves was stepped up even further. The
Catholic monarchs privileged the "letrado" messianic vision of a religiously, geographically, and politically unified Spain and stifled the more
pluralistic "caballero" point of view.

Fernando and Isabel had come to power in a context where their
claims to the throne were much disputed. Former partisans of Isabel,
who had believed that she could be manipulated, were disaffected by her
marriage to Fernando. Supporters of Juana, the daughter of the previous
ruler, Enrique IV, were still a threat. The Catholic monarchs proceeded
to undermine the claims to the throne of Juana's supporters by insisting
that her father had failed to properly discharge his monarchical duties.
Above all, the monarchs' propagandists said, Enrique IV was tolerant of
minorities to the extent that he was even willing to lose the Christian
Castilian identity that ought to be the monarchy's ensign.[35] Propagandists pointed correctly to the fact that Enrique dressed in Eastern clothing and employed Muslims as bodyguards (although as W. Phillips 1978,
87, points out, these guards were all converts to Christianity). Moreover,
they complained that the reconquest had completely stalled under his
leadership. Enrique's sexuality was also questioned in the attempt to justify the Catholic monarchs' rule. Either because of impotence or because
of homosexuality, he was accused of being unable to produce a legal heir
(Juana was said to be the daughter of the king's favorite, Beltrán de la
Cueva). The move to legitimate the Catholic monarchs' political power
was therefore irrevocably linked to attacks on sexuality and on any
degree of religious tolerance and cultural diversity.

As the reconquest drew to a close, the spaces within which women
could assert themselves were also further limited. Medieval Castile's
more powerful women lost many of their prerogatives—for example, the
independent administration of large landholdings, the ability to give

---

35. See Pulgar 1943; Nader 1979, 33.

gifts, the right to inherit, and authority over minor children.[36] With expansion nearly complete, the need for women to repopulate newly conquered Muslim territories sharply decreased. So, too, did women's opportunities in frontier towns.[37] In religious life as well the position of women weakened, and with the waning of the Castilian Middle Ages, a more strident tone of antifeminism prevailed in popular proverbs and ballads.[38] The eleventh through thirteenth centuries could by no means be characterized as an El Dorado for women in Castile, but an increase in antifeminist legislation and behaviors coincided with the various initiatives to further inhibit minorities from the fourteenth century on. The reconquest period ended with the completion of Christian hegemony, involving a closed and orthodox society where Jews and, shortly thereafter, Muslims were forced to choose between baptism and exile, and where Christian women's rights were sharply curtailed.

A book that draws on medieval Castilian literature cannot consider equally representations produced by men and those produced by women, neither in written representations nor, in the case of the medieval oral tradition, songs and compositions. The works of very few Castilian women are known, and those known are, in general, not extensive: one, an autobiography of some nine pages, is the *Memorias* (memoirs) of Leonor López de Córdoba; another consists of three poems attributed to Florencia Pinar in the *cancioneros* (lyric collections) of the period.[39] Teresa de Cartagena, a nun, is an example of a woman who wrote more extensive texts, the *Arboleda de los enfermos* (The grove of the sick) and the *Admiraçion operum dei* (Wonder at the works of God).[40] Surtz's recent book on *Writing Women in Late Medieval and Early Modern*

36. For discussion, see Llorca (1990, 60); Mirrer 1992, 1–17.

37. See Dillard 1984, 220.

38. As Surtz 1995, 17, points out, fifteenth-century Castile was the site of a vigorous anti- and profeminist debate (described in detail by Ornstein 1942), "in which the attackers of women had recourse to nearly every misogynist cliché, while the champions of women sought to defend them with the appropriate arguments." However, the extent to which the debate related to the lives of real women needs further study. See Combet 1971 for discussion of proverbs.

39. A few more poems are attributed to Florencia Pinar in one of the *cancioneros* but not in the others. See Deyermond 1983, 44–45, on this and for discussion and general background on these women writers.

40. For a recent study of Teresa de Cartagena, see Seidenspinner de Nuñez 1993. Translations of the titles of Teresa's works are from Deyermond 1983.

Spain (1995) discusses two other nuns who also wrote during the period, Constanza de Castilla and María de Ajofrín.

In this book, I examine these works by women and indeed argue that they may plausibly be seen as works of female resistence. Reading "contrapuntally"—to borrow a term from Edward Said's work on *Culture and Imperialism* (1993)—I propose that these texts be used to extend our understanding of women's exclusion from medieval Castilian narrative. I discuss, for example, women writers' frequent reliance on linguistic innovation and the discourse of hagiography as ways to enter the official, masculine world of letters and learning. Yet, given the available corpus, the main thrust of this book unavoidably is representation by male authors.

I do not claim here to undertake an exhaustive study of all the female and "feminized" images in medieval Castilian literature. Such well-known representations as the dutiful, noble Christian wife of the epic *Cantar de mio Cid* (Song of My Cid) are not, for example, examined in this book. I do, however, argue that such images as that of Jimena, the Cid's wife in the *Cantar,* also bear traces of the dominant-"other" struggle that so characterized the surrounding society. Jimena, for instance, is explicitly instructed by her husband on what attitudes and beliefs she ought take toward Muslims. She is taught to view war against the infidel as a window of opportunity; to dominate, not to fear, Muslims (e.g., the Cid reassures her that the Muslims' drums, which make her fearful, will soon hang in the church as trophies of Christian victory and dominion); and to strip "other" men of their maleness, viewing them not as men but as objects to be appropriated as her own (e.g., the Muslims are said to be no more than wealth to be taken as dowries for the Cid's daughters).

I have, in my work, been greatly influenced by Foucault's model of power, which involves "a multiple and mobile field of force relations, wherein far-reaching, but never completely stable, effects of domination are produced."[41] But the studies of anthropologists who have worked in

---

41. Foucault 1980, 102. See also Foucault 1983, 220:

In effect, what defines a relationship of power is that it is a mode of action which does not act directly and immediately on others. Instead it acts upon their actions: an action upon an action, on existing actions or on those which may arise in the present or the future. . . . A power relationship can only be articulated on the basis of two elements which are indispensable if it is really to be a power relationship: that "the other" (the one over whom power is exercised) be thoroughly recognized and maintained to the very end as a person who acts; and that, faced with a relationship of power, a whole field of responses, reactions, results, and possible inventions may open up.

the Mediterranean region (e.g., Pitt-Rivers, Denich, Brandes, Gilmore, and J. Schneider) and of linguists who have worked on relations between "women's" language and power (e.g., Lakoff and also O'Barr and Atkins) will figure most prominently in my analyses. From anthropology I have taken the notion of a constant testing of men's strengths and weaknesses through women's sexual behavior. From linguistics, I have derived a methodology that allows me to move away from a conceptualization of gender as an individual attribute and to describe instead complex relationships—sensitive to gender in the context of setting, role, social class, and religion—among protagonists/speakers in a variety of literary texts. My analyses probe two categories conventionally linked to relations of power between men and women in society: *strengtheners* and *weakeners*. Strengtheners, conventionally linked to power, dominance, superiority, and, in general, "men's" language, include threats, imperatives, pejorative expressions/insults, and the future tense of assertion. Weakeners, typically associated with powerlessness, and, traditionally, "women's" language, include polite expressions/flattery, meek/self-effacing utterances, naive utterances, hedges (e.g., subjunctive/conditional expressions and negatives), and utterances of hopelessness. While connections between behavior in speech, on the one hand, and gender and power relations, on the other, of course need to be reviewed with much care,[42] I

---

42. See Brown 1980, 113. There are many recent empirical studies by contemporary linguists that note correspondences between sex and language behavior. Bell (1984), for example, found woman's speech to be more polite and to include more questions. Mulac, Lundell, and Bradac (1986) found evidence of the "Gender-Linked Language Effect"—i.e., females rated higher on sociointellectual status and aesthetic quality, males higher on dynamism. Kriedberg, reported by Berko-Gleason (1975), found that males used the imperative more than females did. Gender-based studies of literary texts have also claimed to find differences in the speech reported for women and men. Cerquiglini (1986), e.g., notes a "formulaic feminine lament" in the elements *mar* (in an evil hour) and *lasse* (alas), which recur throughout Old French texts. Whetnall (1984, 139) says that, in the early manuscript *cancioneros,* "ladies speak their distress with a directness that, as far as one is able to generalize about such a vast quantity of verse, seems to be absent from corresponding poems from the man's point of view." Kramer (1975, 205) finds in fiction a relationship between, for example, "lady-like appearance and behavior . . . and lady-like terms of address—those given and those received."

Indeed, numerous studies show that people draw conclusions about the sex of speakers from the way they speak (see, e.g., Silva-Corvalán 1986). But these "linguistic stereotypes," as Labov calls them (1972b), do not always correspond to the facts. The results of studies by Brotherton and Penman (1977) did not support some of the popular stereotypes about women's speech; Haas (1979) found no feature of spoken American English used exclusively by one sex or the other; and Brouwer (1982) found only a few differences between the language used by women and that used by men in Amsterdam. See also, for further disbelieve that close examination of communicative strategies in literature may offer new possibilities for a wider cultural interrogation of gender roles.

I also draw, in this book, on recent work in feminist theory (e.g., by Irigaray) and in feminist psychoanalysis oriented by object relations, as well as on a number of recent feminist studies of women in literature (e.g., by Bal, Franco, and E. J. Burns). Interpretations of symbolic meaning, however, have to be done carefully and with as much knowledge of history as possible. It would therefore be inadequate to simply apply contemporary critical modes of analysis to the specifics of gender in medieval Castile. My approach has thus been shaped as much by the specifics of gender in the society as by twentieth-century theory.

Though medieval Castile and its literature may be remote in time from the modern world, the Spanish Middle Ages in fact provides a locus for understanding many modern issues. Spanish culture, which, as Paul Julian Smith points out (1992, 219–20), takes cultural difference (between Christian, Jew, and Muslim) as its starting point, offers theory an important example of a "field of enquiry in which cultural identities are quite explicitly founded on originary differences which power seeks in vain to erase."

Indeed, no culture reminds us more of the provisional nature of national, religious, and sexual identity than does that of medieval Spain. Thus, this study explores the gendering of subjects in a society much like many in the twentieth century— composed of people of diverse and often competing cultural backgrounds, a society—much like many in the modern world—in which national identity is bound up in military might, and in which the rhetoric of a "new world order" has given "others" the option of either conversion to the dominant system of beliefs or annihilation.

---

cussion, Bradac 1984, Rakow 1986, F. Johnson 1986, Trieste 1986, and Roman et al. 1994.

I do not here address all aspects of the controversial issue of "men's" versus "women's" language (e.g., biological issues, such as voice pitch).

Part 1
Other Women: Female Muslims and Jews

1

Of Muslim Princesses and Deceived Young Muslim Women

Among the many images of woman found in the literature of medieval Spain and France, one stands out for the privileged treatment it received from singers and writers of the period. It is the image of the young Muslim princess offered up to male Christian protagonists as consolation in times of need, as fulfillment of sexual desire, and, newly converted to Christianity, as a trophy of war and a token of Christian dominion.

The ballad *Pártese el moro Alicante* (The Muslim is leaving Alicante), provides one example of the type.[1] A representative text from the oral-traditional corpus of *romances* (known collectively as *romancero*) so significant within the national literature of Spain (the oral texts were later recorded in *cancioneros* [lyric collections], *pliegos sueltos* [chapbooks], and printed ballad collections), it is also one of a specialized group of texts known as *romances fronterizos* (frontier ballads), which are specifically linked to efforts toward stimulating the completion of reconquest.[2]

The text, which derives from the epic legend of the *Siete Infantes de Lara,* tells first of the pleasure a Muslim king takes in discovering that his warriors have defeated and killed a group of prominent Christians. The king's pleasure then turns to pity when he finds that the dead Christians are the sons of his Christian prisoner, Gonzalo Gustos, a nobleman.

The text depicts a *morica* (young Muslim woman) whom it identifies, simply, as the sister of the Muslim king, Almanzor. The *morica* is described in the text by the phrase *doncella moça y loçana,* which is comprised of three terms that thoroughly, yet succinctly, cover the terrain of

---

1. My source for *Pártese el moro Alicante* is the *Silva de varios romances* (1557). I have also consulted Menéndez y Pelayo's discussion of the text (1914, 11:chap. 33) and Menéndez Pidal's discussions (1953, 1:203–5; 1934).

2. For further discussion of the *romances fronterizos,* see Menéndez Pidal 1953, 1:301–16; 2:6–12.

the image. *Doncella* (the woman who has known no man)[3] makes clear the *morica*'s virginity; *moza* (young woman, serving girl)[4] conveys her youth as well as her submission; and *lozana* (ripe, lusty, fertile)[5] confirms her sexual ripeness. The king offers his sister to his Christian captive as consolation for the deaths of the Christian's seven sons, the *siete infantes de Lara*. Like the *jeunes sarrasines* (young Saracen women) described in many medieval French chansons de geste (epic cycles), the *morica* of *Pártese el moro Alicante* is a gift.[6]

It is, essentially, the *morica*'s sexual ripeness that the king gives away; her "gift" is her virginity and her fertility. This much the text makes clear in its yoking together of the terms *doncella* and *lozana,* for it is the assumptions underlying this particular conjunction that impart to the *morica* her special potential as an object of exchange. Virginity, much prized in a young woman, makes her valuable. It also makes her capable of being given away, for virgins, exclusively the property of their fathers or their brothers,[7] may be freely exchanged, unlike other women.[8] This explains why the *morica* is unnamed in the text, existing solely as Almanzor's sister. On the literary level, the powerlessness of her situation is reflected by her namelessness.[9] It also explains why the verbal expression of the *morica*'s willingness to "serve" Gonzalo Gustos is accomplished in a speech act performed not by the *morica* herself but by the king instead. Indeed, the curious pronouncement that Almanzor

mandó a una morica
lo sirviesse *muy de gana*

(*Silva* 11 verso, emphasis mine)[10]

---

3. See *Diccionario de Autoridades* 1969, 3–4:336.

4. See Corominas and Pascual, 1980, 4:172.

5. See *Diccionario de Autoridades* 1969, 3–4:433.

6. See, for discussion of this topic, Bancourt 1982, de Combarieu 1979, Knudson 1969, and Daniel 1983.

7. In the absence of fathers, brothers generally functioned as guardians of virginal sisters.

8. Widows, e.g., were legally permitted to choose their own partner should they decide to remarry. They thus could not normally be "given away" by brothers or fathers. See also Mauss 1967, in which the author discusses the exchange of women.

9. See Bal 1988, 23, for discussion of this topic.

10. I have added accent marks throughout but, unless otherwise noted, haved not edited the texts cited.

[commanded that a *morica* serve him (the Christian captive, Gonzalo Gustos) *very willingly*]

can only be explained in relation to the social entitlement of a brother or a father—or a king[11]—over the distribution of unmarried/virginal sisters and daughters.

The king's performance of the *morica*'s will in the speech act that accomplishes her exchange not only demonstrates the young virgin's lack of autonomy but also highlights her exclusion from the public discourse surrounding her "gift." Her absolute silence in the text is in stark contrast to both the lengthy speeches of Gonzalo Gustos and the pronouncements of Almanzor. Yet the virginal *morica* is described in the work as "hungrily curing" Gonzalo Gustos's suffering:

Esta le torna en prisiones
y *con hambre le curava.*

(*Silva* 11 verso, emphasis mine)

[She went to him in his prison cell
and *cured him hungrily.*]

The eroticized portrayal of the *morica,* ready for sexual pleasure with a Christian, appears to suggest that, though the young virgin may be submissive with respect to the public ritual of her exchange, she is not entirely without initiative or capacity when it comes to the private aspect of her "gift." The text describes her as taking power as she dominates Gonzalo Gustos's public display of distress and anger with her own private—and silent—show of passion:

con esta Gonçalo Gustos
vino a perder su saña.

(*Silva* 11 verso)

---

11. While a king may exercise power over all of his subjects, he is not normally entitled to give *married* women away—to do so would clearly be considered tyrannical and unjust. His rights vis-à-vis other men's sisters and daughters would also be complicated by notions of justice and good government. Thus the king's expressed familial relationship with the virginal *morica* appears to legitimate his authority over her exchange in this *romance.* Perhaps this is why the *romance,* as well as the *Crónica de 1344* version, differs from the account in the *Estoria de España* (History of Spain), where the *morica* is identified as a *fija dalgo* (noblewoman). See Deyermond 1988, 769–70. I have used Menéndez Pidal's *Leyenda* (1934) as a source for the *Crónica de 1344* and *Estoria de España* texts of the *Siete Infantes.*

[with her (the *morica*) Gonzalo Gustos
came to lose his ire.]

The *morica*'s description as *lozana* (fertile) suggests another feature of
the Muslim princess: her ability to bear children—a condition that would
appear untested in a virgin, but that is, nevertheless, a key aspect of the
young woman's "gift." After all, the *morica* will bear Gonzalo Gustos
the son who will avenge the deaths of the *siete infantes:*

que della le nasció un hijo
que alos hermanos vengará.

(Silva 11 verso)

[and from her was born to him a son
who will avenge the brothers (the *siete infantes*).]

The peculiar conjunction of virginity and fecundity that characterizes
the "gift" of the *morica* in *Pártese el moro Alicante* is in fact familiar
from other literary representations of women. While it is classically virginal women who are given away in literature (and, indeed, in life),[12] fertility is clearly in these texts an integral, albeit paradoxical, part of the
woman's "gift." Mieke Bal has written on this subject in relation to the
reproduction of the "sons of Benjamin" in the Book of Judges. Bal comments (1988, 70),

> Even in a case like this one, where the issue at stake is primarily repro-
> duction of a tribe threatened with extinction, there can be no question
> of using married women, although they may be more fertile. Nor can
> the *'almah,* the young, recently married but not yet pregnant woman,
> apparently do the job.

Bal cites, in partial explanation of Judge's insistence on women's virginity, Freud's discussion of "the demand that a girl shall not bring to her
marriage with a particular man any memory of sexual relations with
another" (Freud 1973, 193; Bal 1988, 52). In Judges,

---

12. Note the traditional marriage ceremony, in which the bride, given away by her
father, wears white, a symbol of virginity.

[b]oth the rival males as well as the memory of them has to be "utterly destroyed." So great is, in this male (*zachar*) view, the importance of the history of the people, that the marriageable women have to be "pure" of memory, perpetuating only the sons of Benjamin (Bal 1988, 70).

In *Pártese el moro Alicante,* there is, as in Judges, a pressing need for a woman who is "pure" of memory to perpetuate a nearly extinct family different from her own. Like many Castilian ballads of the reconquest period, the text draws on Christian-Muslim hostilities. Describing the imprisonment of a Christian and the delight of a Muslim king on discovering that his warriors have slain prominent Christians—

aunque perdió muchos moros
piensa en esto bien ganar

(Silva 10 recto)

[even though he lost many Moors (in the battle)
he believes that in this (the slaying of the *siete infantes*) he wins
    much]

—it plays out a Christian hegemonic ideal: to wipe out even the memory of Muslim presence in Spain. Presupposing that the son born of the *morica* and Gonzalo Gustos will perpetuate the Christian family of his father and half brothers, it assumes that the boy will identify with Gonzalo Gustos and the *siete infantes* and not with his Muslim mother and uncle (the information that the *morica*'s son, Mudarra, is a Christian is in fact expressly given in other versions of the story[13]). The future of the *morica*'s son lies assuredly with Christians and Christianity because the *morica* herself carries no trace of a Muslim man. Her virginity guarantees her son's projection as a Christian in a Christian world.

Indeed, the text's representation of the *morica* as a young virgin given by a Muslim king to his Christian captive for sexual pleasure and procreation of Christians figures into the entire dynamic of Christian-Muslim hostilities of the reconquest period. What may at first glance appear to be a gesture of cross-religious sympathy—the Muslim king generously

---

13. The *Crónica de 1344* (Menéndez Pidal 1934, 286) reads, "llamaron Mudarra Gonçales, que fue después muy buen christiano e a servicio de Dios" [they called him Mudarra Gonçales, who was later a good Christian who performed in the service of God].

makes a present of his own sister as consolation to a grieving Christian—on closer inspection demonstrates Christians' desire for the total possession of Spain. Again, the *morica*'s virginity comes into play. As Freud goes on to declare in his discussion of "the demand that a girl shall not bring to her marriage . . . any memory of sexual relations with another,"

> [it] is, indeed, nothing other than the logical continuation of the right to exclusive possession of a woman. (Freud 1973, 193; Bal 1988, 52)

The *morica*, a stand-in for Muslim Spain, is to be possessed exclusively by Christians.[14] Thus the representation of the *morica*, whose eroticized portrayal in the text makes her easily accessible—indeed welcoming—to Christians, touches on another detail of Christian-Muslim hostility. This is the presumed "right" of Christians to Muslim Spain, played out in the stereotype of the Muslim woman who invites, legitimates, and satisfies Christian desire.

And yet the text recognizes, in its depiction of the *morica* as an object of exchange between a Muslim king and a Christian captive, some obstacles to Christians' exercise of this right. Muslims were not simply passive subordinates, unable to assert themselves within the dominant culture. Up until the close of the reconquest, they continued to oppose Christian hegemony, winning battles, if not the war, against the Christians. Thus the text posits the giving away of the king's sister—in a culture where respectable women were (and still are) kept secluded by men—as part of an imaginary strategy to overcome male Muslim resistance, enabling Christians to fulfill their desire and to take possession.

Indeed, the text not only dissolves male Muslim resistance but also takes revenge on those who opposed Christian dominion, making the women of even the highest rung of Muslim aristocracy accessible to Christians. This is made clear in the fact that the king is portrayed as a collaborator in his own sister's debauchment; he hands her over as a concubine to a Christian. The image of the *morica* hungrily "curing" Gonzalo Gustos only confirms this imaginary Christian fiat.[15]

It is interesting to note that, while the encounters between Christians

---

14. In the *Crónica de 1344* version the equivalence is even clearer, as the Muslim woman must be taken by force.

15. See Daniel 1983, 73, for discussion of this topic. Only in the case of female slaves did Muslim men give women away as gifts—never in the case of upper-class women. See also Bancourt 1982, 2:663.

described in the *Siete Infantes* reflect actual historical events, the "gift" of the *morica* and the birth of her son, Mudarra, are inventions.[16] The concubinage of the *morica* had to be dreamed up to justify the push toward hegemony, entailing Christian right to Muslim Spain: Male Muslims' failure to properly protect what was theirs—whether young women's virtue or their own territories—legitimized Christian possession, and the young Muslim virgin's exercise of her childbearing capacities on behalf of a Christian man who was not her spouse (unlike that same exercise by the Christian *wife* of Gonzalo Gustos, who bore the *siete infantes*)[17] vindicated Christian hegemonic ideals by demonstrating that Muslims themselves reject Muslim values.

The *morica*'s depiction as an object of Christian desire—an object that must be possessed—is a theme in fact echoed in many Castilian ballads that detail the events of reconquest. In these texts, such spectacular Muslim architectural structures as the Alhambra and the *mezquita* (mosque) and such wondrous cities as Granada—the "bride" King Juan II hopes for in the famous ballad of *Abenámar*—are all subject to Christian appropriation. This theme—found, too, in the medieval French chansons de geste,[18] where *jeunes sarrasines* converts are possessed by Christians and reproduce Christians—similarly reinforces the notion of Muslim women rejecting Muslim dominion.

The story of the *morica* in the ballad is related to, but not identical to, that recorded in the epic version of the tale—now lost, but reconstructed on the basis of prosified versions of the text written into the thirteenth-century *Primera Crónica General* (First General Chronicle) and the *Crónica de 1344* (Chronicle of 1344).[19] In the *Crónica de 1344*, the sense that the *morica* is a harbinger of Christian orthodoxy—of a society into which only Christians and a Christian God figure—is made even clearer than in the ballad. The *Crónica*, for example, reports the Muslim princess's pregnancy as specifically receiving God's blessing, despite its extramarital, non-Church-sanctioned origins:

e así tovo Dios por bien que de aquel
ayuntamiento fincase ella preñada de un fijo.

                                              (*Crónica de 1344*, 286)

---

16. See, e.g., Menéndez y Pelayo 1914; Deyermond 1988, 769–74.
17. For discussion of the Christian wife, Doña Sancha, see Deyermond 1988.
18. See Augier 1975 for discussion of this topic.
19. See Menéndez Pidal 1934.

[and thus God considered it good that
from that union she be impregnated with a son.]

God's pleasure, the text suggests, can only be at the prospect of the *morica*'s *Christian* offspring.

Two further details in the *Crónica de 1344* also distinguish this text from the ballad. These details, too, offer evidence that Muslims were not simply passive subordinates within the dominant culture, that Muslims presented obstacles to Christian hegemony. The first is the Muslim princess's characterization as a less-than-willing concubine to the Christian. In the *Crónica*, the *morica*, far from silently consenting and submitting to her being given to a Christian, loudly and articulately protests against it. To her brother's command that she console Gonzalo Gustos she responds,

> así yoguiesen agora todos los christianos de España.
> > (*Crónica de 1344*, 285)

[thus might now lie all the Christian men of Spain.]

She has to be threatened with beheading by her brother before she agrees to go to Gonzalo Gustos:

> si non set ende çierta que non faredes vuestra pro,
> . . . mandarvos he cortar la cabeça.
> > (*Crónica de 1344*, 285)

[if you indeed will not do it of your own accord,
. . . I will order your head to be cut off.]

The *morica* also has to be taken forcibly (raped) by the Christian:

> e lançó por ella mano e yogó con ella.
> > (*Crónica de 1344*, 286)

[and he seized her and lay with her.]

The *Crónica*'s *morica* is depicted, too, as an able storyteller. The chronicler specifically notes that, though clever and convincing, her stories are lies (he remarks, for example, that the story she tells Gonzalo Gustos about a previous marriage is untrue (*Crónica de 1344*, 286). Thus, in both her depiction as unwilling to collaborate with Christians (as did her brother, the Muslim king) and her portrayal as capable of deceit, the *Crónica*'s *morica* is, like strong Muslim men, an obstacle to Christian dominion. Yet, because of the means through which the *morica*'s resistance is ultimately dissolved (i.e., rape), she symbolizes not only Christian overcoming of such Muslim obstacles but also the right of Christians to use force in this endeavor. Hence, unlike the ballad, in which the birth of the *morica*'s son is imaginarily sanitized as the offspring of a willing Muslim "gift," the *Crónica* makes it clear, through its description of the woman's rape, that Mudarra is the product of a hideous, but presumably necessary and legitimate, Christian violence against the infidel.

The *Romance de la morilla burlada* [Ballad of the deceived young Muslim woman] is, like *Pártese el moro Alicante*, a *romance* set on the frontier. Although, as Menéndez Pidal notes (1953, 2:11), the ballad does not directly concern the war against the Muslims, the hostilities between Muslims and Christians are evident in the text's description of the willingness of a Muslim woman to harbor a Muslim murderer from Christian justice.[20] The ballad, printed in several *cancionero* collections (including the *Cancionero de Londres* [London collection of songs and poems], compiled between 1471 and 1500; and the *Cancionero general* [General lyric collection] of 1511) as well as in *pliegos sueltos*, also

---

20. Critics have understood the *Morilla burlada* to be a text that sympathizes with the Muslim point of view. This is primarily because, on the one hand, the ballad makes use of Arabic linguistic constructions and words in the course of its narrative and, on the other, the speaking persona of the work is a Muslim woman who has been raped by a Christian. These critics either posit an Arabic source for the text (an explanation of the work's recourse to the syntax and lexis of a foreign language) or view the work as an example of Christian compassion in the midst of even the most hostile of circumstances. An alternative view expressed in the critical literature is that the text constitutes a Muslim woman's defense against charges of willingly engaging in sex with a Christian. (Aguirre [1972] takes the work to be a defense, by the Muslim woman, against the charge that she actually invited the Christian to a sexual encounter with her.) But the Christian's depiction as capable of deciphering and mastering the cultural code of the Muslims may more plausibly be explained as an assertion of Christian superiority over the enemy. Seen against the backdrop of frontier warfare, where resourcefulness and mental dexterity were crucial for victory, Arabic syntax and lexis demonstrate Christian prowess in outwitting the infidel (not textual indebtedness to an original Arabic source), and the Christian's deceit indicates the type of weapon necessary for promoting the efforts of the reconquest.

shows how Muslims were able to assert themselves within the dominant Christian culture, presenting obstacles to Christian hegemony up to the close of the reconquest.[21] The text tells of an encounter between a Muslim woman and a Christian man who disguises himself as a Muslim. It reads as follows:

> Yo me era mora Morayma,
> morilla de un bel catar;
> Christiano vino a mi puerta,
> cuytada por me engañar.
> Hablóme en algaravía,
> como aquel que la bien sabe:
> —Ábras me las puertas, mora,
> si Alá te guarde de mal.
> —¿Cómo te abriré, mezquina,
> que no sé quien te serás?
> —Yo soy el moro Maçote,
> hermano de la tu madre,
> que un christiano dexo muerto;
> tras mí venía el alcalde.
> Si no me abres tú, mi vida,
> aquí me verás matar.
> Quando esto oí, cuytada,
> comencéme a levantar;
> vistiérame una almexía,
> no hallando mi brial;
> fuérame para la puerta
> y abríla de par en par.
> 　　(*Cancionero de Romances [Anvers 1550];* Wright 1987, 111)

> [I was called Moorish Moraima,
> young Mooress of a lovely appearance;
> A Christian came to my door,

---

21. See Menéndez Pidal 1953, 2:44–45. Dynastic struggle and conflict between the monarchy and the nobility had diverted attention from the efforts of the reconquest from the mid–thirteenth century to the accession of the Catholic Monarchs, as contending factions drew strength from intermittent alliances with the Muslims of Granada. However, centralizing movements of the later fifteenth century demanded completion of the reconquest.

cuytada,[22] to deceive me.
He spoke to me in Arabic,
as one who knows it well:
—Open your doors to me, Mooress,
if you wish Allah to protect you from evil.
—How can I open it to you, wretched me,
if I don't even know who you are?
—I am the Moor, Mazote,
brother of your mother,
I've just left a Christian dead,
and the deputy is coming after me,
If you don't open up, my life,
right here you will see me killed.
When I heard this, *cuytada,*
I began to get myself up;
I dressed myself in a tunic,
not finding my gown;
I went toward the door
and opened it up wide.]

The text's protagonist, another beautiful, young Muslim woman, actively collaborates in the Muslim cause, spontaneously conspiring to protect a man whom she believes to be a murderer of Christians (only opening her "doors" to him—note the sexual connotation of the plural form in his plea to her—when she becomes convinced that he truly needs asylum from Christian justice). Her portrayal vindicates Christian violence; she not only seeks to prevent Christian dominion but is truly dangerous to Christians. Thus, as in the *Crónica de 1344,* Christian deceit (presumably rape) of a Muslim woman suggests a kind of symbolic revenge. The *morilla*'s body is appropriated, just as Muslim territory and possessions are to be appropriated.

The text's portrayal of a rather unencumbered exchange between the Christian and the young Muslim woman (via doors accessible to outsiders) is a central part of this imaginary strategy, for Muslim insistence on women's seclusion—indeed invisibility—is well known. Realized sartorially in the veil[23] and architecturally in special buildings and domestic

---

22. Following Lemaire (1986), I have not translated the word *cuytada.*
23. The veil was introduced for Muhammad's wives during the prophet's lifetime, but its use had spread down the class structure by the Middle Ages.

areas for women that are guarded by eunuchs,[24] Muslim women's isolation was nearly complete, broken only by the *ajimeces* (windows with pointed arch) that permitted those inside to observe the street and by indirect entryways open only to "respectable" people.[25] But the young Muslim woman of the *Morilla burlada* is not only accessible; she is also an actively desiring and representing subject—the text's speaking persona who guides the audience through the text and describes herself in clearly sexual terms. In this portrayal, another fiction is revealed; in the *Morilla burlada,* the authentic female voice is appropriated (like the *morilla* herself) by a male Christian Castilian—a *juglar* (singer/composer) who introduces his own conception of woman's desire into the ballad. This conception appears to be, as Irigaray has declared in another context (1985, 32), a desire to be "as much as possible like man's eternal object of desire"—more specifically, in the texts of medieval Castile, *Muslim* women's desire to be as much as possible like *Christian* men's object of desire.

Thus, from the start, the *morilla* stresses her Muslim identity—already sexually charged in the medieval context[26]—repeating the lexeme *mor* (*mora, Morayma, morilla*). She calls attention, too, to her beauty, describing herself with the phrase *bel catar.* A third descriptor, *cuytada,* used twice in the work, may also underscore her sexuality. This term, Lemaire suggests, may be linked to women's active, subject position in traditional medieval women's song—that is, the corpus of literature belonging to the medieval European, oral, female-composed tradition of love poetry (e.g., Iberian *cantigas de amigo* [songs in which a young woman sings about her lover]).[27] A derivative of the Latin verb "to cook, to burn, to disturb or perturb,"[28] *cuytada,* Lemaire argues (1986, 729), is

> the key-word in the semantic field of words and expressions related to "love" such as: to die of love, to say love, to sing of love, love that gives no rest, to be in love, to be joyous, anxious.

In the *Morilla burlada,* the Muslim woman's expressed choice of a more revealing garment over a more modest one (i.e., the substitution of

24. In the case of the less well-to-do, closed-off female areas.
25. See Departamento de Arabe e Islam 1983, 186.
26. See Aizenberg 1984.
27. On medieval women's love song as an authentically female tradition, see, e.g., Deyermond 1983, 27–28. On the term *cuytada,* see Lemaire 1986, 729.
28. See Lemaire 1986, 729.

the *almexía* [tunic] for the *brial* [gown]), as well as her act of opening her doors, not just a bit, but wide, provide a similar kind of symbolism—a symbolism that may motivate the term *cuytada* as a sign of the *morilla*'s active and burning, yet anxious, desire for the Christian who rapes her. Indeed, the association of the *morilla*'s discourse, through the descriptor *cuytada*, with sexual initiatives taken by women in medieval women's song—and with the symbolic expression of women's erotic fantasies— may yield an image of the *morilla* as an anxiously desiring and *demanding* (in the Lacanian sense) female,[29] with the well-defined aim of sexual satisfaction.

The presumption of superiority suggested in the text's appropriation of women's desire echoes the presumption of superiority in frontier Christians' appropriation of Muslim buildings and territories. Underlying the social space within which the Muslim woman imaginarily interacts with the Christian are the actual geographical domains that underpinned the military and cultural contest between the two groups in the final years of reconquest. In its overlay of antifeminist with anti-Muslim discourse, the text thus compresses two hegemonic ideals: to defeat the Muslims (the text poetically enunciates Muslim defeat in the rape of a Muslim woman—the *morilla* becomes the metaphorical equivalent of actual geographical possession of land) and to vindicate Christian violence against "others" (the text vindicates Christians' show of force in its portrayal of the victim as a lascivious, *demanding morilla* who formulates her own desire and is imaginarily liberated by the Christian from the strict guardianship of her male Muslim kin).

Those who study contemporary Spanish ballads have begun to stress the association between women, both as protagonists and as receptors, and the *romancero* genre. That the *romancero*, which has been perpetuated largely by women during the modern period and which often deals with topics related to women,[30] might be a female-centered and female-empowering tradition has been suggested by, for example, Anahory-Librowicz (1989, 324), who finds that women's singing of texts descriptive of indecorous female behavior may actually permit them "expresión a su propia fantasía" [expression of their own fantasy]. Similarly,

---

29. I.e., Lacan's *demande*. Lacan links the concept of "demand" with "need" (*besoin*) and "desire" (*désir*). See also Lemaire 1986, 730.

30. See Armistead 1978, catalog-index 1:32, which lists eight categories based on erotic motifs.

Catarella (1990, 332) understands the *romancero novelesco,* where women may be "both the speakers . . . and the spoken-about," as "functioning through and for women."[31] These perspectives suggest that even seemingly antifeminist texts might empower women, opening up new options for them.

While not a great deal is known about the reception of the *romancero* in the Middle Ages, there is much evidence to suggest that the texts were well known and popular among all social groups, including women.[32] Thus the portrayals of young Muslim women in medieval epic and ballad as actively desiring and outspoken—dominated and silenced only through the use of physical force—might be seen, despite their primary function as a locus for the fulfillment of male Christian desire, as capable of decentering monological meanings.[33] Indeed, that such images might open the texts up to contestations of feminine powerlessness from a female audience is further developed in part 3 of this study. For in the case of depictions of medieval Castile's more powerful Christian women, women's important function in literature as reader (and occasionally author) as well as patron and literary theme clearly afforded them a significant role in both interpretation and resistance to subordination.

---

31. See also Barugel 1990, 185–86.

32. Two articles on the *romancero* (Anahory-Librowicz 1989 and Catarella 1990) have discussed the importance of women as receptors for the texts. Both these articles, however, deal with the modern oral tradition. Women's role in the reception of the ancient tradition has yet to be established. For a discussion of ballad reception in the sixteenth century, see Orduña 1989.

33. It is beyond the scope of this chapter to speculate about the difference the dating of different versions of the text might have had on these issues. It is interesting to note, however, that the earlier *Estoria de España* version of the story contained in *Pártese el moro Alicante* suggests mutual love between the Muslim princess and the Christian—"et amarse ell uno al otro" [and each one loved the other] (*Estoria de España,* 220)—whereas the later *romance* and the *Crónica* do not. This variation may be an index of a change in attitude toward pluralism in later reconquest Spain.

2
The Beautiful Jewess: Marisaltos in Alfonso X's *Cantiga* 107

There is in the words 'a beautiful Jewess' a very special sexual signification. . . . This phrase carries an aura of rape and massacre.

—Sartre, *Anti-Semite and Jew*

The type of discourse used in *Pártese el moro Alicante* to render its *morica* speechless and powerless, making her a "gift" to be exchanged between two men, and in the *Morilla burlada* to represent its *morilla* as an actively desiring woman and a vindication of Christian violence is strikingly similar to the discourse used to depict Jewish women in the texts of the late reconquest period. Here another mode and venue for the expression of Christian dominion are encountered, with the repeated image of the beautiful Jewess, like that of the young female Muslim, living up to the assumption of "other" women's sexual availability.

It is, for this reason, not as surprising as some have suggested that the literature yields so many depictions of beautiful Jewesses. The society that accorded Jews a subordinate status, subjugating Jewish religious beliefs and requiring Jewish people to live within boundaries circumscribed by Christians,[1] used this image to reiterate the weakness of Jew-

---

Some of the ideas presented in this chapter have been developed in my article on "The Jew's Body" (Mirrer 1994a). Permission to cite materials from that article has been obtained from the Purdue Research Foundation.

1. See Carpenter 1986, 283. Alfonso dedicates an entire title of the *Siete Partidas* to legislation involving the Jews ("De los judíos" [Concerning the Jews], *Part.* 7, Title 24). He specifies the crucifixion of Christ as both motivation and justification for the subordinate condition of Jews:

E la razon por que la eglesia e los emperadores e los reyes e los otros principes sofrieron a los judios bevir entre los cristianos es esta: por que ellos beviessen como en cativerio pora siempre e fuess remembrança a los omnes que ellos vienen del linaje daquellos que crucificaron a Nuestro Señor Jhesu Christo (*Part.* 7, Title 24, Law 1).

ish men, making public the sexual initiatives taken by their women.
Thus, despite offical abhorence of, and harsh penalties for, interreligious
sexual comingling, medieval Castilian literature offers numerous examples of the beautiful Jewess who even engages in an intimate relationship
with a male Christian.[2] So compelling, in fact, is the link the texts make
between female Jews and sexual imagery that even works that specifically
entail anti-semitic attitudes (e.g., those that defend their characters
against charges of Jewish ancestry [i.e., "impure blood"]) eroticize the
Jewess. *Entre la gente se dice* (Among the people it's said), a *romance* discussed in chapter 5 of this study, claims that the illegitimate son of a
queen and her brother-in-law was placed in the care of "the exceptionally
beautiful" daughter of a "beautiful Jewess":

> A una ama le ha encargado
> hermosa es a maravilla
> Paloma tiene por nombre
> según se dice por la villa
> hija es de un tornadizo
> y de una linda judía.

> [He has placed him in the care of a servant
> she is exceptionally beautiful
> Paloma is her name
> according to what people say
> she is the daughter of a convert
> and a beautiful Jewess.]

[And the reason why the church and the emperors and the kings and other princes suffered Jews to live among Christians is this: so that they should forever live in disgrace
and be a reminder to men that they come from the line of those that crucified our lord
Jesus Christ.]

2. In this regard, see Aizenberg 1984, 189, in which the author cites the *Castigos e documentos* (126–27):

... guardate non quieras pecar ... con judia, que es de aquella generaçion de los que
escupieron a Jesu Cristo, tu sennor, en la faz.

[take care and do not desire to sin ... with a Jewess, for she is of the same lineage as
those who scorned Jesus Christ.]

See also Carpenter 1986 and Bagby 1971.

Two fates usually befall the beautiful (in Spanish, *linda* or *hermosa*)[3] Jewess in the medieval Castilian works. One, as Aizenberg (1984, 189) and others have pointed out, is her happy conversion to Christianity; she is saved from official sanctions against sex with a Christian when she cries out for aid from the Virgin Mary and promises lifelong devotion to the Christian faith. The other is the tragic heroine's death; she is killed when her sexual fantasies with a Christian materialize (e.g., the famous legend of the *pozo amargo* [bitter well], in which the beautiful Jewess Rachel ends her life when her affair with a Christian lover is discovered).

Alfonso X el Sabio, "Alfonso the Learned" (1221–84; king of Castile 1252–84), offers one important and enduring example of the former type in his *Cantigas de Santa María* (Songs of St. Mary), a collection of more than four hundred hymns and miracles of the Virgin Mary written in the Galician-Portuguese language.[4] *Cantiga* 107 chronicles the story of Marisaltos, a beautiful Jewess who is hurled from a cliff by her male coreligionists. While the *cantiga* does not specify Marisaltos's crime, the text's description of her as a "Jewess found in error and caught" [judea achada que foi en err' e fillada] and its use of the word *coytada* (or *cuytada;* discussed in chap. 1 as having possible sexual connotations) to identify her with women in a similar predicament strongly suggest that her punishment results from extramarital relations with a Christian.[5] Prior versions of the story of Marisaltos (in particular, that of the thirteenth-century chronicler, Rodrigo de Cerrato),[6] likely to have been known by the text's audience,[7] make even clearer the sexual nature of her crime, specifying that Marisaltos had been accused of extramarital relations with a Christian man. As Marisaltos falls to the ground, the *cantiga* reports, she calls out to the Virgin for help. Landing safely and unscathed, she rushes to be baptized at the Virgin's church and remains to the end a devoted Christian. The text reads as follows:

---

3. See Aizenberg 1984.

4. There is a long bibliography on the *Cantigas* that goes beyond the scope of this chapter. One much-discussed question concerns Alfonso's authorship of the work—i.e., whether he actually wrote the *cantigas* (or at least some of them) or simply approved them. Another question regards the extent of Alfonso's involvement in the miniatures that accompany the texts.

5. As is discussed later in this chapter, Marisaltos's crime is not specified in Alfonso's version of the story, but it is probably understood on the basis of other versions of the well-known miracle.

6. For Cerrato's description, see Fita 1886, 376.

7. The popularity of the story is well attested by its many versions, from the Middle Ages to the modern period. See, for discussion, Tinnel 1988–89.

Como Santa Maria guardou de morte hũa judea que espenaron en Segovia; [e] porque sse acomendou a ela non morreu nen se firiu.

Quen crever na Virgen Santa,
ena coita valer-ll-á

Dest' un miragr', en verdade,
fez en Segovi' a cidade
a Madre de piedade,
qual este cantar dirá
Quen crever na Virgen Santa . . .

Dũa judea achada
que foi en err' e fillada
e a esfalfar levada
dũa pena qu' i está
Quen crever na Virgen Santa . . .

Muit' alta e muit' esquiva.
E ela diss': "Ai, cativa,
como pode ficar viva
quen daqui a caer á,
Quen crever na Virgen Santa . . .

Senon se Deus xe querria!
Mas tu, Reỹa Maria,
u crischãyde fia,
se tal es com' oy ja
Quen crever na Virgen Santa . . .

Que accorre-las coytadas
que ti son acomendadas,
ontre toda-las culpadas
val a mi, ca mester m' á.
Quen crever na Virgen Santa . . .

E sse ficar viv' e sãa,
logo me fare[i] crischãa
ante que seja mannãa
cras, u al non averá."
Quen crever na Virgen Santa . . .

Os judeus que a levaron
na camisa a leixaron
e logo a espenaron,
dizendo: "Alá yrá!"
Quen crever na Virgen Santa . . .

Mais pois dali foi cauda,
da Virgen foi acorruda;
poren non foi pereçuda,
pero caeu long' alá
Quen crever na Virgen Santa . . .

Jus' a pe dũa figueira,
e ergeu-sse mui ligeira-
ment' e foi-sse sa carreira
dizendo: "Senpre será
Quen crever na Virgen Santa . . .

Bẽeita a Groriosa,
Madre de Deus preciosa,
que me foi tan piadosa;
e quena non servirá?
Quen crever na Virgen Santa . . .

E chegou aa eigreja
daquela que senpre seja
bẽeita, u mui sobeja
gente viu, e diss': "Acá
Quen crever na Virgen Santa . . .

Vĩid' e batiçar-m-edes,
e tal miragr' oyredes
que vos maravillaredes,
e tod' om' assi fará."
Que[n] crever na Virgen Santa . . .

E tan tost' aquela gente
a batiçou mantenente;
e foi sempre ben creente
da que por nos rogará
Quen crever na Virgen Santa . . .

A seu Fillo grorioso
que nos seja piadoso
eno dia temeroso
quando julgar-nos verrá
Quen crever na Virgen Santa . . .[8]

[How Holy Mary saved from death a Jewess that they precipitated in Segovia; because she commended herself to her (Mary), she didn't die nor was she injured.

Whoever believes in the Holy Virgin
can count on her when in anguish

A miracle about this, truly,
was made in the city of Segovia
devoted to the Mother,
as this song will tell
Whoever believes in the Holy Virgin . . .

It related to a Jewess found
in error and caught
and taken to the edge
of a peak that was there
Whoever believes in the Holy Virgin . . .

It was very high and very frightening.
And she said: "Oh, miserable me,
how can anyone stay alive
who falls down from here
 Whoever believes in the Holy Virgin . . .

If God himself doesn't want it?
But you, Queen Mary,
in whom all Christianity believes,
if all is as I have heard already
Whoever believes in the Holy Virgin . . .

That you come to the aid of all those anguished women
who are commended to you,

---

8. The text is from Alfonso X el Sabio 1981, 1:405–7. The translation is my own.

then among all the guilty ones
help me, because I need it.
Whoever believes in the Holy Virgin . . .

And if I remain alive and well,
then I will become a Christian
before morning comes
tomorrow, to be sure."
Whoever believes in the Holy Virgin . . .

The Jewish men who took her
left her in her slip
and then threw her over,
saying: "There she goes!"
Whoever believes in the Holy Virgin . . .

But when she fell from there,
she was helped by the Virgin;
for this reason she did not perish
but fell away from there (the rocks),
Whoever believes in the Holy Virgin . . .

Just at the foot of a fig tree,
and she stood up very easily
and went on her way,
saying: "May she always be
Whoever believes in the Holy Virgin . . .

Blessed the Glorious,
precious Mother of God,
who was so merciful to me;
and who will not serve her?
Whoever believes in the Holy Virgin . . .

And she arrived at the church
of the one who should always be
blessed, where many, many
people saw her, and she said: "Here
Whoever believes in the Holy Virgin . . .

Come and baptize me,
and you will hear a miracle
that will make you marvel,

and every man do thus."
Whoever believes in the Holy Virgin . . .

And so quickly those people
baptized her right away;
and she was always a true believer
in the one who will pray for us
Whoever believes in the Holy Virgin . . .

To her glorious Son
that he be merciful to us
on the fearful day
when he comes to judge us
Whoever believes in the Holy Virgin . . .]

Critics, otherwise divided on the general question of the extent of
Alfonso X's anti-Semitism, agree that the story of Marisaltos presents the
Jewish woman in an unequivocally positive light. Lasry (1987, 301)
notes its "striking non-racist neutrality," and Bagby (1987, 242) comments that, of some thirty of the two hundred seventy-three narrative
cantigas to feature a Jew or Jewess,

> [o]nly *Cantiga* 107, concerning the miracle of Marisaltos, makes no
> negative reference whatsoever; the subject is, in this case, a woman.
> Thus we see that only as a convert to Christianity and as a woman is
> the Jew to be seen in a positive light.

Also, the six miniature panels with prose captions that accompany the
text (see, e.g., fig. 1) have been seen by critics as presenting the Jewess
with none of the caricatured "Jewish" features (e.g., hooked nose) of the
graphic depictions that accompany some of the other *cantigas*. Bagby
writes (1971, 687), "In all six panels of the miniature she is drawn as a
beautiful woman with a kind face." Yet, as Hatton and Mackay note
(1983, 194), Jewish women, unlike Jewish men, were in fact never *physically* distinguished (from Christian women) in the work's miniatures.
It is true that Marisaltos's depiction differs from the transparently
anti-Semitic portrayals of Jews in other *cantigas*—for example, *Cantiga*
25, which rehearses the familiar stereotype of the Jew as greedy; *Cantigas*
3 and 109, which show the Jew in league with the devil; *Cantigas* 4 and
6, which play on the theme of the Jew as a murderer of children; and

Cantiga 108, which proffers Jewish babies born with their heads on backward as examples of the consequences of Jews' failure to accept Christian doctrine (see fig. 2).[9] Yet the text's portrayal of the Jewish woman is in fact embedded in a negative depiction of Jews. For example, the language of *Cantiga* 107 strongly suggests sexual promiscuity (other versions indicate more clearly that she is prone to have sexual relations with Christian men). In addition, male Jews are willing to immodestly display her in front of Christians. This willingness is made clear in the miniature that accompanies the text, which depicts Marisaltos as publicly paraded by her male coreligionists, her voluptuous nude body clearly visible underneath the sheerness of her slip. Indeed, in the panels, the erotic image of the Jewess is offered up to the text's Christian audience.[10] Thus Marisaltos's public display entails also what Alloula has, in another context (1986, 5) called "the practice of the right of (over)sight"—a practice that male Christian Castilians arrogated to themselves.[11] As I will later discuss, male Jews would never have really undressed their women in front of Christians—or, for that matter, in front of Jews either. Thus Marisaltos imaginarily dissolves male Jewish resistance as well. Her stereotypical depiction as a beautiful, sexually attractive Jewess placed on display by male Jews symbolizes, in a variety of ways, male Jewish weakness vis-à-vis the Christian community. Jewish women's sexuality is uncontrolled; worse still—as is made plain in other versions of the story—Jewish women have sexual relations with their Christian adversaries, so male Jews cannot even ensure that the offspring of Jewish women remain part of the Jewish community. Moreover, even in their belated attempt to curtail women's sexuality, Marisaltos's male coreligionists are shown to be ineffectual, for, because she is saved by the Virgin, they fail in their bid to carry out a death sentence for her.

Marisaltos's representation in Alfonso's *Cantigas* evokes, too, the much-studied medieval link between sex, violence, and piety attested to

---

9. Hatton and Mackay (1983, 193) believe that this text presents an ambivalent picture of the Jew and is thus not particularly anti-Semitic. Yet it is difficult for me to conceive of stronger evidence for religious intolerance than the child's deformity, which, more than any other sign (e.g., a yellow badge or distinctive clothing), graphically, publicly, and permanently manifested Jewish difference.

10. Although not much is known about the audience for the text, Keller (1987, 11) theorizes that it might have been displayed along with tapestries, jewels, and other valuable artistic items in the treasuries of cathedrals. Moreover, Alfonso's last will and testament decrees that the *cantigas* be sung on the feast days of the Virgin Mary in the church where his body was interred. See Keller and Kinkade 1984, 9.

11. Alloula (1986) is writing of French colonialism in Algeria.

even today. In the contemporary Pero-Palo festival of Villanueva de Vera (Cáceres), for example, "Pero-Palo" (an effigy of Judas), is carried around on a pole and periodically spun about by young women in a maneuver called the *judiada* (Jews' own deed)—before being blown to bits by a firing squad.[12] The image of the purified, Christian Marisaltos who renders ineffectual Jewish men's punishment similarly entails the mocking of male Jews by young women. Indeed, Marisaltos's story, like the Pero-Palo ritual, uses young women to underscore male Jews' impotence in the face of the dominant religion, imaginarily expunging them. In the text, Jewish men are silenced; in the miniature, they disappear from view. Thus the Jewess's portrayal is a sign not so much of the gentle proddings toward conversion carried out by Christians concerned about the state of Jewish souls[13] but of the extreme religious intolerance that initially led the text to strip Jewish men of their control over Jewish women and their power to carry out their own justice, imaginarily fulfilling a dream of Christian orthodoxy some two and a half centuries before it actually became a reality.

Marisaltos's well-defined function in the text specifically relates to the alien and subordinate position of both Jews and women in medieval Castile. Her portrayal condenses anti-Semitic with antifeminist attitudes, for she is presented as the object of a fury that is sexually, as well as religiously, charged. A speaking persona who describes herself as in disgrace ("Ai, cativa," she cries) and who associates herself with the term *coytada* (or *cuytada*)—a term, as discussed in chapter 1, that may signal women's active, burning, and anxious sexual desire—she is made an example of by her men for taking sexual initiative with a Christian, sentenced to the horrible—and unusual—punishment of death-by-precipitation (the victim is not only hurled from a cliff but is lacerated with sharp rocks on the way to the ground).[14] A Jewish woman who actively desires sexual satisfaction, she is the subject of an "error" ("foi en *err*' 'e fillada"; emphasis mine) that collapses sex with religion (the lexeme *err* is specifically used, too, in the *Cantigas* to denote Jewish refusal to accept the Christian faith—e.g., in *Cantiga* 108, the Jewish baby born with his head on back to front is a sign "polos judeus tirar de seu *erro*" [for the Jews to pull back from their *error*] (emphasis mine). Finally, Marisaltos is a sexually

12. See T. Mitchell 1988, 97.

13. See Hatton and Mackay 1983.

14. See Cerrato's description in Fita 1886, 374–75. Lasry (1987) points out that this punishment was unusual.

wayward Jewess who becomes, as a Christian, chaste.[15] The beautiful Jewess who converts to Christianity is thus a metaphor for the triumph of Christianity.

Alfonso's *Cantiga* 107 is one of many versions of the Marisaltos story. The miracle is reported also by a thirteenth-century chronicler, Rodrigo de Cerrato (who claims that, along with other witnesses to the miracle, he himself saw the woman) and by others from medieval to modern times.[16] In Cerrato's version—and in other versions[17]—Marisaltos is innocent. Moreover, while the Jewess's punishment is meted out by her coreligionists in *Cantiga* 107, in other versions the wife of her Christian lover accuses her, and Christian judges favoring the dominant religion sentence her. Finally, *Cantiga* 107, unlike other versions of the story, never specifies Marisaltos's crime. For most critics, either the woman's sin was already so well known by Alfonso's audience that its details did not warrant rehearsal, or the punishment described in the text so clearly "gave away" the woman's crime that it did not require any further description. (There is, too, the association of Marisaltos with the term *coytada,* which may identify her as among those women having a well-defined aim of sexual satisfaction.)

Yet one salient detail remains static in Alfonso's report and in other reports, including Cerrato's, that perhaps reveals why Alfonso did not need to specify Marisaltos's crime or wonder about her guilt. This detail is the undressing of the Jewess and her description as clad only in a slip as she drops from the cliff. Cerrato's version reads:

preter camisiam exuentes omnibus vestibus . . . [18]

[removing all her clothing except her slip . . .]

Alfonso's version reads:

na camisa a leixaron.

[(they) left her in her slip.]

Cantiga 107, line 37

---

15. Marisaltos's chastity is assumed at the end of the *cantiga,* which notes that she remained a pious devotee of Christianity. Other versions of the text specify her chastity. See Fita 1886.

16. See Fita 1886 and, more recently, Tinnel 1988–89, the latter of which discusses the Mallorcan tradition.

17. See Fita 1886.

18. This line is from Fita's transcription of the original Latin document. See Fita 1886, 374–75.

Lasry (1987, 304) has claimed that the detail of the slip is an allusion to Mishna, the Jewish oral law transmitted as decrees and regulations, local laws, and penalties, which forbade women to be punished with their clothes off. She quotes,

> When [the accused] was four cubits from the place of "stoning" [i.e., precipitation], they removed his clothes . . . but the Sages say: A man is stoned nude, but a woman is not stoned nude.[19]

But the theory of Mishnaic allusion could not explain the presence of the detail of the slip in Cerrato's version, which makes it clear that Marisaltos was judged and sentenced according to Christian law, by Christians. More importantly, since Mishna specifically stipulates that the female victim of stoning must remain dressed—not surprisingly, in the context of traditional male Jewish insistence on women's modesty— it could not explain the Alfonsine phrase, "na camisa a *leixaron*" [(they) *left* her in her slip] (emphasis mine), which makes it clear that the woman was, indeed, undressed (at least partially) by her coreligionists. Of course, the miniature accompanying the text leaves no doubt as to whether Marisaltos's modesty was or was not maintained by her men, plainly disclosing Marisaltos's nudity.

It is thus likely that the detail of Marisaltos's clothing derives not from a gesture toward female modesty in Jewish oral law but, on the contrary, from the stereotyped erotic appeal of the Jewess.[20] An irresistible, and hence immutable, element not only in Cerrato's and Alfonso's portrayals but also in those of later transmitters of the legend (though not in that of the fifteenth-century converted Jew Alfonso de Espina, who omits the detail),[21] Marisaltos's immodest appearance is relevant in explaining Alfonso's certainty of Marisaltos's guilt. Relevant, too, is the fact that the beautiful Jewess is universally known to be a loose woman; the term *judía* (Jewess) alone would tend to incriminate her. Viciously sexual in its semantic field, *judía* is virtually a synonym for *harlot,* as Thompson (1987, 18–19) illustrates with a well-known example from a later period that draws on the traditional association between the two terms:

---

19. Lasry cites Danby 1933, 390; Sanhedrin 6:3. She translates Sanhedrin.

20. See Snow 1977, in which the author underscores the relationship between portrayals of minorities in the *cantigas* and stock medieval portraiture. Marisaltos would thus appear in the cast of the beautiful Jewess who excites men's lust.

21. See Fita 1886, 376–77.

Pues tales los hombres son:
cuando no han menester,
somos su vida, su ser,
su alma, su corazón;
    pero pasadas las ascuas,
las tías somos judías,
anda el nombre de las Pascuas.

                    Lope de Vega, *Fuenteovejuna* 1. 3.267–71

[that is how men are:
when they need us
we are their life, their being,
their soul, their heart;
    but once the embers die down
nothing but Jewesses are we,
and the name, "harlot" (literally, feast day)[22] gets around.]

Why Alfonso, unlike Cerrato and others, depicts Marisaltos as the target of Jewish, not Christian, law remains a vexed question, particularly as the penalty for the Jewess's crime—that is, death—is rather exceptional in relation to the authority of rabbinical courts in the Middle Ages.[23] Lasry (1987) reports that only in the case of an informer who threatened the existence of the Jewish community did Jewish courts authorize the taking of a life.[24] Might it be that the Jewish woman who slept with a Christian was—within the context of a dominant culture that confiscated Jews' land; imprisoned Jewish tax-farmers; arrested Jews in their synagogues; and put to death the male Jew who engaged in sexual relations with a Christian woman, while providing no civil penalty for male Christians who had sex with Jewish women[25]—de facto a threat to Jewish existence? There is much to suggest this in Jewish literature from the Middle Ages to the modern period, where the beautiful Jewess who has sexual relations with a non-Jew has long ceased to become an instrument of Jewish survival (in the mold of Queen Esther) and has instead become a symbol of the fragility of the Jewish community. Perhaps Alfonso's version of Marisaltos in fact plays out his recognition that the

---

22. I have used Thompson's translation (1987).
23. See Lasry's personal communication in Tinnell 1988–89.
24. See also Tinnell 1988–89 for Lasry's personal communication on this subject.
25. See Trivison 1988, 121; Carpenter 1986; Aizenberg 1984.

threat from within (symbolized by Marisaltos, who is intimate with a male Christian) could be far more destructive to the Jewish community than the threat from without.[26] And King Alfonso, whose laws, even when drafted for political ends, were frequently couched in religious terms,[27] may in fact have seen a strategic use for the symbolism of the beautiful Jewess in the struggle for Christian dominion in Castile. For *Cantiga* 107 clearly demonstrates that Jews who aided the goal of orthodoxy through voluntary "purification" were immune from Jewish justice and were embraced, rewarded, and given a place of honor in Christian society. In this the text also weakens male Jewish social and political power, even limiting their authority over the Jews themselves.

---

26. Indeed, the history of the Jews in Spain has graphically shown that this was often the case. See, e.g., Selke 1986, in which the author discusses the disastrous impact that information relayed by an insider had on the seventeenth-century Majorcan crypto-Jewish community.

27. See Carpenter 1986, 283.

Part 2
Other Men: Male Muslims and Jews in Ballad and Epic

3

Muslim Men in the Ballad

Do not weep now like a woman for what you could not defend like a man.
—Legendary admonishment of Boabdil, the last Muslim king in Spain,
by his mother as he cast a glance backward on his lost kingdom

The literary texts of medieval Castile are suffused with the praise of men who act aggressively, are sexually assertive, and speak menacing language. Indeed, such traits and attitudes appear to have been considered ideal for men in the society; in popular as well as in learned texts masculinity is proved not through biology but through force, intimidation, and the use of threatening language.[1]

The notion that manliness involves—much more than anatomy—acts of aggression, is in fact at the heart of a well-known story by Juan Manuel (1282–1348), a medieval Castilian Christian writer and statesman. Juan Manuel relays the puzzling advice given to the count of Provence by the Muslim sultan Saladin to "marry [his] daughter to a man," explaining, in the course of the tale, that what Saladin meant by "man" was a male willing, able, and ready to use the sword.[2] In another story, Juan Manuel makes even clearer the concept that manhood must be proved through aggressive behavior. He tells of a Muslim bridegroom who demonstrates his masculinity by "taming" his new bride. This bridegroom commands, threatens, and insults his dog, cat, and horse, then hacks them to pieces for their disobedience, all to show his wife how he reacts when his orders are disobeyed. Indeed, a significant consequence of the bridegroom's violent behavior in this story is the silencing of the

Some of the ideas presented in this chapter have been developed in Mirrer 1994b. Permission to cite materials from that article has been obtained from the University of Minnesota press. On the epigraph opening this chapter, see Buetler 1986, 177.

1. For an interesting discussion of manhood as different from simple anatomical maleness, see Gilmore 1990, chap. 1.

2. See Manuel 1987, 157–67. Here, I have used this 1987 edition, edited and translated by England, to facilitate references for nonspecialists.

bride. Prior to her husband's aggression, this woman had been portrayed as "fierce and truculent" [*fuerte y brava*] (Manuel 1987, 217). By the close of the tale, she wordlessly obeys her husband's every order, including, apparently, the one to sleep with him.[3] The stories told by Juan Manuel, as well as those told by many other medieval Castilian male Christian writers of the thirteenth through fifteenth centuries, drew on Arabic sources and Islamic customs known and admired throughout medieval Spain.[4] Their characterizations reflect masculine ideals shared by Christians and Muslims alike, for Christian writers appropriated Muslim culture to the extent that it affirmed precisely those qualities prized by Christian men like themselves.[5] It is, for this reason, not surprising that Juan Manuel, a Christian, used Muslim men to purvey the masculine ideal of aggression.[6]

Yet in the depictions of Muslim men found in oral-traditional Castilian texts that specifically treat Christian-Muslim military conflict (i.e., the reconquest), this trait is almost entirely absent.[7] The texts do sometimes point to a common store of prized qualities—Christians, for instance, admire the beauty of Muslim architecture.[8] But male-com-

---

3. For an interesting discussion of this story, see Sandoval 1989.

4. Eastern literary traditions were heavily relied on by Christian writers in Spain throughout the medieval period. For discussion, see Menocal 1987.

5. This much is clear from the remarks Juan Manuel, e.g., makes at the end of each of his tales. The stories end with the comment that the author found "good" or "truth" in them and that is why he included them in his book.

6. The sexual aggression of Muslim men is in fact proverbial in Spanish culture, even in the modern period. See Gilmore 1987, 129, where an informant is quoted as saying, "Everyone knows . . . that they [Moors] have sexual organs twice the size of Europeans. They are all satyrs." See also Viera 1985 for a discussion of the medieval Catalonian tradition of the Muslim's inordinate desire for sexual satisfaction.

7. The best-known epic text, the *Cantar de mio Cid*, was composed c. 1207. While not a great deal is known about the reception of it and other texts of the frontier, it is widely theorized that the *Cantar de mio Cid* encouraged men to take active part in the reconquest by emphasizing the possibilities for financial gain in warfare. For an important study of this aspect of the work, see Duggan 1989.

The emphatic distinction of Muslim from Christian men in epics and ballads resonated in late medieval ordinances that legislated special signs of "difference" to be worn by Muslims—e.g., the yellow "capuche" and turquoise "moon." See Díaz-Plaja 1984, 23.

8. The famous *Romance de Abenámar* (Wright 1987, 106; C. Smith 1971, 125) exemplifies this. In *Abenámar*, King Juan II of Castile is reported remarking, in reference to the beautiful buildings of Granada, "¿Qué castillos son aquellos? / ¡Altos son y relucían! [What castles are these? / They are tall and are shining!]. My examples here are from Wright's and C. Smith's editions of Spanish ballads (1987 and 1971, respectively). Because I do not in this chapter cite the texts in full (with the exception of *Junto al vado de Xenil*), I have used editions that facilitate reference for nonspecialists: Wright provides translations of the texts and Smith's notes and comments are in English.

posed, Christian epic texts (e.g., *Cantar de mio Cid*, c. 1207) and frontier ballads (composed in the fourteenth and fifteenth centuries) almost never looked to Muslims or to Islamic culture for examples of culturally exalted masculine practices and attitudes. Indeed, in these texts, Muslim men—like the women in Juan Manuel's stories[9]—have only the most limited access to such behaviors.

Though the Muslims were, at the time of frontier ballad composition, at or near the nadir of their power, they nevertheless could be a formidable enemy, capable of winning battles, if not the war, against the Christians. Indeed, that an independent Muslim state (Granada) continued to exist in Spain until 1492 shows how strenuously Muslims resisted Christian conquest to the end.

Yet, in the critical literature, Muslim men's frequent depiction in the texts as defeated or "docile"[10] witnesses to the strength and military superiority of the Christians has generally been said to reflect friendly, or mutually respectful, relations between Christians and Muslims, even in the midst of heated battle, when many of the texts were composed—a kind of cross-religious sympathy[11] (or even *maurophilie* [maurophilia][12]) as opposed to the cross-sexual antipathy of Juan Manuel's stories. But it is almost always Muslim, not Christian, men who are "friendly" in the texts.[13] In, for example, the ballad of *Pártese el moro Alicante*, discussed in chapter 1 of this study, Muslim men console their Christian captives by offering them their sisters as concubines. In other frontier ballads, Muslim men speak with great courtesy to Christians who seek to divest them of their holdings (in the *Romance de Abenámar* [Ballad of Abenámar], for example, the Muslim Abenámar, is expressly courteous when the Christian King Juan seeks to take the city of Granada from the Muslims [C. Smith 1971, 125–27; Wright 1987, 106–7]). Muslim men address their Christian opponents as "amigo" (e.g., in the ballad *En los campos de Alventosa* [In the fields of Alventosa; C. Smith 1971,

---

9. Aggressive women, in Juan Manuel's stories, are the consequence of men who fail in their duty to dominate.

10. This is Burshatin's term (1984).

11. Wright (1987, 236) calls this cross-religious sympathy "normal" in frontier ballads. There is a long bibliography on the subject that goes beyond the scope of this chapter. Burshatin (1985) offers an excellent evaluation of some of the more salient features of the *maurophilie* argument.

12. See Cirot's influential article (1938).

13. Only rarely are Muslim men portrayed as equally, or more, aggressive than their Christian opponents. E.g., in the ballad of *Alora*, a Muslim outsmarts and kills the Christian *adelantado*, Diego de Ribera (C. Smith 1971, 127; Wright 1987, 107).

147–49]), and they weep sorrowfully when their Christian captors set them free (e.g., in the epic *Cantar de mio Cid*[14]). Even the Cid's famous Muslim "friend," Abengalvón, appears to have been selected as a prototype of Muslim generosity and loyalty toward Christians. Though he is introduced with the epithet *amigo de paz*, the *amigo* in this phrase probably does not have the modern connotation of personal friendship, but rather that of "ally."[15]

Christian men, however, threaten, insult, intimidate, and act violently toward Muslim men freely. In the *Cantar de mio Cid*, they enslave them;[16] in other frontier texts, they starve them (e.g., in *De Antequera partió el moro* [The Moor left Antequera; C. Smith 1971, 118–21; Wright 1987, 101–3]) or rape their women (e.g., in the *Romance de la morilla burlada*, discussed in chapter 1 of this study). Although Muslim kings, such as Almozorre of the historically inspired *Poema de Fernán González* (Poem of Fernán González), may be described as wielding great power over other Muslims, that their power is limited to coreligionists underscores the superiority of Christians whose might and authority extend well beyond their own membership. And these Muslims are always powerless against the Christians, who almost inevitably defeat them.

Why did the epic and frontier ballads so often deny Muslim men the aggressive, or "manly," traits and attitudes that Muslim, as well as Christian, culture so valued? And why, indeed, did the texts rely so heavily on masculine ideals to distinguish Muslim from Christian men? It was, after all, religious, not sexual, difference that fueled the reconquest.[17]

An answer to these questions appears to lie, at least partially, in the nature of reconquest itself. It became clear in the later Middle Ages that the fight against the Muslims involved not only the process of conquering

---

14. In the *Cantar de mio Cid*, the Moors of Alcoçer weep as the Cid leaves the city he has taken by force. These Muslims had been made to serve their Christian captors (lines 851–56). To facilitate references for nonspecialists, I have used C. Smith's edition of the *Cantar de mio Cid* (1972), which has notes in English.

15. See Lacarra 1980, 200.

16. E.g., *Cantar de mio Cid*, lines 617–22 (C. Smith 1972).

17. Indeed, there are traditional Spanish texts that directly address the religious aspect of hostilities in reconquest Spain. The Judeo-Spanish ballad *El idólotra de María* [The idolatry of Mary], for instance, speaks of the superior power of the Jewish faith in its story of a Christian ship captain who prayed to the Virgin Mary for relief from turbulent seas and drowned, while his Jewish sailors prayed to God on High and were saved. See, for examples, Benmayor 1979.

territories on the margins of an expanding society but also the problem of dealing with a conquered enemy. As MacKay notes (1977, 4):

> From the eleventh century onwards the frontier was not simply one of relatively empty territories being occupied and colonised. The lands in question were held and defended by the Muslims, and since not all of them withdrew or were forced to withdraw in the face of Christian advances, the course of the reconquest raised problems of assimilation or rejection of cultural and religious minorities.

Possible solutions to the problem of dealing with the conquered Muslims were, over time, increasingly found in three principal domains: religious orthodoxy, racial and—through the use of metaphors—animal distinctions, and masculine ideals.

Evidence of the first solution—that is, the militant Christian goal of religious orthodoxy in the region—can already be found in thirteenth-century documents, where a stepped-up insistence on the links between military and religious ideals (described, but not generally emphasized, in the works of previous centuries) clearly portends the end of any kind of cultural pluralism.[18] In late medieval chronicle and literary reports of Christian victory, new terms and images appear, including descriptions of ritual religious "cleansings" of towns taken from the Muslims. The *Primera Crónica General,* for example, composed during the reign of Alfonso X, describes the manner in which even the memory of Muslims was obliterated from Córdoba after Christian conquest in 1236:

> On the feast day of the apostle Peter and Paul the city of Córdoba . . . was cleansed of all the filthiness of Muhammad and given up and surrendered to King Ferdinand. King Ferdinand then ordered the cross to be put on top of the chief tower where the name of the false Muhammad was wont to be called upon and praised; and then the Christians began to shout with happiness and joy: "¡*Dios, ayuda*!"[19]

The *Primera Crónica General* and other late medieval documents provide evidence, too, of the second domain—that is, racial distinction. Embellishing and reinforcing the central stereotype of Muslims as

---

18. Barkai 1984, 219–23, discusses this in detail.
19. I have used here MacKay's translation (1977, 60) of the passage from the *Primera Crónica General* (2:733–74).

"false," with a special focus on the dark color of their skin, these texts portrayed Muslims as a fearsome "black" people to be overcome by white Christians wearing white clothes.[20] Muslim women were *moras* (black women),[21] lexically identified with the name *mora*, given by Castilian farmers to black cows (hence, the implication also of Muslims' bestiality).[22]

In late medieval literary works, such as the mid-thirteenth-century *Poema de Fernán González*, as well as in historical texts, such as the *Primera Crónica General*, the use of animal metaphors to distinguish between Muslims and Christians similarly "solved" the problem of the conquered Muslims. In these works, Muslims were "sheep" or "lambs" to be slaughtered by Christians, who fought like lions and wolves. In the *Poema de Fernán González*, for example, the count advises his soldiers, "Et non devemos espantar porque ellos son muchos, ca pueden tres leones que diez mil ovejas, et matarien treinta lobos treinta mil corderos" [And we shouldn't be afraid because there are many of them (Muslims), for three lions can kill ten thousand sheep; and thirty wolves, thirty thousand lambs] (chaps. 639, 672). Indeed, the association of Muslims with sheep acquired a folkloristic quality in the newly proverbial Muslim cowardice; the *Primera Crónica General* notes that Muslim mothers had only to mention the Christian caballero to stop their children from crying:

> Et tomaron del tan grant miedo los moros que non osava uno salir nin otro entrar; et quando algun ninno llorava, dizienle: "cata Melendo," et non osava mas llorar
>
> (Alfonso X 1955, chap. 1057)

> [And the Moors had such great fear of him (the Christian caballero) that one didn't dare to go out nor the other to enter; and when some child cried, they said to him, "Look, Melendo,"[23] and he didn't dare to cry any more.]

---

20. See Barkai 1984, 223, for discussion.

21. The word *moro* derives from the Latin *maurus,* meaning "inhabitant of Mauritania." However, by allusion to the dark-colored skin of Mauritanians, the term was applied also to black horses and to other black animals. Eventually it referred more generally to people of African descent. See Corominas and Pascual 1980, 4:151.

22. See Barkai 1984, 223, for discussion.

23. This name is meant to be typically Muslim.

The reliance of epic and frontier ballads on masculine ideals to distinguish Muslim from Christian men constitutes a third—and, in this literature, dominant—solution to the Muslim "problem." As in other texts of the period, the epic and frontier ballads draw parallels, or connections, between Muslims' personal qualities and reconquest military/religious goals. Repeatedly linking male Muslims to their mothers (as in the ballad of *Reduán* [C. Smith 1971, 116–18]),[24] and portraying them as polite, rather predictably defeated, and incapable of "making good" on threats of rape against Christian women (as in the ballad *Moricos, los mis moricos* [Moors, my little Moors]; [C. Smith 1971, 116]), the texts imaginarily disqualified male Muslims—as did such animal metaphors as "sheep" and "lambs"—from holding or attaining positions of power in Castile.[25]

Proverbial associations—perpetuated in the folklore and speech of Spain and other countries to the present day—frequently bind masculine to military values, military to sexual conquest, and powerlessness to women. Gilmore (1990, 12–14), for example, has discussed the connection between military prowess and "manliness," pointing out that many societies test "manliness" by placing men at risk on the battlefield or in confrontation with their fellows. Pleck (1987, 21) notes that male sex-role identity is frequently seen to be demonstrated when men are militaristic—apparently manifesting the sex-appropriate traits that validate or affirm their biological sex. In the late medieval literature, associations similar to those discussed by Gilmore and Pleck guarantee positions of power to male Christians alone. Epic and frontier ballads that focus specifically on the war between Muslims and Christians repeatedly link "manliness" to the military superiority of the Christians. Manliness is, moreover, proffered as a quality that increases in proportion to the number of Muslims defeated: in the *Cantar de mio Cid,* the Cid's beard flourishes with every successful campaign against the infidel, and Minaya Alvar Fañez speaks "a guisa de varón" [in the fashion of a man], when, laden with booty taken from the Muslims, he approaches King

---

24. King Boabdil of Granada is the most prominent example of the identification of Muslim men with their mothers. Christian men are associated with their fathers (e.g., in *Por aquel postigo viejo* [Through the old city gate; Wright 1987, 45–46] and in the ballads concerning the Cid—e.g., *En Santa Gadea de Burgos* [In Santa Gadea de Burgos; C. Smith 1971, 96–99]).

25. Similar tactics were used elsewhere in the ballad. King Pedro I of Castile, e.g., was also thrust into the "feminine" sphere (said to have been under the influence of his mistress) in an attempt to disqualify him from rule. See my discussion of the *Romance de Doña Blanca* in chap. 5.

Alfonso.[26] In such ballads as *Día era de San Antón* (It was St. Anthony's Day; C. Smith 1971, 129–31), young Christian men "prove" themselves in anti-Muslim raids, and a truly "great" man is one with whom the Muslims fear doing battle, as in the ballad *Dadme nuevas, caballeros* (Give me news, knights; C. Smith 1971, 131–33).

This concept of "real" or "great" men as warriors is also demonstrated in Brandes's study of contemporary Andalusia. Brandes notes that popular jokes frequently link military and sexual conquest. He gives two striking examples—both uttered by male informants: "Spain conquered America not by the sword, but by the prick"; and "America was conquered by Spaniards who were carrying the cross in one hand and the prick in the other" (Brandes 1980, 92).

Likewise, in the epic and frontier ballads, the language of militarism is often couched in a sexual idiom.[27] In the ballad *Día era de San Antón,* for example, defeated Muslim men are presented to Christian warriors' girlfriends as tokens of love. In such texts as the ballad of *Alora* (C. Smith 1971, 127–28), Muslim-controlled cities are cast as women and addressed with flirtatious language or "seduced," and in such texts as the ballad of *Alhama* (Wright 1987, 112–14), Muslim leaders are shamed through Christian appropriation of their daughters.

Brandes's study shows too that the connection between masculinity and militarism is frequently made through the enforced "feminization" of enemies. Brandes speaks of men who prove dominance over rivals by forcing them to adopt a "feminine" role, citing, as one example, the harvest ritual *hacer las facas del rey,* in which male genitals are obscured.[28]

An examination of the language and imagery of the epic and frontier ballads suggests a similar phenomenon. Male Christian poets at times

---

26. C. Smith 1972, line 1350.

27. Gilmore's studies of contemporary southern Spain show a related phenomenon—the language of sex is couched in a military idiom:

A man makes conquests; a woman is prey; she capitulates; battles are won or lost; a rejected suitor is defeated, and so on. Andalusian notions of sexuality, then, are deeply steeped in the mentality and language of forceful assertion, competition, and conflict, of waging campaigns, that is, aggression. (1987, 126)

28. In this ritual, described by Brandes (1980, 154–55), the genitals of one's masculine opponent are obliterated by covering them with mud. Brandes comments (155): "To eliminate a man's genitals symbolically is to emasculate him and thereby to emphasize one's own comparative potency." Throughout his study, Brandes stresses that dominance is proved through the emasculation or feminization of enemies.

perform a kind of symbolic conversion of Muslim men and their holdings into women to demonstrate, as in Brandes's study, supremacy. The texts, for instance, term cities held by Muslim rulers potential "brides" of Christian kings (in *Abenámar,* King Juan II proposes to the city of Granada). The texts also focus on feminine aspects of the clothing worn by Muslim men, such as the finely embroidered caps with veils that cover the men's faces (e.g., in the *Romance de Antequera* [C. Smith 1971, 118–21; Wright 1987, 101–3]);[29] they associate Muslim cities lost in battle with (female) loss of honor (e.g., in *Reduán*);[30] they diminish Muslim men in size;[31] they speak of soon-to-be-taken Muslim strongholds in terms of female marital conditions (e.g., as in *Abenámar,* as brides, matrons, and widows); and they tell of Muslim towns, transformed into women through personification, that powerful Christian men surround and penetrate with artillary fire (e.g., in *Alora* [Wright 1987, 107–8]).

One further explanation for the texts' emphasis on sexual symbolism lies in the works' implication of Christianity in the culturally exalted masculine ideal of aggression. Through its association with brave and usually victorious soldiers—not to mention such fighting clerics as the *Cantar de mio Cid*'s Bishop Jerome and the frontier ballads' Bishop of Jaén—Christianity dramatically surfaces in the texts as the more "muscular," "manly," or potent faith (a familiar enough characterization in works of a more recent vintage).[32] Indeed, in the epic and frontier ballads, Muslim submission appears as a metaphor for the dominion of Christianity, as well as for the mastery of those who fought for its supremacy.

In a frontier ballad dating from the final years of reconquest,[33] a Muslim king of Granada wins at chess against his opponent, the Christian *adelantado* (frontier governor) Pedro Fajardo. The king's prize is sup-

---

29. Indeed, Muslim clothing, rich in color and texture, was at times worn interchangeably by men and women. See, for discussion, Ahmed 1992.

30. In the *Romance de Reduán,* the Muslim king's mother speaks of the "honor" of Granada, a Muslim city about to be lost to the Christians (C. Smith 1971, 116–18; Wright 1987, 100–101).

31. As is discussed later in this chapter, the "rey chico" becomes the "rey chiquito" (Wright 1987, 116–18).

32. Gilmore (1990, 18) discusses the suggestion of the nineteenth-century English publicist Thomas Hughes and his colleagues, who argued also for the "manliness" of Christ and Christianity.

33. This text is from the *Cancionero de Romances 'sin año'* (Ballad collection with no date; c. 1548). I have used the version in C. Smith 1971, 133–34.

posed to be the Christian city of Lorca, but when he claims it, the *adelantado* refuses to give in. Instead, he tells the king to "shut up" [calles, calles] and vows military action against the Muslims should their leader persist in his demand for the city. Surprisingly, the Muslim king makes no complaint against his opponent's failure to honor the terms of the game. Indeed, he reacts with good grace, respectfully assuring the *adelantado* of his intention to drop the matter entirely, and complimenting him on his chivalry:

> Allí hablara el rey moro,
> bien oiréis lo que decía:
> "No juguemos más, Fajardo,
> ni tengamos más porfía,
> que sois tan buen caballero
> que todo el mundo os temía."

> [Thus spoke the Moorish king,
> well will you hear what he was saying:
> "Let's not play anymore, Fajardo,
> nor have any more arguments,
> for you are such a good knight
> that everyone lives in fear of you."]

The conciliatory image of the Muslim projected onto the resolution of this ballad is striking for its placement in a work that suggests, through the metaphor of the game, that Muslims still "play"—and indeed win—in the war with the Christians. The point appears to be that Muslims know their gains will not be tolerated by Christians. Once stepping "out of line," they quickly make amends, reverting to the submissive behavior appropriate to the weak and vulnerable, and employing politeness strategies that aim to disarm real physical threats posed to them. In fact, the text represents the Muslim king as using the very same politeness strategies that women use in cultures where unsubmissive female behavior is not tolerated by men (e.g., where women are beaten for threatening men's reputations).[34] The king, like such women, uses language to convince his addressee of his appreciation for his addressee's strength and of his respect for his addressee's "face"; he takes special care not to offend

---

34. See Brown 1980 for discussion.

the *adelantado*, for he knows he is vulnerable to the Christian's reprisals. The Muslim king's speech also echoes medieval courtesy books that exhort women to speak temperately and in a conciliatory manner, as opposed to the many medieval documents that prescribe an aggressive linguistic behavior for men.[35]

The categories "weakeners" and "strengtheners," applied to the speech of the Muslim king and the Christian *adelantado* in tables 1 and 2, indeed show a predominance of powerless features in the Muslim king's speech. (As discussed in the introduction to this study, strengtheners have typically been associated with powerful—and, traditionally, "men's"—language;[36] while weakeners have typically been associated with powerless—and, traditionally, "women's"—language.[37]) These features underscore the Muslim king's position of powerlessness with respect to the Christian.

To some critics, the powerless speech of the Muslim is proof of the friendly and respectful relations that obtain between the text's protagonists. Wright, for example, comments (1987, 235): "The two sides respect each other, but feel they have to hold on to what is theirs. . . .

TABLE 1.   Strengtheners (powerful language) in *Jugando estaba el Rey Moro*, by Religion of Principal Speaker

	Principal Speaker	
Strengtheners[a]	Rey Moro (Muslim)	Fajardo (Christian)
Threats[b]	—	2
Imperatives[c]	—	2
Pejorative expressions/insults	—	—
Future tense of assertion	—	—
Total	0	4

[a]The subcategories of strengtheners are not mutually exclusive. I have therefore assigned instances to the category in which they most clearly fall and have specified in the notes to each category which instances have been placed in the category.

[b]que aunque me la ganases / no se te daría
que defenderían

[c]calles
calles

35. See Bornstein 1983 for discussion.

36. Strengtheners include threats, imperatives, pejorative expressions/insults, and the future tense of assertion.

37. Weakeners include polite expressions/flattery, meek/self-effacing utterances, naive utterances, hedges (e.g., subjunctive/conditional expressions), negatives, and utterances of hopelessness.

Peaceful relations are maintained." Wright takes the fourth line of the text, which, in indirect speech, notes the Muslim king's "love" for the Christian *adelantado*—"con amor que le tenía" [with the love that he (the Muslim king) had (for the Christian adelantado)]—as further evidence of a great friendship between the pair.

Yet only the Muslim appears respectful and friendly in the work, and only the Muslim attempts to maintain peace. As tables 1 and 2 show, powerful features dominate the speech of the Christian, who uses commands and threats to intimidate his Muslim opponent. Thus, while the Muslim king is depicted as respectful, the Christian *adelantado* is portrayed as aggressive and militant; nowhere does he express a friendly, respectful, or loving attitude toward his adversary.

Far from suggesting relations of friendship and solidarity in the text, the powerless features used by the Muslim king reflect a perceived lack of power vis-à-vis the Christian *adelantado*. His polite language only serves to emphasize his own position of vulnerability and inferiority. It may be at first glance surprising that the text should choose to portray a king, of all Muslims, as weak and inferior. The king, after all, represents the pinnacle of his faction's power structure—a point the text in fact develops through its report of the protagonists' nonreciprocal use of titles: the Muslim is addressed by the *adelantado* as "Señor rey," while the *adelantado* is addressed by the Muslim simply as "Fajardo." But the text repre-

TABLE 2.   Weakeners (powerless language) in *Jugando estaba el Rey Moro*, by Religion of Principal Speaker

	Principal Speaker	
Weakeners[a]	Rey (Muslim)	Fajardo (Christian)
Polite expressions/flattery[b]	2	—
Meek/self-effacing utterances[c]	2	—
Naive utterances[d]	1	—
Hedges	—	—
Utterances of hopelessness	—	—
Total	5	0

[a]The subcategories of weakeners are not mutually exclusive. I have therefore assigned instances to the category in which they most clearly fall and have specified in the notes to each category which instances have been placed in the category.

[b]que sois tan buen caballero
que todo el mundo os temía
[c]no juguemos más, Fajardo, / ni tengamos más porfía
[d]la villa de Lorca es mía

sents the Muslim king's access to the powerful ranges of speech as limited by physical, not social, factors. The emphasis on his social status indeed underscores this limitation, for if a Muslim king is powerless to withstand a Christian's threats, so too must be his people.

By representing the Muslim king as submissive, vulnerable, and powerless, the text demonstrates his—and all Muslim men's—difference. It makes clear that, in a society that valued men for their aggressive and militant behavior, the conciliatory or docile Muslim man had, to borrow a term Irigaray uses to talk about women, no "proper" place.[38] Moreover, the Muslim king's difference, grounded as it is in spoken language, could not have been made plainer than in an oral genre, such as the *romancero*, where a performer could easily have exploited the distinctiveness of protagonists' speech styles. One can only imagine the modulations of voice (falsetto, exaggerated rhythmicity, etc.) that fifteenth-century *juglares* might have used to underscore their representation of the *rey moro* not as a "true" king—that is, a manly warrior worthy of respect—but instead as a "wimp," culturally relegated to a secondary status relative to Christian men.

King Boabdil of Granada [Emir Muhammad b. 'Ali], nicknamed the "Rey Chico" (Little King) by Christians, was the last Muslim king in Spain. When Boabdil sought to exploit his demoralized Christian enemy after this group's resounding and humiliating defeat in Ajarquía (1483), he was captured. A strategic decision was made by the Christians to ransom Boabdil back; the Muslims were in the midst of a civil war, and the King's absence mitigated factional strife, thus strengthening Muslim forces. In a move viewed with dismay and hostility by Granadan Muslims, Boabdil's mother arranged and paid for his release. The Arabic source for the story concludes that the entire event was a shameful disaster for the Muslims, and that it led ultimately to the ruin of their homeland.[39]

In the Castilian court, much was made of Boabdil's humiliation at the hands of the Christians. One of the salient issues was whether the Muslim king should be made to kiss the hand of King Ferdinand when leaving the Christians.[40] The frontier ballad tells the following story:

38. See Irigaray 1987, 121.
39. See Harvey 1990, 278. Harvey cites Bani Naṣr 1940, 12.
40. See Harvey 1990, 278–83.

Junto al vado de Xenil
por un camino seguido
viene un moro de cavallo,
en polvo y sangre teñido,
corriendo a todo correr   5
como el que viene ahuydo.
Llegando junto a Granada
da gran grito y alarido,
publicando malas nuevas
de un caso que a contescido;   10
"Que se perdió el rey chiquito
y los que con él han ydo,
y que no escapó ninguno,
preso, muerto o mal herido,
que de quantos allí fueron   15
yo sólo me he guarescido
a traher nueva tan triste
del gran mal que ha succedido.
Los que a nuestro rey vencieron,
sabed, si no havéys sabido,   20
que fue aquel Diego Hernández,
De Córdova es su apellido,
alcayde de los donzeles,
hombre sabio y atrevido,
y aquel gran Conde de Cabra   25
que en su ayuda avía venido.
Éste venció la batalla
y aquel trance tan reñido,
y otro Lope de Medoça,
que de Cabra havía salido   30
que andava entre los peones
como león bravo metido.
Y sabed que el rey no es muerto
mas está en prisión rendido,
yo le vide yr en trahilla   35
en acto muy abatido.
Llevan lo drecho a Lucena,
junto a donde fue vencido."
Llorava toda Granada

con grande llanto y gemido;   40
lloravan moços y viejos
con algazara y ruydo;
lloravan todas las moras
un llanto muy dolorido;
unas lloran padres, hijos,   45
otras hermano o marido,
lloran tanto cavallero
como allá se huvo perdido;
lloravan por su buen rey,
tan amado y tan querido,   50
prometen todas sus joyas
para que sea redemido,
sus exorcas y texillos,
atutes de oro subido.
Con esto y otras riquezas   55
fue rescatado y trahido
el rey chiquito a Granada
y en su possessión metido.[41]

[At the ford of the river Xenil
on a crossing path
comes a Moor on horseback,
stained with dust and blood,
riding as fast as he can   5
like one who is fleeing.
Approaching close to Granada
he sends out a great cry and alarm,
conveying bad news
about an event that has taken place;   10
"The tiny king is lost
and those who went with him as well;
no one escaped at all,
they're either captured, killed, or badly wounded;
of those who went over there   15

---

41. Text is from Wright 1987, 116–18. Wright uses the version in Timoneda's *Rosa española*, 67–69.

I alone remain
to bring the sad news
about the great misfortune that has befallen us.
Those who vanquished our king,
you should know, if you didn't already,   20
included that Diego Hernández,
De Córdova is his surname,
deputy of the royal household,
a skilled and daring man;
another was that great Count of Cabra   25
who came along to help.
This one won the battle
and the perilous struggle and fight;
another of them was Lope de Mendoça,
who had come from Cabra   30
and plunged in among the infantrymen
to fight like a fierce lion.
And know that our king is not dead
but lies defeated in prison instead;
I saw him led round on a leash   35
in a very humiliating state.
They took him straight to Lucena,
near to where he was vanquished."
All of Granada was crying
with great tears and wailing;   40
young boys and old men were crying
clamoring and making noise;
all the Moorish women were crying
a very sorrowful cry;
some cried for fathers, sons,   45
others for a brother or husband;
they cry for all the many soldiers
that had been lost there;
they were crying for their good king,
so beloved and revered;   50
they promise all of their jewels
in order to ransom him back;
they gave up their belts and bracelets,
and all their ornaments of gold.

With these and other riches   55
they rescued and brought back
the tiny king to Granada
and he was placed again in their possession.]

In the ballad, Boabdil's capture and its aftermath are described in the
large segment of direct discourse spoken by an unidentified Muslim soldier (lines 11–38). This soldier's discourse relies heavily on evaluative
devices to reinforce the point of view of his story.[42] As in the case of the
powerless features that characterized the Muslim king's language in
Jugando estaba el rey moro (The Muslim king was playing chess), the
evaluative devices employed by the soldier in *Junto al vado de Xenil* (At
the ford of the River Xenil) ensure a representation of Muslims as
weak—unable both to stand up to Christians and to measure up to the
masculine/military ideals valued by both cultures.

Consider, for example, the soldier's initial announcement of his king's
defeat. This announcement is evaluated in a long string of clauses that
emphasize the resounding humiliation of the Muslims' loss. A double
negative and quantifiers stress that not one of the king's men, except for
the soldier himself, escaped imprisonment, death, or grave injury ("y que
no escapó ninguno, / preso, muerto, o mal herido, / que de quantos allí
fueron / yo sólo me he guarescido . . .," lines 13–16). Positive evaluation,
however, characterizes the soldier's description of the Christian victors.
Such titles marked for high social status and power as "alcayde" [deputy]
(line 23) and "conde" [count] (line 25) stress the victors' membership in
Christian nobility; the citing and repeating of their names and surnames
("Diego Hernández," "de Córdova," "de Cabra," "Lope de Mendoça")
reinforce their prestigious identity. Moreover, attributives and comparators that positively evaluate the skill and daring of the noble Christians,
such as the description of one as "hombre sabio y atrevido" [a skilled and
daring man] (line 24) and the comparison of another to a fierce lion
("como león bravo" [like a fierce lion], line 32), highlight the aggression
and military superiority of those who won the battle.

In stark contrast to the victorious, brave, and noble Christians is the
defeated Muslim king. The soldier, in his evaluation, focuses particular

---

42. Labov 1972a identifies a number of evaluative strategies in narrative, including rep-
etitions, ritual utterances, negatives, futures, modals, comparators, attributives, apposi-
tives, conjunctions, and causals. This language, he argues, enters into the narrative for the
purpose of explicating or evaluating a particular action.

attention on the abject state of the Muslim ruler. He reports, for example, that the king lies subdued in prison ("está en prisión rendido," line 34). The soldier stresses, through the repetition of words relating to the king's humiliation, the lowliness of the ruler's appearance and condition. He reinforces his description by insisting that his words are no exaggeration: he claims he has firsthand knowledge of the king's circumstances, declaring, "Yo le vide yr en trahilla / en acto muy abatido" [I saw him led round on a leash / in a very humiliating state] (lines 35–36).

To most critics, the evaluative devices employed in the soldier's discourse serve to engage audience sympathy for the Muslims, for they draw attention to their plight and that of their leader.[43] But the text, which goes on, in indirect speech, to describe the Christians' ransoming of the king to the Muslims, who bankrupt themselves buying their humiliated leader back, in fact makes the Muslims look ridiculous without in the least diminishing the valor of the Christian victors. The king whom the Muslims are so keen to have back is, after all, not much of a king. Though the Muslims mourn his captivity, his presence is rather sorry and diminutive. Indeed, the text repeatedly assigns him an epithet designed to exaggerate his small size, thereby diminishing him even further. He is called in the work not simply the "Little King" (Rey Chico), as he was commonly known by Christians, but the *tiny* king ("rey chiquito" or "rey chiquillo"): "fue rescatado y trahido / el rey chiquito a Granada" [the tiny king was rescued and brought back to Granada] (lines 56–57). Moreover, in the Muslim soldier's discourse, the king is also referred to as "rey chiquito": "Que se perdió el rey chiquito" [The tiny king has lost] (line 11). That the text makes the Muslim soldier call the king by his "Christian" name further establishes the fiction of its "Moorish point of view"; only to Christians was Boabdil known as the "Little King." Indeed, nowhere in the description of this event is the Muslim side of the story apparent, although critics have been quick to insist that it is (an insistence that suggests, rather unfortunately, that Christian *juglares* knew more about Muslims' response to the event than the Muslims themselves).[44] Indeed, it is curious how Muslim ambivalence about Boabdil and his ransoming is entirely absent from the text's dynamic.

---

43. Wright comments (1987, 241), "We might expect a Spanish poem to gloat over the Muslim distress . . . but there is no hint of such an attitude in the text."

44. Even such a work as Harvey's recent book on Islamic Spain (1990), which stresses the Muslim point of view and recognizes Christian propaganda in many chronicles of the period, refuses to see the frontier texts as anything but evenhanded when it comes to representing Muslims. See Harvey 1990, 222.

Through its negative evaluation of the Muslim king's physical attributes and its positive evaluation of the Christian warriors' social status and military capabilities, *Junto al vado de Xenil* succeeds in presenting two distinct and contrasting images of men during the reconquest. The "manly" image belongs primarily to male Christian Castilians; the "docile" or "tamed" image is reserved primarily for male Muslims. That the text makes a Muslim man articulate this distinction appears to be part of its strategy for reassuring its Christian audience that the threat of "other" men has been reduced. Muslims, once tamed, also sing the praises of Christians.[45] Once again, one can only imagine how contemporary *juglares* might have intervened in the text during performance. They could could easily have used gestures, along with modulations of voice, to make clear the contrast between the "manly" noble Christians, who won the battle, and the defeated little Muslim king, led round by the neck on a leash.

Less than a decade and a half after the emir's release—and in clear violation of the specific conditions of Muslim surrender in 1492—the Muslim population of Castile was offered the choice of expulsion from Spain or conversion to Christianity.[46] It is difficult, in this context, to understand how frontier epic and ballad, which figured so prominently in the reconquest project, could be understood as works of mutual recognition; as part of a genre, as many critics would have it—including those truly sensitive to the Muslim position toward the end of reconquest—where "villains are absent . . . as are weak men and cowards" and where "both sides are imbued with the same admirable moral qualities, both respect the same chivalric code of conduct" (Harvey 1990, 222).

---

45. See Godzich 1986, xiii.

46. This edict was published by the Catholic monarchs in 1502. For discussion, see Fletcher 1992, 166–69.

4

Jewish Men in the *Cantar de mio Cid*

We are now in a position to understand the anti-Semite. He is a man who is afraid.

—Jean-Paul Sartre, *Anti-Semite and Jew*

In epic and ballad literature of the reconquest period, male Muslims are not the only men depicted as lacking in aggressive, masculine qualities. Jewish men, too, are often accorded the sexual status and identity of the powerless. Indeed, representing "other" men in the epic and frontier ballads was in general a matter of limiting access to the traits and behaviors considered ideal for men in medieval Castile.[1]

The epic *Cantar de mio Cid* (c. 1207; hereafter abbreviated *CMC*),[2] one of Castile's earliest and most treasured texts, is a case in point. The work narrates some two decades of events in the life of a noble Christian military leader from Castile, Rodrigo Díaz de Vivar, or the *Cid*. When the text begins, the hero has been denounced by enemies and exiled by his king, Alfonso VI. In the course of the text, he conquers Valencia, thus extending Christian Castilian dominion to the Mediterranean Sea. Defeating vast numbers of Muslims and plundering their wealth, the Cid manages eventually to win his way back into the king's good graces.

Among the most salient and memorable characters in the text are two Jewish men—moneylenders called "Rachel" and "Vidas." These men are tricked into making a six-hundred-mark loan to the text's impoverished

---

Some of the ideas presented in this chapter have been developed in my article on "The Jew's Body" (Mirrer 1994a). Permission to cite materials from the article has been obtained from the Purdue Research Foundation.

1. This applies to the representation of non-Castilians in the literature as well. Two salient examples are found in the depiction of Ramón Berenguer and the *infantes* of Carrión in the *Cantar de mio Cid*.

2. For a summary of opinions on the date of composition for the *CMC*, see Lacarra 1980, 224–54; Deyermond 1987a, 20–22.

Christian hero, who fills two chests with sand[3] and, claiming they contain ill-gotten riches, offers them to the Jews as collateral. Initially described as gleeful, rejoicing at the very thought of the Cid's illicit treasure in their possession—

> Gradan se Rachel e Vidas / con averes monedados,
> ca mientra que visquiessen / refechos eran amos
>
> (lines 172–73)

> [Rachel and Vidas are pleased / with their money
> because as long as they lived / they would both be rich]

—the pair later appear angry, for they have been made fools of by the text's Christian hero, who fails to repay them, despite his clear ability to do so.[4] Desperately seeking to recover their lost money, they even offer to forgo the interest on their loan:

> Desfechos nos ha el Çid / sabet, si no nos val;
> soltariemos la ganançia, / que nos diesse el cabdal.
>
> (lines 1433–34)

> [The Cid has undone us / you know, if he does not aid us;
> We will forgo the interest, / if he gives us back the capital.]

But there is no evidence in the text that the Jews are ever repaid. When last heard from, Rachel and Vidas make an empty threat to seek the Cid out in Valencia:

> . . . dexaremos Burgos, / ir lo hemos buscar.
>
> (line 1438)

> [. . . we will leave Burgos, / and go to look for him.]

C. Smith (1965, 527) comments that the pair here show themselves up in a ludicrous position, for Valencia "is several hundred dangerous miles

---

3. The Cid is helped in this endeavor by his vassal Martín Antolínez.
4. There is a long bibliography on this subject. See, e.g., C. Smith 1965 and, more recently, McGrady 1985.

away across wild and mostly Moorish-held territory, and the Jews are not only elderly, but comfort-loving townsmen."

The *CMC*'s episode of the sand-filled chests is of folkloric origin.[5] Thus, like the story of the seductive Muslim princess in the *Siete Infantes* legend, the moneylending Jews originate in the precincts of fiction rather than history. Yet, also as in the case of the seductive Muslim princess, the Jewish moneylenders are crucial to a story otherwise based, at least loosely, on historical events. Indeed, Rachel and Vidas's loan provides a main catalyst for the text's narrative, for it is the Jews' money that enables the Cid to embark on his quest for wealth and vindication in mostly infidel territory.[6]

The episode of the sand-filled chests and the second appearance of Rachel and Vidas in line 1430b also provide the text with a substantial measure of comic relief. As Trachtenberg has noted (1961, 13), the Jew, in the Middle Ages, could be a comic as well as a vile creature. The caricatured presentation of Rachel and Vidas offers no exception, fully exploiting the stereotype by supplying a "humorous" example of two greedy usurers who fall prey to a Christian's hoax. Such a stereotype of course also underscores the cleverness of Christians who are able to outsmart "others." The strategy here is similar to that discussed in chapter 1 of this study with respect to the young Muslim woman tricked by a Christian into opening her doors to him (in the *Romance de la morilla burlada*).

A great deal has been written about the pair of Jews from whom the Cid borrows, but never repays, six hundred marks. Much of the critical discussion has centered on the question of whether or not the portrayal of Rachel and Vidas bears witness to anti-Semitism in the text and/or in

---

5. See McGrady 1985, 526 n; Menéndez Pidal 1913, 28–30; Uriarte Rebaudi 1972 [1973], 215–30.

6. Aizenberg asks (1980, 485 n. 28):

Could the Cid's non-payment of the loan to Raquel and Vidas also be an anachronism related to papal bulls of the twelfth and thirteenth centuries exempting crusaders from their obligation to pay usury on debts incurred? Peter the Venerable, Abbot of Cluny, who had visited Spain in the 1140's and was the author of anti-Moslem and anti-Jewish works, wrote in a letter to the King of France that the Jews engage in no useful occupation, but obtain their wealth through the trickery they exercise against Christians. Hence, he suggested: ". . . let their money be taken away. Thus, by the right hand of Christians, aided with the funds of the blaspheming Jews, the audacity of the unbelieving Saracens might be conquered."

Aizenberg cites here Synan 1967, 76.

the surrounding culture. A number of arguments have rejected anti-Semitism as a factor in the pair's representation. Sola-Solé (1976, 11), for example, has argued that anti-Semitism was not an issue at the time of the text's composition: "la armonía entre las tres castas . . . era bastante perfecta" [the harmony between the three castes . . . was almost perfect]. But anti-Jewish sentiment in Spain was in fact so prevalent during the late Middle Ages[7] that it is difficult to conceive of it as not having had some effect on the rather stereotypical depiction of the Jews as selfish, money-loving, oily, and persistent.[8] As McGrady notes (1985, 522–23),

> It is precisely this medieval delight in anti-Semitic satire that accounts for the painstaking detail indulged in by the author: had the Cid defrauded a couple of ordinary merchants, there would have been no point in showing Rachel and Vidas avariciously counting their money (101), expressing their desire for usury (123), denying the loan without security (139–40), and drooling at the prospect of becoming the owners of gold worth far more than the loan, should the Cid not redeem his pledge within the appointed time (170–73).

Indeed, the portrayal of Rachel and Vidas in the *CMC* appears wholly motivated by a desire to make the pair unmistakably *recognizable*—in the sense outlined by Sartre in *Anti-Semite and Jew* (1948, 10)—*as Jews*. Endowed with all of the defects with which tradition has endowed the Jews in general, the two moneylenders are specifically marked as "others" in Christian Spain.

Yet, while the Jews' representation was surely driven by the culture's pervasive anti-Semitism, it was also motivated by a desire to construct—and reconstruct—an image of a dominant Christian culture. If Rachel and Vidas have a particular psychological identity and social role in the *CMC* because they are Jews, they also have a specific cultural script. While the Cid and his Christian vassals earn riches in an aggressive war against the Muslims, Rachel and Vidas stay at home, passively collecting interest on their loans.[9] Thus the Jews are excluded from participating in

---

7. Sola-Solé (1976) bases his argument on a rather early date of composition for the text (1140), which is not now widely accepted. See Lacarra 1980, 222–54; Deyermond 1987a; Duggan 1989. For a discussion of anti-semitism in Spain, see, e.g., Baron 1952.

8. See Diz 1988 for a discussion of stereotyping in the Jews' characterization.

9. A result, as Aizenberg (1980, 479–80) and others have pointed out, not so much of objective factors but of theological, social, and economic myths about Jews that operated in medieval Europe from at least the time of the First Crusade of 1096.

medieval Castile's culturally exalted practice of war against the Muslims. De facto, they are prevented, too, from the pursuit of medieval Castilian society's chief confirmation of manhood—that is, the demonstration of "manly" qualities of daring, strength, and bravery on the battlefield. Forced to adopt a passive, domestic role in an aggressively militant environment, the CMC's Jews are portrayed in a manner that reinforced male Christians' sense of themselves as powerful, manly, and superior.

The narrow correspondence between the Jews' depiction in the CMC and male gender dominance in medieval Castile is, in fact, supported even by the names assigned to the pair in the text. As Salomonski notes (1956, 216), *Vidas* harks back to the biblical *Hawwā,* or "Eve":

Die Geschichte des Namens *Hayyīm* beggint . . .
mit der Erschaffung der Welt, d.h. mit Hawwā 'Eva'.

[The history of the name *Hayyīm* (Hebrew for Life—in Spanish, *Vida*) begins . . . with the beginning of the world, that is with Hawwā 'Eve'.]

And *Rachel* is, of course, the name of the matriarch of Israel.

The names *Rachel* and *Vidas* have, in fact, long been something of a puzzle for critics. *Rachel* has been taken as evidence of scribal error (e.g., a misinterpretation of the male Hebrew name *Roguel*), as evidence of Rachel's female identity (e.g., that she is Vidas's wife), and even as evidence that the pair is not Jewish but Christian Castilian.[10] Yet, if the names *Rachel* and *Vidas* indeed are meant to designate male Jewish characters, as most critics believe they are,[11] then, rather than an error in scribal transmission,[12] the assignment of feminine-type names to the Jews may have been an intended further touch of humor in their characterization. One can only imagine the hilarity with which such crossnaming

---

10. There is a lengthy critical debate on the origins and significance of the names *Rachel* and *Vidas*. See, for some salient examples, Salomonski 1956, Cantera Burgos 1958, Sola-Solé 1976, and Garci-Gómez 1975, 85–112. Garci-Gómez's opinion (1975) that the moneylenders are not Jewish is not widely held.

11. Apart from the argument about whether or not medieval Jewish women would actually have engaged in moneylending activities on an equal footing with their husbands, as the CMC suggests the pair does, it seems to me that, were Rachel and Vidas not both men, it would be rather unlikely for Martín Antolínez to address them jointly with the hearty and familiar expression *los mios amigos caros* (my dear friends). Neither would the pair likely be referred to by the Cid as "*don* [sirs] Rachel e Vidas" (lines 155, 159).

12. I believe that the name *Vidas* is also marked as feminine. This would legislate against the theory of scribal error in the use of the feminine name *Rachel*.

would have been met during performance. Moreover, the names, while humorously accentuating the Jews' behavior—behavior that, as England suggests (1980, 55), inherently "pairs" the Jews with the feminine through the text's implication that it is unacceptable precisely because of its association with female comportment[13]—may also have condensed anti-Semitic with antifeminist sentiment. *Rachel* and *Vidas* are in fact typical Jewish names, repeatedly called on in Spanish literature to signal the Jewish identity of characters.[14] Indeed, the names may be an important expression of the metaphoric chains linking male Jews with women, for they symbolically project the feminine onto the pair's image.

In a similar manner, the names *Rachel* and *Vidas* may be a kind of *signe victimaire* (ritual sign of the victim), in Girard's sense (1978, 1982)—that is, a mark of the Jews' "difference" that provoked Christian enmity.[15] The feminine/Jewish names are, after all, in sharp contrast to the "curious" choice, noted by Diz (1988, 450–51), of military-type epithets assigned to the Cid and his vassal immediately before introducing the Jews—

> Fablo mio Çid / el que en buen ora çinxo espada:
> ¡Martin Antolinez / sodes ardida lança!

(lines 78–79)

> [My Cid spoke / who in good hour girded the sword:
> "Martín Antolínez, / you are a brave lance!]

—a metaphoric expression, perhaps, of the fact that the Christians' enmity toward the Jews ("el enemigo metido en la casa" [the enemy at

---

13. Such a "pairing" is also alluded to in C. Smith 1965. Smith notes (524) that,

> as objects of ridicule and as sufferers at the hands of the Cid, the Jews are on a par with other important characters in the poem: with the Count of Barcelona, portrayed as a blustering, effete aristocrat, and with the Infantes de Carrión, depicted as juvenile, cowardly and villainous.

These other characters are, like the Jews, aliens in Christian Castile (the Count of Barcelona is Catalonian and the *infantes* of Carrión are Leonese), and their depictions are similarly "feminized." For further discussion of "pairings" in the text, see Deyermond 1973.

14. When Lope de Vega, e.g., wants to dramatize the Jewishness of his female protagonist in a play written well after the expulsion, he uses the name *Raquel* (Rachel). See Swietlicki 1988. Garci-Gómez (1975, 85–112), however, does not view the names as particularly Jewish. See also, Garci-Gómez's more recent study (1993).

15. See T. Mitchell 1988, 58–59.

home]) is at least on a par with their enmity toward the Muslims ("el enemigo declarado que le ocupa la tierra" [the declared enemy who occupies
their land]) (Diz 1988, 452).

Male Jews were, in fact, routinely stripped of their markers of masculinity and symbolically transformed into women in medieval Castilian
literary, legal, and folkloric texts. The popular notion that sodomy originated with the Jews (validated in late medieval theological writing—e.g.,
in the declaration of the *Libro llamado alborayque* [Book called Alborayque; 1488] that "La sodomía es venida de los judíos. . . . De los judíos
vino a los moros, a los malos cristianos . . ." [Sodomy came from the
Jews. . . . From the Jews it went to the Muslims, to bad Christians . . .]),[16]
the equivalence in thirteenth-century legal works between the word *Jew*
and such sexual epithets as *cornudo* (cuckhold),[17] and the proverbial
image of the Jew as coward (e.g., the saying "Muy cobardes, más que
judíos" [Very cowardly, even more so than Jews])[18] all link images of
male Jews to the praxis of patriarchy—that is, the dominion of men over
women and of certain, more "manly" groups of men (i.e., Christian
Castilians) over others in medieval Castile.

Indeed, there was in Spain, as well as in other parts of Europe, a long-
standing legal, political, medical, and doctrinal tradition of associating
male Jews with certain homosexual practices and/or feminine attributes.
Many scholars of the Middle Ages have noted, for example, that in
medieval Christian writings, the medical ailment most often attributed to
Jewish men is menstruation.[19] The early thirteenth-century Castilian
"Disputa entre un cristiano y un judío" (Debate between a Christian and
a Jew) asserts a similar kind of link between male Jews and women. This
text admonishes a Jew:

Ond, quando bjen uos mesuraredes, fonta uos i iaze & muy grand; que
la boca de uestro rabi que conpieça uestra oración, feches cono de
muier; & de mas sabedes que la barba y las narizes an y mal logar. E
de mas ueedes qual fonta de sugar sangre de tal logar.

16. For an edition of the *Libro*, see López Martínez 1954, 391–407. See also Thompson
1987, 17.

17. E.g., "Qui dixier a otro cornudo o fududinculo o gafo o judío a traidor alla mulier
puta o çeguledora o gafa pectet çinco moravetís" (*Fuero de Usagre*, 1907, 72; cited in
Thompson 1987, 14).

18. For discussion, see Thompson 1987, 15.

19. See, e.g., Strack 1909, 202. Strack describes, among other instances, a 1494 document from the city of Tyrnau that mentions, as part of an explanation of Jews' need for
Christian blood, that both male and female Jews menstruated.

[Whereas when you think well upon it (you will see that) you commit an outrageous act that lies herein; that the mouth of your rabbi who begins your prayers, you make it into a woman's cunt; and even more you know that the chin and the nose don't belong there. And even more you see what an outrage it is to suck blood from such a place].[20]

There is another, as yet unexamined, symbolic arena in which Jews may have been linked with the feminine in the medieval world. Trachtenberg (1961, 44–53) discusses in detail the medieval association of Jews with the Devil and his attendant symbols, particularly the horns. The miniatures that accompany Alfonso X's *Cantigas* make this association clear, picturing, for example, a devil with an enormous "Jewish" nose (see fig. 3). In folklore, horns are, of course, also symbolic of the man who is made a cuckold—in Brandes's persuasive interpretation (1980, 90–91), the man who is transformed symbolically into a woman:

. . . to be cuckolded is to be transformed symbolically into a woman. The horns, originally associated with or belonging to the woman, are placed upon the head of a man, thereby feminizing him.

In Brandes's study, the horns "represent the harmful, devilish dimensions of the feminine character." The horns, Brandes notes, are "given" by *women* to men (e.g., in Spanish one might say, "Pobrecillo, que no sabe que su mujer le está metiendo los cuernos" [Poor guy, he doesn't know that his wife is putting the horns on him]),[21] and hence they *come* from women. Thus, Brandes argues, a *she*-goat (not a he-goat, as Pitt-Rivers says [1977, 116]) is the animal implied in the act of cuckolding—an argument Brandes supports by noting the close association, in folklore, of goats with womankind, and also by noting that female goats, unlike female sheep, have horns. This type of symbolic link between women and the Devil is mirrored in medieval depictions of Jewish men. As Trachtenberg notes (1961), male Jews were commonly represented with horns and/or in association with the goat as either a favorite domestic animal or a favored mount. Moreover, apart from the horns, a supposedly typical feature of male Jewish physiognomy that is constantly stressed in prints and in folktales is the goat's beard, or goatee—a characteristic associated particularly with the *female* animal, as the female-linked Spanish equiva-

20. Castro 1914, 176. I use here Goldberg's translation (1979, 102–3).
21. See Brandes 1980, 90.

lents, *perilla* and *barbas de chiva,* suggest. In this regard, too, as Hatton and MacKay (1983, 194) note in their observations on the miniatures of the *Cantigas de Santa Maria,* physical caricature affects only *male* Jews; physically, Jewish women and children are wholly indistinguishable from Christians. Thus, women, Jews, and the Devil all appear to be metaphorically united as one as "creature[s] of an altogether different nature" (Trachtenberg 1961, 18)—that is, "others."

The medieval tradition of associating male Jews with homosexuality, or with the feminine, seems to have drawn at least partially on a desire to project Jewish men into the discourse on politics and law as effeminate, hence disqualifying them for positions of power and authority in society. Though Boswell 1980 does not suggest this, he does note (1980, 15–16) that

> the fate of Jews and gay people has been almost identical throughout European history, from early Christian hostility to extermination in concentration camps. The same laws which oppressed Jews oppressed gay people; the same groups bent on eliminating Jews tried to wipe out homosexuality; the same periods of European history which could not make room for Jewish distinctiveness reacted violently against sexual nonconformity; the same countries which insisted on religious uniformity imposed majority standards of sexual conduct; and even the same methods of propaganda were used against Jews and gay people—picturing them as animals bent on the destruction of the children of the majority.

In this context, it is significant that the *CMC* tends to stress precisely those aspects of Rachel and Vidas's characters that are most at odds with features exalted within the mainstream male Christian Castilian domains of politics, religion, and history. In a culture shored up by the praxis of male gender dominance, this type of characterization (like that of the Muslim princess and the beautiful Jewess) could only argue for the Jews' exclusion from positions of power and authority.

Rachel and Vidas's speech, appearance, and behavior, for example, are clearly distinguished from that of male Christian Castilians and, indeed, are often "paired" with that of women and non-Castilian Christian male characters.[22] The two are made to speak a classically "power-

---

22. See also C. Smith 1965, England 1980, and Deyermond 1973.

less" language, characterized by speech in unison—a technique used also in the representation of the Cid's cowardly Leonese (i.e., *non*-Castilian) sons-in-law[23] and his daughters, Elvira and Sol. The Jews are even described initially as *together as one* ("en uno estavan amos," line 100), and only once does one speak alone. The two also use such naive utterances as the proverbial expressions "non duerme sin sospecha / qui aver trae monedado" [he who has money with him / sleeps uneasily] (line 126) and "Non se faze assi el mercado, / si non primero prendiendo / e despues dando" [Business is done / first by taking / then by giving] (lines 139–40), and they revel in expressions of extreme flattery, which include gestures of respect and appreciation for Christians' "face" (e.g., Rachel exclaims, "Ya Campeador / en buen ora çinxiestes espada!" [Ah, Great Warrior / in a good hour you girded your sword!] [line 175]). Rachel and Vidas also employ empty threats (e.g., when the Cid fails to repay the loan, the pair threaten to come after him, even though the text has made clear that their locus of activity is the home: ". . . dexaremos Burgos, / ir lo hemos buscar" [We will leave Burgos, / and go look for him] [line 1438]), and they use the type of epithets aptly characterized by Walsh (1990, 2) as "the flattery of the desperate" (e.g., they call the Cid's vassal, Minaya Fañez, "cavallero de prestar" [worthy knight] (line 1432) as they attempt to use him to recover the Cid's bad debt).

Rachel and Vidas's dissonance with the text's sharply physical sense of masculinity is perhaps most forcefully represented through descriptions of the Jews' physical behavior. In the space of a short, thirty-line interview with the Cid (lines 152–82), for example, the pair kiss the hand of the newly exiled Christian warrior four times. The first three instances are described as actual gestures; the fourth is a verbal "kiss," given the Cid by Rachel at the end of the interview—he says, "Cid, beso vuestro mano" [Cid, I kiss your hand] (line 179). While kissing the hand of a superior is not an unusual activity in the *CMC*, it is, in the case of the Jews, exaggerated. Elsewhere in the work, one kiss per interview usually suffices.[24] The text thus appears to take particular satisfaction in the

---

23. See Fernández Jiménez 1982, 48.

24. The Cid's followers, e.g., each kiss his hand a single time, as they join his company (line 298). The Cid's wife, Doña Jimena, also kisses his hand—once, as the couple prepares to part (line 265); a second time, some seventy lines later, when they actually do part (line 369); and then in a few, scattered reunions throughout the text, with one kiss per occasion. When the Cid's vassal Alvar Minaya Fañez brings gifts to King Alfonso on behalf of the Cid, he makes a verbal representation of the action. He tells the king that the warrior kisses both his hands and his feet (e.g., lines 879, 1322–23) and his hands alone (line 1338). Yet,

pair's act of submission, using the repeated gesture of the kiss to demonstrate Rachel and Vidas's subordination to the Christian warrior.

But the exaggeratedly submissive behavior of the Jews in the text also distinguishes the pair from other subordinates in the work. For the Jews are not the Cid's vassals, and it is clear that their gesture does not stem, as does that of other characters, from this type of hierarchical relationship. Indeed, it appears that, in the *CMC*, only productive hierarchical relations, such as those obtaining between the Cid and his vassals, are appropriate for men (vassals, for instance, kiss the hero's hand as an entrée to productive, income-earning labor on the battlefield). Thus, the Jews, who engage in the pursuit of unearned profit (Walsh [1990, 10] notes that they are described counting their wealth ["en cuenta de sus averes," line 101] as if that were their perpetual exercise), appear "unmanly." This point is stressed in Rachel's "verbal" kiss, which is a prelude to his request for an ornate, exotic *gift* from the Christian warrior: "una piel vermeja / morisca e ondrada, / Cid, beso vuestra mano / en don que la yo aya" [a crimson skin, Moorish and prized / Cid, I kiss your hand / that I might have it as a gift] (lines 178–79). Indeed, the gift Rachel asks for—a crimson skin—underscores the Jews' "unmanliness" so persuasively that one modern critic, Sola-Solé (1976, 15), has found in it indisputable evidence of Rachel's "feminine psychology" and, hence, female sexual identity:

¿Cabe realmente mayor indicio de feminidad? ¿No se define y delata aquí Raquel a sí misma al pedirle al Cid que, como regalo de tierra de moros, le traiga una piel morisca, bermeja y preciada? ¿No sería una señal contundente de psicología femenina?

[Is there, in fact, any greater sign of femininity? Does not Rachel here define and delineate herself in asking that the Cid bring her a prized,

---

in these sections of the text, the actual physical act of kissing the king's hands is accomplished in a single gesture alone, by Minaya (lines 894, 1320). The only segment of the *CMC* in which the text is comparably saturated with hand kissing is the interview between the Cid and King Alfonso, as the latter pardons the former. But here, as the text makes clear, there are specific reasons for such behavior relating to the special, overdetermined nature of the occasion. The Cid kisses the king as would anyone a ruler; he kisses the king to assure him that he, once suspected of treason, is respectful and loyal; he kisses the king because he is relieved by the news of his pardon; and he kisses the king to show that he is grateful to the ruler, who, having once banished him, now honors him (line 2025 and passim).

crimson Moorish skin as a gift from the land of the Muslims? Would not this be a convincing indication of feminine psychology?]

That it is masculine, not simply Christian, beliefs and attitudes the Jews depart from in the text is made clear in the work's express affirmation that the attitudes and ideals of the Cid and his vassals belong specifically to men. The Cid, for example, has to "instruct" his wife and daughters—who are, of course, Christians—in these attitudes, for as women, they are ignorant of them. The women, for instance, "learn" from their men to view war as a window of opportunity (with respect to the Muslim invasion of Valencia, the Cid tells the women, "ca todo es vuestra pro" [for all this is your profit] (line 1664); they "learn" not to fear Muslims but to dominate them (the Cid reassures the women that the Muslims' drums, which make them fearful, will soon hang in the church as trophies of Christian victory and dominion [lines 1666, 1668]; they "learn" to dehumanize "other" men, for these are not truly men but alien objects to be appropriated as their own (the Muslims are no more than wealth to be taken as dowries for the Cid's daughters [lines 1648–50]).

In this context of exalted male aggression and extroversion, the "otherness" of the Jewish men could not have been plainer. Over and again the text makes the point that the Jews' locus of activity is the home, while that of Christian Castilian men is the battlefield. It dwells on the image of the Jews returning to the enclosed spaces of their residence after they agree to make a loan to the Cid, laying a carpet on the floor, and then placing a fine white sheet on top of it—all to make a comfortable "bed" for the silver coins they throw out (lines 182–84). It is no wonder Martín Antolínez, the brave Christian Castilian warrior, is so anxious to leave the Jews' house for the Cid's tent in the countryside ("Grado exir de la posada" [He was glad to leave their house] (line 200). The text also stresses Rachel and Vidas's sedentary behaviors and eagerness to profit from, but not engage in, war. One can only picture the contortions of singers as they described how the Jewish men strained themselves, not in glorious battle as "real" men ought, but in lifting the sand-filled chests they stupidly believed held great treasure.[25] One can picture also the

---

25. The lines, "non las podien poner en somo / mager eran esforçados" (lines 171–72) are generally understood to mean, "they could not lift them, although they were strong." However, the syntagm *eran esforçados* could also lead to a reading of the lines as, "they could not lift the chests although they exerted themselves." I believe that the phrase ought

ironic representation of Rachel and Vidas as they repeatedly rejoice over the expectation of profit—profit they would never receive, because, unlike "real" men who battled Muslims for their money, they had done nothing to earn it.

By the end of the *CMC*, the Jewish men are silenced. Their final plea for the Cid to repay them—even without interest—is ignored, and they speak no more in the work, although it is only less than half over at this point.

The episode of the sand-filled chests and the second appearance of Rachel and Vidas in the *CMC* function as a medium for representing male Jews, while discriminating against them. Usurping their signifying and representing functions, these segments of the text even override Jewish men's historical reality; the description of the male Jews and their activities (like the seduction of the *morica* and the birth of her son, Mudarra, in the *Siete Infantes*) is based solely on a stereotype. Indeed, the clichéd image of the Jewish moneylenders screens reality with the mediations of anti-Semitism to the extent that it is impossible to grasp any "real" object that the characters might designate at all.[26]

And yet, male Jewish culture of the Middle Ages entailed many values similar to those held by male Christian Castilians. Male Jews certainly did not consider themselves to be effeminate and, in fact, strictly observed many of the masculine ideals reserved for male Christian Castilians in the *CMC*.[27] The reality of medieval Jewish men may also have presented some obstacles to male Christian dominion. Bello long ago suggested this (1881):

Esta historieta de las arcas de arena fue inventada sin duda para ridiculizar a los judíos, clase entonces mui rica, poderosa i odiada.

[This little story of the sand-filled coffers was no doubt invented in order to ridicule the Jews, in those days a rich, powerful, and despised class.]

---

to be interpreted the latter way in the *CMC*, for surely that interpretation fits better with the picture of the two Jews conveyed elsewhere in the text. See *Diccionario de la lengua española* (1992, 625).

26. See Said 1985 for a related discussion with respect to modern "orientalism."

27. See Brundage 1987, 51–57, for a description of some sexual attitudes in traditional Judaism.

Thus, one plausible explanation for the Jews' "feminization" in the text may be in the fear evoked in the dominant masculine community by the specter of male Jews' power and emanating from the Jews' "otherness." As the studies of Brandes (1980) and others have suggested, in the popular arena—for which the *CMC* was originally destined—men's preferred mechanism for dealing with threats from male enemies has long been to strip them of their markers of masculinity. In the *CMC*, "feminized" images of male Jews may, imaginarily, have done just that. The characterization of Rachel and Vidas surely renders Jews powerless and, ultimately, speechless. In this manner, too, the work shored up male Christian Castilian identity, formulating the Jews' future exclusion from Spain.

Part 3
Men's Language, Women's Power: Representing Christian Women

5

Queens in the Ballad: *Landarico* and *Doña Blanca*

Images of lawless, reckless, and lascivious upper-class Christian matrons appear across a broad spectrum of literary texts in late medieval Castile. These women, who wield enormous amounts of power, use commands, threats, and pejorative expressions when addressing men of all social classes.

Reconquest politics often shape these images of powerful Christian women, even though the texts do not always deal explicitly with the reconquest. As in the case of Muslims and Jews, powerful Christian women are perceived as symptoms of a social and political crisis that must be overcome to shore up male Christian Castilian control. Indeed, the images depend on the same sociosymbolic field described in parts 1 and 2 of this study and likewise aim to sustain the dominant group against religious and sexual antagonisms.[1]

That images of powerful Christian women appear and reappear throughout the late Middle Ages is at first surprising and perplexing;[2] a rich array of doctrinal, legal, literary, political, and popular sources collaborated during the period to offer a view of women as fundamentally subordinate to men. Even the most exceptional women, including the Virgin Mary, were made subordinate in these sources,[3] and the decision-making power of even the highest-placed noblewomen was frequently challenged. While, for example, females' right of succession to the throne

---

1. My use of the term *symptom* here is borrowed from Zizek (1989, 126–27). The application of Zizek's concept of "a disfigured representation of social antagonism" (126–27) to my study was brought to my attention through my recent reading of an unpublished paper, "'Lazarillo de Tormes' and the Picaresque in Light of Current Political Culture," kindly made available to me by its authors, David Castillo and Nicholas Spadaccini.

2. But see Irizarry 1983 on "Amazons." See also Mirrer 1995b.

3. While, e.g., the male apostles were granted the power to absolve sinners in the *Siete Partidas,* Alfonso X's ambitious legal project of the thirteenth century, the Virgin was not (*Part.* 1, Title 6, Law 26).

was recognized in Castile, it was often contested, abrogated, or criticized. (In Aragon, Pedro IV [1336–87] had tried to name his daughter as heir to the throne, but there was such strong opposition that he withdrew the designation, and women, thereafter, were effectively excluded).[4] Although writers sometimes idealized early examples of independent noblewomen whom they depicted as obtaining objectives without renouncing femininity (for example, Berenguela, the wife of King Alfonso VII [1126–57], who, left on her own, was said to have defended Toledo with the only arms she had at her disposal—her dignity, the display of her retinue of women hoisting up musical instruments, and some choice words that confused the enemy), contemporary women who acted independent of men were subjected to special criticism. One salient example is Catalina of Lancaster, queen of Castile 1390–1406 (coregent for her minor son, Juan II), who was derided for her attempts to exercise authority and diminished in writing by male contemporaries.[5] Another is Leonor López de Córdoba (b. 1362/3), a noblewoman whose influence at court was deplored (along with that of the Jew Ferrand López de Saldaña) by the famous biographer Fernán Pérez de Guzmán (1965, 34). Leonor rose to prominence without the help of her husband, a victim of the fourteenth-century civil war who sought in vain to regain his fortune.

Medieval courtesy books, meant to serve as guides for behavior in the real world, persistently stressed that upper-class women should exercise modesty in gesture and in speech, reserving the powerful ranges of behavior for men alone.[6] In the domestic setting, a wife was by law considered to owe her husband obedience, respect, and fidelity in return for the protection, support, and control he afforded her—even when the wife belonged to a higher social class than her husband. These reciprocal obligations, as Dillard has pointed out (1984, 93), made the ideal conjugal relationship hierarchical in principle—a view reflected in the *Fuero Juzgo*,[7] which prohibited marriage between an older woman and a younger man, on the assumption that such a marriage would be "against nature" (Book 3, Title 1, Law 4), that is, a transgression of the "natural" power relations between women and men.

Other works confirm, through outright misogyny or through argu-

---

4. See O'Callaghan 1975, 432, for discussion.

5. Pérez de Guzmán (1965, 9) notes that Catalina looked as much like a man as a woman.

6. See Bornstein 1983 for discussion.

7. The *Fuero Juzgo* was a law code promulgated in the seventh century, but influential throughout the Middle Ages.

ments claiming to be divine in origin, similar notions of women as essentially subordinate to men. The thirteenth-century *Libro de los buenos proverbios* (Book of Good Proverbs), for example, exhorted, "Would that all trees bear such fruit," in response to the sight of a woman's burned corpse hanging from a tree (Goldberg 1983; al-Ibadi 1970). And James Brundage (1987, 425–28) cites a string of doctrinal works of the medieval period that invariably conclude, "women were created for the subordinate role of assisting men to carry out the divine plan."

Medieval Castilian works that focus on the subordination—and, indeed, the suppression—of women appear to play out what anthropologists have described as an ever-present undercurrent of fear in the dominant community, a fear that the forces of dominant-"other" struggle will work to undermine the dominant community's coherence.[8] This fear, which in medieval Castile translated into hostility, punitive sanctions, and the exclusion of authentic women's narrative, accounts for both the centrality—in the world of direct domination—of military force to control those defined as "other" and, in the cultural sphere, the use of language to legitimize the dominant group. Yet the anthropological explanation, while useful in uncovering and interpreting the dynamic of domination in medieval Castilian society, only serves to sharpen the great contrast between the subordination and suppression of women described in general by many texts (in particular by the volumes purposefully written during the period to restrict the legal rights and behavioral practices of women) and the examples the literary corpus provides of women whose behavior and, above all, speech suggest power and authority.

Because it is primarily texts composed by men that mediate the goals and desires of women in the literature of medieval Castile, it is difficult to speculate about how women actually did speak during the period. Some male authors insisted, in prologues and in "asides" to the reader, that they maintained strict fidelity to "real" speech in their works.[9] But this does not mean that female speech in the literature directly reflects contemporary women's language.[10] Nor does it explain why so often the complex of features used by male authors to portray feminine discourse

---

8. See, for example, Pitt-Rivers' and Denich's discussions (1977 and 1974, respectively) of penalties for adultery that respond to men's fears of their own vulnerability and that involve a continual testing of the strengths and weaknesses of men and women.

9. López de Ayala, e.g., declares this in the opening lines of the *Crónica del rey don Pedro*, (1875–77, 400).

10. Bakhtin (1986, esp. 62) provides an interesting analysis of how rejoinders in literature lose their relation to actual reality and to the real utterances of others.

generated a language of power *en boca femenina* (in the mouth of a woman). Even in the case of the more powerful noblewomen represented in the texts, this type of language is surprising; medieval courtesy manuals instructed upper-class women in particular to refrain from strong speech and, in many instances, to maintain complete silence.

Precisely because it was mainly male authors who controlled the speech of women in the literature of medieval Castile, it is reasonable to expect, as has been suggested elsewhere, that they would "portray with broad strokes a female image which the dominant masculine community [found] comforting and reassuring" (Cerquiglini 1986, 189). Why, then, is this not the case; why do we find that so few of the legal and behavioral distinctions between the sexes promulgated throughout the society are reflected in the feminine discourse of the texts?

Two popular medieval Castilian ballads, the *Romance de Landarico* (Ballad of Landarico) and the *Romance de Doña Blanca* (Ballad of Queen Blanche), provide striking examples of noblewomen who wield enormous amounts of power. These texts depict lascivious, reckless, and even criminal queens whose weak or absent husbands allow them limitless access to the discourses of power.

Landarico and *Doña Blanca* are both oral-traditional *romances* dating from the late reconquest period.[11] Their shared theme of female adultery and the social disorder that results from it resonates in a large number of works from the medieval period, even within such disparate genres as the popular proverb and code of law. In this corpus of texts, women, acting independent of men's control, go to extraordinary and illegal lengths both to satisfy their enormous sexual appetites and to hide their illicit affairs (and illegitimate children) from their husbands.

Not a great deal is known about the reception of the *romances* during the Middle Ages.[12] Yet the genre appears to have cut across boundaries of social class—even though the *romances* [ballads] often have as their

---

11. Both texts represent queens who figure centrally in well-known medieval historical works. The queen in *Landarico* is described in the Latin *Gesta Regum Francorum* (Deeds of the Frankish kings) and *De Gestis Francorum* (Concerning the deeds of the Franks); Blanca de Borbón, the wife of King Pedro I of Castile, is discussed in Pero López de Ayala's *Crónica del Rey don Pedro*. The versions used here are from sixteenth-century *pliego sueltos* (chapbooks).

12. Two recent articles on the *romancero* (Anahory-Librowicz 1989 and Catarella 1990) have discussed the importance of women as receptors for the texts. Both these articles, however, deal with the modern oral tradition. Women's role in the reception of the ancient tradition has yet to be established. For a discussion of ballad reception in the sixteenth century, see Orduña 1989.

heroes and heroines members of royalty and nobility.[13] *Romances,* according to the testimony of some fifteenth-century learned writers, were a form of diversion for "people of low and servile condition," or "rustics" [Menéndez Pidal 1968, 2:21], but much other evidence suggests that the texts were well known and popular among all social groups,[14] a view bolstered by the large number of texts cited in works from the fifteenth century onward. Indeed, the genre became a favorite pastime of the royal court, and the same texts appear to have enjoyed wide circulation in both noble and nonnoble circles (Débax 1982, 72).

The ancient version of *Landarico* (the text remains even today as a vital part of the ballad repetoire[15]) tells the story of an adulterous queen whose treachery is discovered by her husband, the king. To avoid punishment, the queen arranges for her husband to be murdered. The text reads as follows:

Para ir el rey a caça   de mañana ha madrugado
entró donde está la reyna   sin la aver avisado
por holgarse yva conella   que no yva sobre pensado
hallóla lavando el rostro   que ya se avía levantado
mirándose está a un espejo   el cavello destrançado.
El rey con una varilla   por detrás la avía picado.
La reyna que lo sintiera   pensó que era su querido.
"Está quedo, Landarico"   le dixo muy requebrado.
El buen rey quãndo lo oyera   malamente se ha turbado
la reina volvió el rostro   la sangre se le a quajado.
Salido se ha el rey   que palabra no ha fablado
a su caça se ha ydo   aún que en al tiene cuydado.
La reyna a Landarico   dixo lo que ha passado.
"Mira lo que hazer conviene   que oy es nuestro fin llegado."
Landarico que esto oyera   mucho se acuytado.
"En mal punto y en mala ora   mis ojos te han mirado
nunca yo te conociera   pues tan cara me has costado

---

13. Armistead and Silverman (1965) discuss the lack of necessary correspondence between the attributes of a *romance*'s protagonists and its receptors' beliefs and attitudes. In particular, they remark on the Judeo-Spanish audience's taste for texts that detail the exploits of Christian Spain's heroes and heroines.

14. See, e.g., Entwistle 1930 for an account of ballads in the work of erudite chronicles.

15. Benmayor (1979) recorded eight Sephardic versions of the text in 1972–73 in Seattle, Washington, and Los Angeles, California.

que ni a ti [hallo] remedio   ni para mí lo he hallado."
Allí hablara la reyna   desque lo vio tan penado.
"Calla calla Landarico   calla hombre apocado
déxame tu hazer a mí   que yo lo habré remediado."
Llama a un criado suyo   hombre de muy baxo estado
que mate al rey le dize   en aviéndose apeado
que sería a boca de noche   quando oviese tornado
házele grandes promesas   y ellos lo han aceptado
en bolviendo el rey dezía   de aquello muy descuydado;
al punto que se apeava   de estocadas le han dado.
"Trayción," dize el buen rey   y luego ha espirado
Luego los traydores mesmos   muy grandes bozes han dado
criados de su sobrino   havían al rey matado.
La reyna hizo gran duelo   y muy gran llanto han tomado
aunque en su coraçon dentro   otra cosa le ha quedado.

(*Pliegos poéticos españoles en la Universidad de Praga* [Spanish
Poetic Documents in the University of Prague] 1960,
2:331–32)[16]

[Because he was going out hunting   the king rose up early in the
morning.
He entered the room where the queen was   without first announc-
ing himself.
He went to relax with her;   with no other purpose in mind.
He found her washing her face;   already having arisen.
She looks at herself in the mirror;   her hair still hanging loose.
The king with a very small rod   tickled her from behind.
The queen when she felt this   thought it was her lover who had
come in.
"Be gentle, Landarico,"   she said, flirting with him as she spoke.
The good king when he heard this   was badly shaken indeed.
At once the queen turned her head,   her blood has frozen with
fear.

---

16. I have reproduced the text here with limited editorial intervention. I have, e.g., added accents and some punctuation for the sake of clarity and, in particular, to make the text more accessible to nonspecialists. Because of its rhyme (-*ado* throughout) and its semi-learned words and expressions, this version of *Landarico* appears to be either a reworking of an oral version or, perhaps, a basis for modern, traditional versions. Concerning *Landarico* and its origins, see Bénichou 1968, 103–8; Armistead and Silverman 1979, 51–52.

The king left the room at that point;   he has not spoken one single
   word.
He has gone out on his hunt as planned,   although he is greatly
   disturbed.
The queen to her lover, Landarico,   reported what had occurred.
"Look now to what must be done   for today our destiny is
   come."
Landarico, when he heard this,   has become very anxious indeed.
"Evil was the moment and hour   when I first lay eyes on you!
Oh that I'd never known you,   so dearly has it cost me!
I [find] no solution at all,   not for you and not for me."
In this way spoke the queen   after seeing him so afflicted:
"Shut up, shut up, Landarico—   shut up you cowardly man;
Leave to me what must be done.   I will find a way to fix things."
She calls on one of her servants,   a man of very low station;
she tells him to kill the king   as he dismounts from his horse,
which would be as nighttime fell   when from the hunt he
   returned.
She made him many great promises,   and they were all accepted.
When the king was returning, they said,   he did not suspect a
   thing.
As soon as he stepped off his horse   he was struck with blows
   from a sword.
"Treason!" the good king cries   and then he falls down dead.
Afterward the traitors themselves   gave a very great hue and cry
servants of the king's nephews, they said,   had murdered him.
The queen made much of her grief   and has shed very many tears,
though down deep in her heart   something quite different was
   lurking.][17]

What *Landarico* in fact describes are the consequences of women's
excessive power. The text shows how independent women like the queen
wreak havoc on the state. Unfettered by the primary authority of her husband, who goes off on a hunt instead of immediately exacting punishment for his wife's adultery, the queen in the text exploits her residual
authority. She humiliates her lover, a man of lower social rank who,
albeit late in the day, recognizes his folly and is prepared to accept blame

---

17. Unless otherwise stated, all English translations from Spanish texts are mine.

for it; she bargains with a lowly servant, enticing him to treasonous action against a legitimate ruler; she sees to it that unlawful coupling ultimately triumphs over legally and religiously sanctioned marital relations.

Because the queen's husband, as king, also represents the state, the text makes the point that ruinous political consequences result when women are given access to the discourses of power. For not only is the legitimate head of the family dishonored in this work, but the legitimate head of the state is disfranchised. His murder deprives him of his right to rule and deprives his subjects of their right to be governed with reason and justice. His death leaves the state in the vulnerable position of having no one to see to it that order is maintained. Indeed, criminals go free in this headless community—a result seen plainly in the suggestion at the end of the text that the queen escapes unscathed from her misdeed.

In the text's first lines there is, on the one hand, an immediate establishment of sex roles based on traditional assumptions about men and women. Male activities are given as aggressive and as centered outside of the home (the king is shown initially as preparing to go out on a hunt; the king uses a short rod [penis?] to tickle his wife, the queen). Female activities are presented as nonaggressive and home-centered (the queen's hair is hanging loose—a style appropriate only to the bedroom; the queen is described as responding with flirtatious language to her husband/presumed lover when he tickles her with the rod [penis?]). Indeed, the portrayal of the female protagonist in the work suggests that the queen has deliberately been made recognizable as a "real" woman;[18] her special capacities as queen neither erase nor obscure the cultural markers of her gender.

On the other hand, a close examination of the language styles of the text's principal speakers—the queen and her lover, Landarico[19]—demonstrates that it is the female speaker (the queen) who uses powerful language; the male speaker (Landarico) uses powerless language. Tables 3 and 4 show the frequency distribution of Strengtheners and Weakeners, or powerful and powerless features, in the rejoinders of the two protagonists.

As tables 3 and 4 show, each language style—that is, powerful and powerless—is used consistently and exclusively by the speakers, who are

---

18. She is not, e.g., represented in the fashion of Juan Ruiz's *serranas* (mountain women), who, while physically strong and verbally aggressive, are expressly portrayed as aberrant.

19. The king speaks only one word (¡Traición!) in the text.

male and female. The text thus describes a pattern of linguistic practices in which female speech is not characterized by the linguistic markers generally seen to constitute the language of powerlessness (e.g., hedges,[20] hesitations,[21] or polite expressions[22])—that is, the language that women, even today, are supposed to speak. Power, as reflected in the linguistic choices attributed to the male and female protagonists in the text, is thus not a condition patterned along traditional sex lines. As some recent investigations in sociolinguistics have suggested, powerful and powerless language features appear not as a priori characteristics of men's or women's speech, but rather as features distributed throughout language

TABLE 3. Strengtheners (powerful language) in the *Romance de Landarico*, by Gender of Principal Speaker

	Principal Speaker	
Strengtheners[a]	Landarico (male)	Queen (female)
Threats	—	—
Imperatives[b]	—	5
Pejorative expressions/insults[c]	—	1
Future Tense of Assertion[d]	—	1
Total	0	7

[a]The subcategories of strengtheners are not mutually exclusive. For example, *calla* is both an insult and an imperative. I have therefore assigned instances to the category in which they most clearly fall and have specified in the notes to each category which instances have been placed in the category.
[b]mira
calla
calla
calla
déxame
[c]apocado
[d]habré

20. I.e., forms that reduce the force of assertion, making room for exceptions or avoiding commitments (O'Barr and Atkins 1980, 101). Some examples in Spanish would be *un poco, algo, un tanto*, subjunctive/conditional forms, etc.
21. I.e., "pause fillers" or "meaningless particles." Some examples in Spanish would be *pues, bueno*, etc.
22. For an interesting discussion of power and women's language, see O'Barr and Atkins 1980. There has been a great deal of resistance in recent feminist writings to the equation "women's language = powerless language." One of the central issues involved is the definition of power, which, for many theorists, must be revised to reflect the distinction between the public sphere (where men generally hold power) and the domestic sphere (where women may be powerful). See Rosaldo and Lamphere 1974 and Erler and Kowaleski 1988. For more on the "women's language" controversy, see n. 42 of this study's introduction.

that under certain specific conditions may apply equally to the speech of both sexes.[23]

Because it is a queen who speaks in *Landarico*, it is tempting to suggest that the view of gender and social relations presented in the *romance* is class-marked and to stress position in the social hierarchy (i.e., social class) at the expense of gender in explaining women's powerful language. Some recent work in medieval women's history has certainly tended in this direction, considering noblewomen apart from other women in the discussion of power and authority (e.g., Rosenthal 1987). Yet, while the repeated use of the word *queen* leaves no room for doubt about the social class of the ballad's female protagonist, *Landarico* also goes to some lengths to insist that it is, above all, a woman speaking in the work. It is, for instance, certain that the different male and female sex roles given in the culture outside of the text—irrespective of social class—undergo no transformation whatsoever in the work. And that the king, whose position in the social hierarchy is surely superior to the queen's, is practically silent in the text further suggests that language style in the ballad cannot be attributed to social position alone.

The specifically powerful tone of the queen's utterances appears, therefore, to have more to do with the "problem" of women who are allowed to wield enormous amounts of power than with the class-

TABLE 4.   Weakeners (powerless language) in the *Romance de Landarico*, by Gender of Principal Speaker

Weakeners[a]	Principal Speaker	
	Landarico (male)	Queen (female)
Polite expressions/flattery	—	—
Meek/self-effacing utterances	—	—
Naive utterances	—	—
Hedges	—	—
Utterances of hopelessness[b]	3	—
Total	3	0

[a]The subcategories of weakeners are not mutually exclusive. I have therefore assigned instances to the category in which they most clearly fall and have specified in the notes to each category which instances have been placed in the category.

[b]en mal punto y en mala ora / mis ojos te han mirado
nunca yo te conociera / pues tan cara me has costado
que ni a ti [hallo] remedio / ni para mí lo he hallado

---

23. See, in particular, O'Barr and Atkins 1980.

marked language of kings and queens. The message of the text is the adverse consequences of such females.

In *Landarico*, a woman, allowed access to the discourses of power, uses her authority to disgrace and dishonor her surrounding male community. While she relies on commands, deprecatory expressions, and the aggression of a future tense to say what she will do to escape her crime with impunity, the men around her are either silent, as is the king when he learns of his wife's adultery, or reduced to defending themselves with powerless language (e.g., Landarico relies on utterances of hopelessness).

This, in the context of medieval Castile, is a topsy-turvy, imaginary world. It stands on its head the concept of woman as subordinate—at least in marriage and in government, two of the most sensitive areas of medieval society. But this does not appear to be, as some have argued with respect to other worlds of role reversal (in particular, the carnival), a world that undermines the status quo by widening behavioral options for women.[24] On the contrary, the text attempts to limit women's behavioral options, showing that they ought not be allowed "on top."[25] For *Landarico* reports a woman speaking in a powerful way to show that women's power is dangerous and should be suppressed. Forcing a displacement of the deep determinants of medieval Castile's repressive discourses—that is, the instability of relations between men and women[26]—the text cautions against such freedoms as would allow the imagined goals and desires of women to be realized. Thus the text becomes a vehicle for expressing the dreaded consequences of a culture in which women are not prevented from speaking powerful language: the structure of the family as a mechanism for guaranteeing the conservation of wealth and property is dismantled, factions occur within the ruling classes, daily occupational routines are disrupted, and so on.

As in other medieval Castilian texts, it is the authoritative woman who is disruptive and subversive (Doña Lambra, discussed in the introduc-

24. Davis (1975) discusses this phenomenon. For other views on this theme, see Fenster 1987, Weissburger 1988 and 1989, and Westphal-Wihl 1989.

25. It is interesting to note in this context the continual questioning of the legitimacy of the power of queens in medieval Castile. See Estow 1992.

26. For a discussion of this instability from an anthropological point of view, see Denich 1974 and Pitt-Rivers 1977. Both discuss the continual testing of the strengths and weaknesses of men through women's sexual behavior in Mediterranean communities. See also Foucault 1980—his model of power involves "a multiple and mobile field of force relations, wherein far-reaching, but never completely stable, effects of domination are produced" (102)—and Eagleton 1983, 73.

tion, is another prominent example of this type). Submissive women (e.g., Jimena, the dutiful wife in the epic *Cantar de mio Cid*) do not appear to threaten the social order. Authoritative men, however, are depicted in the texts as upholding the traditional hierarchy. It is their weaker counterparts—men like the nearly silent king in *Landarico*—who cause, through their inaction, social and political disaster.

Although *Landarico* fails to specify a punishment for the queen, stressing instead that criminals go free in the headless society that results from female acts of lawlessness, the final lines of the text ("aunque en su coraçon dentro / otra cosa le ha quedado" [though down deep in her heart / some other thing was lurking]) do appear to resolve the dominant-"other" struggle, refusing the queen the last word. These lines suggest that the text's powerful female protagonist can never publicly avow her act of authority. Rendering her speechless, the text would also appear to render her powerless. Thus the stereotyped image of the powerful Christian queen, like stereotyped images of Jews and Muslims, helped shore up male Christian Castilian authority. Collapsing female power with reckless and lascivious behavior, it appears to disqualify all women from exercising social or political control.

And yet, though the text manages to silence the queen, it fails to reach a coherent resolution; the queen's behavior is not explicitly punished. Since the text involves adultery, such punishment would entail bringing the queen's body, as well as her voice, under male control. This failure to physically punish the queen is curious because medieval Castilian law and doctrine were clear about the corporal consequences of female adultery. The seventh-century *Fuero Juzgo* (Code of Laws), for example, translated into Castilian during the thirteenth century on the order of Fernando III and given to Córdoba and other cities as municipal law,[27] stated that both the woman's husband and her father had the right to murder her with impunity (Book 2, Title 4, Law 9); the *Siete Partidas* (Seven codes of law), written in the thirteenth century and promulgated in the fourteenth,[28] which summarized Roman and canon law, empow-

---

27. See O'Callaghan 1975, 65.

28. Alfonso X's nephew, Don Juan Manuel, commented that the work "put into Romance all ecclesiastical as well as secular laws" (see Hillgarth 1976–78, 1:100–101 for discussion). The object of the work, as stated in its prologue, was to impose the *Siete Partidas* as the one and only body of laws in the kingdom (see MacKay 1977, 99, for further discussion). By the mid–fourteenth century, the *Partidas* was accepted as such, although the

ered the state to whip the unfaithful wife publicly or to place her in a convent [*Part.* 7, Title 18, Law 15][29]. In *Landarico,* neither the king nor any other male official avails himself of the prescribed punishments. Thus, while *Landarico* clearly cautions against female power, underscoring its disastrous consequences, it also reveals a certain instability and ambivalence when it comes to the fundamental question of how to deal effectively with powerful women.

Landarico's resolution is not, of course, a transparent reflection of the situation of real-life women in medieval Castile. But real women do indeed seem to be at the heart of the text's ambivalence, straining against the boundaries that delineated their participation in the dominant culture. Queens and other noblewomen did in fact have a role to play in the social and political arrangements of the society, and the ballad's ambivalent denouement opens the text up to contestations of feminine powerlessness from an audience that probably included such women.

Thus, though the text's masculinist discourse appears as part of a project to limit women's behavioral options, its ambivalent resolution ends up rehearsing the political and social possibilities for women who could, and did, occupy certain spaces within the medieval Castilian power structure. It is, in this context, interesting to note that as these spaces closed up toward the end of the reconquest period, the indecision that characterizes the medieval *Landarico*'s resolution disappears. Indeed, the

---

validity of urban *fueros* (statutes) and noble privileges was still recognized. Alfonso X, in dating his work by the Hegira as well as by the Christian era, spoke as ruler of all Muslims as well as of all Christians.

29. The preoccupation with women's sexual behavior within marriage manifested in the legal codes probably stemmed from the belief that the married woman, as the bearer of children, was the chief guardian of the family. The *Partidas,* e.g., gives this as the reason for marriage being called matrimony rather than patrimony (*Part.* 4, Title 2, Law 2; Sponsler 1982, 127). They give the same reason to justify strict control over the married woman's sexual behavior. Indeed, the *Partidas* recognized that a woman could become pregnant as a result of an extramarital affair. Thus, when the married woman committed adultery, the entire family structure was at stake. She could produce offspring who might compete with her husband's own legitimate heirs. She might even, in the worst possible scenario, seek to do away with her husband to remarry a lover, and then mistreat or kill her first husband's children (*Part.* 6, Title 6, Law 17).

Since female adultery raised the issues of paternity and inheritance in a way that male adultery did not, the law codes viewed the married woman, but not the married man, as a grave potential threat to the family structure. In medieval Castile, as elsewhere in medieval Europe, the family was a pillar of the established social order. On it rested most of the means for the distribution and conservation of wealth and property, and most of the mechanisms for determining social class, legal rights, and socioeconomic responsibilities.

ambivalent resolution of the text is almost completely absent in versions of the same story produced in later periods and in a now completely closed society. In these later versions, the queen is punished viciously and in no uncertain terms; she is usually beheaded.[30]

The fifteenth-century *Romance de Doña Blanca* tells the story of yet another powerful woman who brings social disorder. The following verses of one popular version of the text show how female adultery jeopardizes the family structure, producing illegitimate offspring and subsequent heirs whose royal and Catholic blood cannot easily be established:

> Entre la gente se dize
> y no por cosa sabida
> que del honrrado maestre
> don Fadrique de Castilla
> hermano del rey don Pedro   5
> que por nombre el Cruel hauía
> está la reyna preñada
> otros dizen que paría
> entre los unos secreto
> entre otros se publica   10
> no se sabe por más cierto
> de que el vulgo lo dezía
> . . . .
> allá le lleva a criar   55
> dentro del Andaluzía
> a un lugar muy nombrado
> quel arena se dezía
> A una ama le ha encargado
> hermosa es a marauilla,   60
> Paloma tiene por nombre
> según se dize por la villa
> hija es de un tornadizo
> y de una linda judía.[31]

---

30. See Bénichou 1968, 104; Benmayor 1979, 71–76.
31. My source for the text is the *Silva de Romances* [1550–51] 1970, 306–7. I have regularized some spelling to make the text more accessible to nonspecialists.

[Among the people it's said,
and not as something that's known,
that by the honored Master
Don Fadrique of Castile,
brother of King Don Pedro,
who goes by the name "the Cruel,"
the queen is pregnant;
others say that she gave birth.
Among some (it's) a secret;
among others it's publicized.
It is not known with greater certainty
than what the masses have said

. . . .

He was taken there to be brought up
deep within Andalusia,
to a very well known place,
Llerena it was called.
He has been given to a servant;
exceptionally beautiful is she.
Palmona is her name,
according to what people say—
the daughter of a convert
and of a beautiful Jewess.]

This and other, similar versions of the ballad—collectively termed here
Doña Blanca[32]—develop the theme of women's sexuality as the root of

---

32. I will refer in this chapter also to the version of the *romance* copied in Durán's
Romancero General (1945, 35–36) from a codex of the second half of the sixteenth century. The corresponding verses of this version read as follows:

　　Entre las gentes se suena,
　Y no por cosa sabida,
　Que d'ese buen Maestre
　Don Fadrique de Castilla
　La Reina estaba preñada;
　Otros dicen que parida.
　está la reina preñada
　No se sabe por de cierto;
　Mas el vulgo lo decía:
　Ellos piensan que es secreto,
　Ya esto no se escondía.

conflict and violence.[33] They tell of the putative pregnancy—and/or childbirth—of Queen Blanca de Borbón (1336–61). The event, the texts say, results from the queen's illicit affair with the king's half brother, Fadrique. Its consequences, which include the charge of impure (i.e., Jewish) ancestry against the presumed descendents of the pair,[34] overlay women's sexual behavior with Christian hegemonic ideals. But, in their particular focus on a queen, the texts also appear to bear out male concern for the social and sexual conformity of the more powerful women in society. In their targeting of an imagined wayward Blanca as the source of social, political, and sexual disorder, they suggest that queens, above all, must be kept subservient, their behavior rigidly controlled by men.

Indeed, in the ballad's depiction of the grave consequences of a queen's uncontrolled female sexuality—for example, fratricide, factions within the ruling classes, uncertain identity of offspring, and so on—is a rather unambiguous call for limitations on powerful wives' ability to act independently—an ability that appears to lead them to deviate from group sexual norms. This perhaps helps to account for the difference between the the queen's characterization in the ballad of *Doña Blanca*—as a powerful matron who speaks powerful language—and in other ballads that represent Blanca as an innocent young woman, her virginity stressed as part of her representation as a powerless young female put to death by a bloodthirsty and despotic husband:

[Among the people it's rumored,
and not as something that's known,
that by the good Master
Don Fadrique of Castile
the queen was pregnant;
others say she gave birth.
It is not known with certainty;
But the masses were saying it:
They think it is a secret,
but this can no longer be hidden.]

I have retained Durán's spelling and punctuation. See, for discussion, Menéndez y Pelayo 1916–24, 8:56–64.

33. This is a persistent theme in the *romancero*. Deyermond (1988) has touched on similar issues in the epic—particularly the relation between female sexuality and conflict.

34. The last three lines of *Entre las gentes se suena* introduce the admiralty of Blanca and Fadrique's child, conferred by King Enrique II: "Y como el rey don Enrique / Reinase luego en Castilla, / Tomara aquel infante / Y almirante lo hacia" [And as King Enrique reigned then in Castile, / that child was taken / and was made an admiral]. The text thus uses the story of Blanca's adultery to press a claim of royal and pure blood for the powerful Almirante de Castilla family. Menéndez y Pelayo discusses this (1916–24, 8:63).

¡Oh Castilla! ¿Qué te hice?
No por cierto traición.
¡Oh Francia, mi dulce tierra!
¡Oh mi casa de Borbón!
Hoy cumplo dieciséis años,
a los diecisiete muero yo.
El rey no me ha conocido,
con las vírgenes me vo.[35]

[Oh Castile! What did I do to you?
Certainly not treason.
Oh France, my sweet country!
Oh my house of Bourbon!
Today is my sixteenth birthday,
at seventeen I will die.
The king has never known me,
with the virgins go I.]

As a concomitant circumstance, the texts point to the indecisive or
weak man whose lack of such "ideal" masculine characteristics as sexual
assertiveness and aggressive behavior enabled women to cause social disorder (e.g., the king who abandons his wife on his wedding night [in
Entre las gentes se suena (Among the people it is rumored)] or who is
under the spell of another woman [*Entre la gente se dice* (Among the people it is said)][36]). It is, the texts show, only in the wake of ineffectual male
leadership in the home as well as the state (Blanca's husband is also king)
that Blanca finds herself free to carry on her affair with Fadrique:[37]

—Yo, desventurada Reina,
Más que cuantas son nacidas,   55
Casáronme con el Rey
Por la desventura mía.
De la noche de la boda
Nunca más visto lo había,

---

35. The source for these lines is Menéndez y Pelayo 1916–24, 8:134–35.
36. *Entre la gente se dice* goes on to talk about María de Padilla, the king's mistress,
making clear that he is in her sway. For discussion, see Cruz 1992.
37. In *Entre la gente se dice*, e.g., there is a lengthy digression that develops the theme
of Pedro's unkingly behavior.

Y su hermano el Maestre
Me ha tenido en compañía.   60

(Entre las gentes se suena)

[I, the luckless queen,
More than any ever born—
They married me to the king
By my misfortune.
From the night of our wedding
I never saw him again,
And his brother the master
Has kept me in his company.]

In the rejoinders of Queen Blanca is an abundance of powerful language features. Like the queen in *Landarico,* Blanca makes use of the command form when addressing her male interlocuter—here, Alonso Pérez, Fadrique's trusted secretary, a man not much farther down the social scale from Blanca. Indeed, Blanca's first words in this text are introduced by the declaration that she *commanded* the secretary to appear before her ("mandóle que viniese"). In the exchange that follows, Blanca repeatedly uses the imperative in her address to the secretary. She commands him to look at the child she thrusts in front of him (presumably the one she shares with Fadrique); to give the child away to be looked after (after the secretary admits the resemblance between the child and Fadrique); and to refrain from telling anyone about it:

Mira, mira, Alonso Perez,
el niño ¿a quién parecía?
. . . .
Pues daldo luego a criar
y a nadie esto se diga

(Entre las gentes se suena)

[Look, look, Alonso Pérez,
the child, whom does he resemble?
. . . .
So give him away to be cared for
and don't tell anyone about it.]

Because Blanca is a queen, it is tempting to privilege social class over gender in explaining women's powerful language. But, as in *Landarico*, sex and social class are linked. Blanca's story is, above all, a *woman*'s story; the problems associated with her extramarital affair and resultant pregnancy relate mainly to her womanhood, not her social status. (Her preoccupation, for example, is with reprisal from her husband—an expected consequence of adultery for medieval women of any station.) But Blanca's use of powerful language occurs specifically as a consequence of the political and social vacuum created by the absence of her husband, the king:

El rey don Pedro está lejos,
y de esto nada sabía.

(Entre la gente se dice)

[King Pedro is far away,
and knew nothing of this (the adultery and child).]

Blanca, like the queen in *Landarico,* is a noblewoman who wields enormous amounts of power. Also like the queen in *Landarico,* she uses her authority to deceive her husband. (She does not have the king killed, but she does demand that the evidence of her adultery be hidden so that he does not hear of it.) As in *Landarico,* too, the queen's power to command men is specifically linked to social disaster. The child she shares with Fadrique is sent off to be cared for by a Jewish woman, thus paving the way for accusations of impure blood against the noble family and for questions about property and inheritance rights.

It is interesting how this and other versions of the ballad of *Doña Blanca* specifically mimic the range of linguistic behaviors characteristic of gossip in their discourse. Gossip may be, as Roland Barthes put it (1977, 169), "murder by language." Hence these texts mark and censure their queen by meticulously avoiding any reference to specific, named persons as their sources. The texts use instead one of gossip's classic self-referential techniques: they begin with the phrases, "entre la gente se dice" [among the people it is said] and "entre las gentes se suena" [among the people it's rumored].[38]

---

38. I have discussed gossip and indirection as modes of representation in Mirrer 1995a.

Gossip is a powerful means of penalizing such improprieties as Queen Blanca's supposed extramarital affair. Indeed, the genre has often been seen to function as an informal device for social control, punishing those who deviate from group ideals and enforcing conformity to community norms through a collective, oral exchange of information.[39] That gossip may be particularly effective in controlling female behavior is apparent in the many examples of women, in anthropological and other literature, whose real or perceived sexual misconduct becomes a subject of gossip, which in turn virtually destroys their community standing. Gilmore's classic example of "Conchita," a young Andalusian woman whose plans for marriage are ruined by gossip that she is pregnant, is a case in point.[40]

In the ballad of *Doña Blanca,* Blanca, too, is a victim of verbal aggression. Her reputation for purity, much touted in other ballads and in written accounts of her behavior that stress her virginity and the fact that her marriage to King Pedro was never consummated,[41] is threatened—perhaps even destroyed—by the gossip conveyed in the opening lines of the texts.

Yet the oral hostility expressed in the report of Blanca's pregnancy and/or childbirth probably does not reflect any true sexual misconduct on the part of the real, historical Queen Blanca. There is no documentary evidence of her pregnancy, let alone childbirth. Moreover, the ballad texts were composed at too far a chronological remove from the events they describe to establish the truth of their accusation. Indeed, the texts appear to have targeted for their gossip a long-dead protagonist, for the ballad's point of reference relates to events that took place well after Blanca's lifetime.[42] All of this suggests that the deep determinants of the texts' discourse had little to do with the reality of their subject.

Why, then, did the composer of the ballad choose to deploy language acts associated with gossip in its opening lines?[43] One possible explana-

---

39. There have been many anthropological studies of gossip. Gluckman's (1963), which is considered seminal, was consulted here.

40. This gossip stemmed from Conchita's public display of sexuality—she was seen necking ("pelando la pelota" [skinning the turkey]) with her boyfriend. See Gilmore 1987, chap. 4, 53.

41. In Pero López de Ayala's *Crónica del rey don Pedro,* e.g., Blanca is a young virgin.

42. *Entre las gentes se suena,* e.g., specifically mentions Enrique II as ruler.

43. González (1984) has studied the importance of opening lines in the *romancero.* His work demonstrates that the openings of ballads may be of great significance to both meaning and textual transmission. It is thus of interest to note that the gossip mode is used at the beginning of the texts.

tion is that the ballad, at least in part, functions to evaluate for a projected female audience the behavior of women who step outside of their narrowly defined gender roles. This hypothesis could be supported by recent studies of the modern ballad tradition that call attention to its intimate association with women—as protagonists, transmitters, and, importantly, receptors of the texts (e.g., Anahory-Librowicz 1989, Catarella 1990, Barugel 1990).[44] The selection of gossip as a mode of representation in the ancient texts might relate to the expectation of female receptors for the ancient tradition as well. Thus, perhaps the works draw on gossip's crucial role in enforcing female social conformity. Gossip—above all a major locus of fear in that it entails the constant monitoring of individuals' actions[45]—might be a useful linguistic resource in cautioning women against engaging in such prohibited sexual behaviors as Blanca's extramarital affair.

Indeed, the texts do appear to insist on female social and sexual conformity. For example, they deliberately highlight Blanca's responsibility for her sexual misconduct and its consequences: "Si esto ha pasado, / Toda la culpa era mía" [If this has happened / All of the fault was mine] (*Entre las gentes se suena*). The ballad's reliance on gossip to caution women against engaging in prohibited sexual behaviors may also illuminate the otherwise puzzling laudatory epithets attached, in all of the ballad's versions, to Fadrique's name (e.g., "buen" [good], "honrado" [honored]). Though, objectively, the man and woman were equal partners in the affair, the texts make it clear that the scandal belongs, in particular, to Blanca. Blanca is in fact reported confirming this, declaring, in *Entre las gentes se suena,* that she, more than Fadrique, will be punished: "Si el rey don Pedro lo sabe, / De ambos se vengaría; / Mucho mas de mí, la Reina / Por la mala suerte mía" [If the king, don Pedro, finds out, he will take revenge on both of us; / Much more on me, the queen / By my bad luck]. Again, Blanca, the chief target of the texts' gossip, effectively carries the burden of responsibility for the social, political, and sexual disorder the ballad goes on to describe.[46] Thus the ballad, in introducing gossip about the now-dead Blanca, draws attention to the continual reappraisal of women's behavior for the benefit of female receptors—demonstrating to them that the revelations might be endless. It also

44. These studies have examined the modern oral tradition in particular, yet they may in a number of respects also be applicable to the *romancero viejo* (ancient ballad).

45. See Black's discussion (1985, 281) of gossip in Tobian folk psychology.

46. See Girard 1972 for discussion of this theme.

shores up male Christian Castilian control, playing on the theme that the instability of male-female relations may generate, in the absence of strong men, women capable of wreaking havoc in society.[47]

Yet, as in the ballad of *Landarico*, an ambivalent and unstable denouement threatens to subvert the various strategies used in the text to argue—particularly in the context of a female audience—for the limitation of women's access to the discourses of power. Failing to specify a punishment for its female protagonist's adultery and subsequent "cover-up," the ballad of *Doña Blanca*, like *Landarico*, provides no coherent solution to the "problem" of powerful women.

---

47. For studies related to this theme, see Pitt-Rivers 1977 and Denich 1974.

6

The Virgin and the Abbess: Gonzalo de Berceo's *Milagros de Nuestra Señora*

> Where Islam dignifies women by shrouding them in veils, Christianity
> removes the veil and offers the Virgin Mary as a model of feminine virtue.
> —Jane Schneider, "Of Vigilance and Virgins"

Gonzalo de Berceo's thirteenth-century *Milagros de Nuestra Señora*
(Miracles of Our Lady; c. 1225) also exposes the danger powerful
women pose to male-dominated society when allowed access to the discourses of power. But, unlike the ballads of *Landarico* and *Doña Blanca*,
Berceo's text provides a coherent strategy for dealing with powerful
women. This strategy, which relates specifically to the realm of religion,
involves nuancing the link between female power and social and political
disorder with an explicit recognition of the "humane" and maternal
aspects of the feminine. The Virgin becomes an object with whom powerful women may identify, but whose status they may never achieve.

The *Milagros de Nuestra Señora* collects some twenty-five brief tales,
each of which rehearses a miracle effected through the intercession of the
Virgin Mary. While almost all of the text's miracles depend on sources
well known in the Middle Ages,[1] there are a number of departures of
style and content that place them specifically in the Castilian context.
Azam (1983, 11) even detects a "utilitarian" aspect of the work, which
he claims results from the fact that "le souvenir de Las Navas de Tolosa
est encore dans toutes les mémoires et la Castille vient à peine de conjurer
le péril islamique" [the memory of (the battle of) Las Navas de Tolosa is
still in everyone's consciousness and Castile has just scarcely emerged
from containing the Islamic peril].

---

1. See Berceo 1967, Introduction, for discussion.

One of the most interesting of the *Milagros*'s departures in the Castilian context is precisely its development of a powerful female image. To this end, the Virgin Mary, the main protagonist of all of the miracles, is depicted as "humane" but also aggressive and authoritative[2]—a portrayal that bears scant resemblance to her passive, obedient, and dependent doctrinal image. This portrayal is somewhat surprising because Berceo, the work's author, was a priest.

To emphasize her authority, Berceo repeatedly attributes to the Virgin such linguistic strategies as commands, threats, and pejorative expressions. She is in particular made to favor speech acts entailing either a conditional (*si-*) clause, followed by a clause in the future tense (with the verb either in the future or in the present but used as a future) spelling out the negative consequences of disobeying her—for example, "del mal si non te guardas, / caerás en peor" [if you don't keep yourself from evil you will find yourself in something worse] (line 261d)—or a future tense clause used alone to function as a reinforcement of her threats—for example, "¡desend verás qé vale / la sanna de María" [in this way you will see how much María's (the Virgin's) fury is worth!] line 231d).

That the Virgin holds authority in her own right is also stressed in the *Milagros*. God, almost as an afterthought and apparently without much will of his own, often acts simply to approve her decrees. This is the case in the miracle of *El Romero engañado por el diablo* (The Pilgrim deceived by the Devil). There the Virgin commands:

> . . . "Yo esto mando   e dólo por sentencia:
> la alma sobre quien   avedes la entencia,
> qe torne en el cuerpo,   faga su penitencia.
>
> (stanza 208)

> [. . . I command this   and give it as a judgment
> that the soul over which   you had a dispute
> should return to its body,   (and) should repent.]

And God rubber stamps her command:

> Valió esta sentencia,   fue de Dios otorgada.
>
> (stanza 209)

---

2. For two interesting discussions of the Virgin's power in Berceo, see Ackerman 1983 and Finke 1978.

[This judgment prevailed;   it was authorized by God.]

God's authority is sometimes even ceded to the Virgin to the extent that there is no mention at all of His intervention. In the miracle of *El pobre caritativo* (The charitable poor man), for instance, the Holy Mother acts completely of her own accord:[3]

Yo so aquí venida   por levarte comigo,
al regno de mi Fijo   qe es bien tu amigo.

(stanza 137)

[I have come here   to take you with me
to the kingdom of my Son,   who is truly your friend.]

In the light of the Virgin's power, male authority appears weakened. Moreover, female authority, embodied in the image of a "humane" Virgin, seems not to be subject to the severity of either man's or God's law. This is strikingly demonstrated in the miracle of *El ladrón devoto* (The faithful robber). Here the Virgin intercedes to save the life of an evil robber (ladrón malo) who prefers stealing to churchgoing ("qe más querié furtar   qe ir a la eglesia," lines 142a–b) but nevertheless believes in the Virgin with all his will ("credié en la Gloriosa   de toda voluntat," line 144c). When the thief is caught by the legal authorities and sentenced to die, the Virgin comes forward on his behalf. She places her hands under the criminal's feet to support him as he hangs, and he survives. When a different punishment, beheading, is attempted (line 155a), the Virgin again intervenes. At this point, her role on the thief's behalf is recognized, and he is set free; no one dares to oppose the Virgin's will ("ellos non querién ir   contra sancta María," line 157b).

While Berceo notes, in the text's resolution, that the faithful robber thereafter parts from his evil ways,[4] there is never any suggestion in the miracle that the man was wrongly accused or that his accusers were wrong to punish him. Moreover, the text makes it clear that the thief was tried in the appropriate legal manner, stressing that, because he was caught red-handed, he could present no defense against the charges:

---

3. See Azam 1983, 14–15.
4. He omits, however, the detail from his Latin model that the robber became a priest (Berceo 1967, 74).

oviéronlo con furto   est ladrón a prender;
non ovo nul consejo   con qé se defender.

(lines 146b–c)

[They had arrested this robber   with stolen goods;
he had no means at all   with which to defend himself.]

Berceo even subtly suggests that the thief may have committed crimes other than theft ("Si facié otros males,   esto no lo leemos, serié mal condempnarlo   por lo que non savemos" [If he committed other crimes,   this we do not read about   and it would be wrong to condemn him for things we know not of], lines 143a–b). In this way, Berceo underscores the man's evil ways and his guilt.

Thus, when the Virgin intervenes to save the thief's life, she does so in the face of legitimate punishment, playing havoc with men's laws and upsetting the official structures explicitly designed to guarantee social order (e.g., the safeguarding of individual property rights). Indeed, the Virgin also appears to flout Christian law in her intervention, for the sinner never repents of his crimes, and hence he ignores the appropriate doctrinal avenues for salvation.

Berceo's representation of feminine power as magisterial and not subject to either men's or God's law goes against the social and symbolic order of the Church. Moreover, the text fails to explain why the Holy Mother had to achieve her results independent of the law, seeing to it that a guilty man (a seasoned criminal, no less) goes unpunished for his crimes. While the criminal's reformed behavior might in the end appear to justify the Virgin's "humanity," in granting the Virgin the power to effect the stay of an execution justified legally and morally (in the medieval world), Berceo's miracle overlays the customary maternal image of the Virgin—which normally endowed her with such powers as comforting, nursing, and succoring—with a more political image traditionally associated with kings, queens, and nobles.

Indeed, the Virgin's imaginary political role suffuses the entire work;[5] her authority ranges, for example, from the precincts of criminal law (she grants clemency to a confirmed thief) to those of race relations (she instigates a full-fledged pogrom against Spanish Jews in the miracle of *Cristo*

---

5. Ackerman (1983, 23) notes that the Virgin's capacity for independent action is implied from the very start of the work in the self-regenerating nature of the field Berceo describes and in his explanation of the image of streams.

y los judíos de Toledo [The Miracle of Christ and the Jews of Toledo]) to those of marriage and the family (she obstructs an arranged marriage designed to ensure the lineage and property rights of a wealthy Italian family in the miracle of *La boda y la Virgen* [The wedding and the Virgin]).[6]

The *Milagros*'s depiction of the Virgin as a politically powerful woman who interferes with men's laws appears to result from Berceo's assimilation of her image to that of the more powerful Christian matrons of the medieval world discussed in previous chapters of this study. Indeed, the Virgin is repeatedly called "Queen" [reina] in the work and endowed with the attributes and symbols of nobility. Like these women, too, her access to the discourses of power is linked to lawlessness, and her authority, represented chiefly in the context of weakening male domination, is characterized by a frightening excess. Her behavior, like that of the queens depicted in the ballads of *Landarico* and *Doña Blanca*, overturns customary hierarchical relations between the sexes. Here, then, would be another link between dominant-"other" struggle and images of powerful Christian women in medieval literature.

Berceo's *Milagros* depicts a woman who assumes authority not only in the realm of politics but in that of religion as well. The Virgin is, for example, coredemptrice—a characterization firmly established by Berceo's striking declaration, in the miracle of *El ladrón devoto*, that she is Christ's partner as well as mother:[7]

---

6. The miracle of *Cristo y los judíos de Toledo* (18) shows how the Holy Mother steps in to resolve one of medieval Castile's most troubling political issues—i.e., the status of Jews in Christian society—instigating a rather violent solution. In the miracle of *La boda y la Virgen,* the Holy Mother participates fully in the political arena, engaging secular law ("la ley del sieglo," line 335b) as she tampers with marriage arrangements specifically designed to ensure the maintenance of family wealth, property, and lineage (she obstructs the financially advantageous wedding of a young man who had earlier "promised" himself to her).

7. This attribution and others like it found throughout the *Milagros* have led Saugnieux (1977) and others to find an explanation for Berceo's image of an independent, powerful Virgin in the influence of seventh- and eighth-century Spanish liturgy, particularly the thought of Saint Ildefonse,

C'est parce qu'il accepte implicitement le principe de la corédemption que Berceo attribue au rôle d'intercesseur de la Vierge la même importance qu'au rôle rédempteur du Christ. Pour lui il n'y a aucune différence entre l'action du Fils et celle de la Mère. (Saugnieux 1977, 38)

Las mannas de la Madre   con las d'El qe parió
semejan bien calannas   qui bien las connoció;
Él por bonos e malos,   por todos descendió,
Ella, si la rogaron,   a todos acorrió.

(stanza 159)

[The ways of the Mother   along with those of Him to whom she
  gave birth
surely conform to each other,   like natures that know each other
  well;
He, for both good and evil ones,   descended on behalf of all of
  them;
She, if they prayed to her,   succored everyone.]

This aspect of the Virgin's image suggests a further explanation for her unusual depiction. As in the ballads discussed earlier, the text may have anticipated an audience that included women, and its distinctive symbolic world may have been motivated at least in part by a concern about medieval society's more powerful females.

Dutton, in his introduction to the *Milagros* (Berceo 1967) and, more recently, Gerli (1992), argue that Berceo's own historical context is responsible for the work's imagery. They suggest that the *Milagros*'s language and images specifically interfaced with pilgrims on their way to Santiago de Compostela, to whom the text would have been read aloud during the journey. Dutton and Gerli propose that Berceo may have used the *Milagros* to draw pilgrims' attention to the Virgin's shrine at his own, economically depressed monastery at nearby San Millán.

It is well known that many women numbered among the visitors to Santiago during the Middle Ages. González Vázquez (1989), for example, cites a number of queens, noblewomen, and female religious whose pilgrimages to Santiago are documented in medieval records. These women include Violante of Aragon (Alfonso X's wife), who visited San-

---

[It is because he implicitly accepts the principle of coredemption that Berceo attributes to the Virgin's role as intercessor the same importance as to Christ's role as redeemer. For him there is no difference between the actions of the Son and those of the Mother.]

I argue, however, that it is more likely, as Dutton, in his introduction to Berceo's *Milagros* (Berceo 1967), and, more recently, Gerli 1992 have suggested, that Berceo's own historical context was responsible for the work's imagery.

tiago in 1260; Saint Pauline, who visited in 1112; and Queen Isabel, who visited in 1450. Women pilgrims also figured among the wealthy and important donors to Santiago in the Middle Ages: gifts of gold, silver, and rich fabrics were presented by such queens as Elvira (in 911), Urraca (in 1117), Catalina (in 1386), Isabel, and others.[8] Indeed, numerous medieval Castilian documents provide evidence of the complex ways in which women were centrally involved, either as donors or as relatives of donors, in the transfer of goods and property to monastic communities.[9] For these reasons, Berceo may have sought to attract women, along with men, through his text. Indeed he may have used the text's imagery specifically to appeal to women, who could imaginarily identify with—but of course never achieve—the powerful female image he offered.[10]

Berceo, whose significance in the domains of religion and society has now been fully recognized, may also have used the text's imagery to address contemporary female behavior, seeking to calm social anxiety during a period characterized by increased social tension between the sexes, particularly in the context of the monastery. As Gold points out (1987, 76), the monastery was one of the key spaces in which medieval women had demonstrated some potential for achieving autonomy. But within the monasteries, women still had to rely on priests, necessarily male, to perform the sacraments and to provide other services that were seen as inappropriate to women in the Middle Ages, including physical labor, business, and travel arrangements. Precisely in the twelfth and thirteenth centuries, medieval monasticism, itself recognizing women's potential for independence, attempted to manipulate the prevailing ideology of female weakness to allow male supervision to undercut nuns' autonomy.[11]

---

8. See González Vázquez 1989, 26–29.

9. There is evidence of high-level support for female monasteries in Castile and for female religious life, with documents from kings, such as Fernando IV, e.g., arranging for the financial underpinnings of the convents of San Bernardo and Santa Clara. See Layna Serrano 1943 for discussion.

10. See Kristeva 1985, 139.

11. As Gold points out (1987, 77) the very term *cura monialium* (the care of nuns) underscores the gender imbalance in medieval monasticism, with nuns seen as in need of the care of men, but with monks capable of a life independent of women. But see Surtz (1994, 2) who notes that, despite Innocent II's papal bull prohibiting women's episcopal jurisdiction (1200), the abbess of the Cistercian convent of Las Huelgas continued to enjoy quasi-episcopal jurisdiction over the towns and churches subject to her monastery until 1874.

Berceo's image of a powerful but "humane" (and maternal), female
with which women could imaginarily identify may have been designed to
establish a measure of equilibrium between the sexes, particularly within
the monastery.[12] His representation of medieval society's real-life virgins,
found in one of the only two miracles in the work to deal with women as
the Virgin's supplicants, is a case in point.[13]

Much of Berceo's version of the miracle of *La abadesa preñada* (The
pregnant abbess) turns on the reversal of gender imbalance. That the miracle's reversal of gender imbalance takes place precisely within the spaces
of the convent is significant. The miracle tells of an abbess's despair on
finding herself pregnant as a result of *una locura* (an act of madness) and,
consequently, threatened with expulsion from her convent. Prayers to the
Virgin bring relief in the form of a painless childbirth and the spiriting
away of the woman's newborn son. Because the abbess's pregnancy and
childbirth miraculously leave no physical trace, she is also saved from
punishment by the supervising bishop who, invited to the convent by
jealous nuns, examines her. The abbess's son, brought up in his early
years by a hermit, becomes a priest himself, eventually succeeding the
supervising bishop.

One of the most striking features of the miracle of the pregnant abbess
is the sisterly rapport—and perhaps even female conspiracy—between
the Virgin and the abbess. Boreland (1983, 23–26), for example, notes
the many significant parallels between the two women in the text, suggesting that the abbess may have been portrayed by Berceo (consciously
or not) in the light of Mary. (The abbess, for instance, recalls the Virgin's
depiction at the Annunciation and Nativity in that she prays alone in her
private chapel, is fearful and needs reassurance, gives birth painlessly and
without a trace of having been pregnant, and bears a son who becomes a
leader of his people.)

Beyond typological connections between the two women is the further
bond of absolute female authority. The abbess, for example, is head of
her convent and hence most advantageously positioned to enjoy any
measure of independence or power available to women in the medieval
female monastery. Further, the Virgin's miraculous intervention renders

---

12. Kristeva (1985, 139) suggests this in her analysis of the Virgin's image as far back
as the sixth century.
13. The other miracle is *La preñada salvada por la Virgen* (The pregnant woman saved
by the Virgin).

her, like her protectress, immune from the severity of men's laws. Finally, the text shows that the abbess, too, is capable of overturning customary hierarchical relations between the sexes.

The text's initial dialogue between the bishop and the abbess gives evidence at the start that the bishop believes in his superiority and his right of oversight in the realm of the convent:

> Empezóla el bispo   luego a increpar
> qe avié fecha cosa   por qe devié lazrar,
> e non devié por nada   abadessa estar,
> nin entre otras monjas   non devié abitar:
>
> "Toda monja qe face   tan grand desonestat,
> qe non guarda so cuerpo   nin tiene castidat,
> devié seer echada   de la socïedat,
> allá por do quisiere   faga tal suciedat."
>
> (stanzas 548–49)

> [The bishop began   then to scold her
> that she had done something   for which she should be punished,
> and that she should not for anything   be an abbess,
> nor should she with other nuns   live
>
> "Every nun who commits   such a great dishonesty,
> who doesn't watch over her body   nor maintain her chastity,
> should be thrown out   of her convent,
> out there wherever she wants   she can do such dirty things."]

When the bishop fails to uncover any wrongdoing on the part of the abbess, he admonishes the nuns who had invited him to examine their superior. This discourse further underscores the bishop's assumed (male) right of oversight in the convent:

> Tornóse al conviento,   bravo e muy fellón,
> "Duennas—disso—fiziestes   una grand traïción;
> pussiestes la sennora   en tan mala razón
> qe es muy despreciada   vuestra relïgión.
>
> Esta cosa non puede   sin justicia passar,
> la culpa qe quissiestes   vos a ella echar,

el Decreto lo manda,   en vos deve tornar,
qe devedes seer   echadas d'est logar."

(stanzas 561–62)

[He turned to the nuns,   angry and outraged,
"Ladies, he said, you have committed   a great treachery;
you have the lady   so wrongly incriminated
that disgraced is   your religion.

This thing cannot be allowed   to pass without justice being done
The guilt that you have wished   to throw on her
The Decree commands that   it come back to you,
you should be thrown out   of this place."]

But the text actually works to examine and, eventually, undermine the bishop's right of oversight—if only temporarily. First, the miracle discloses the greater "humanity" of the feminine, focusing on the sharp contrast between male and female discourses. The bishop's stern accusations against the abbess, for example, are explicitly distinguished from the Virgin's words of comfort to her:

Non ayades nul miedo   de caer en porfazo,
bien vos ha Dios guardada   de caer en ess lazo,
. . . .
non lazrará por esso   el vuestro espinazo."

(stanza 532)

[Do not have any fear   of falling into disgrace
well has God kept you   from falling in this trap.
. . . .
For this reason you will not be hurt   by your thorn.]

Similarly, his tirade against the accusing nuns is distinguished from the abbess's defense of her accusers:

"Sennor—disso—las duennas   non son mucho culpadas."

(line 563d)

["Sir," she said, "the ladies   are not very much to blame."]

Second, the text makes it clear that the feminine—mostly confined, for Berceo, within the limits of the maternal[14]—is inaccessible to men's oversight, specifically showing how the Virgin shields the abbess' maternal condition from the bishop's gaze. And finally, the text metaphorically represents the consequences of the feminine's triumph, depicting the once dominant bishop as humble, "unmanly," and submissive as a result of the Virgin's intervention:

Espantóse el bispo,   fo todo demudado,
disso: "Duenna, si esto   puede seer provado,
veré don Jesu Christo   qe es vuestro pagado,
yo mientre fuero vivo   faré vuestro mandado."

        (stanza 567)

[The bishop became frightened,   he was completely changed;
he said: "Lady, if this   can be proved,
I will see that Lord Jesus Christ   is your protector,
and as long as I live   I will do as you bid."]

Tovóse enna duenna   el bispo por errado,
cadióli a los piedes   en el suelo postrado,
"Duenna—disso—mercet,   ca mucho so errado,
ruégovos que me sea   el yerro perdonado."

        (stanza 571)

[The bishop took himself   to be in error with the lady;
he fell at her feet   prostrate on the floor,
"Lady," he said, "mercy,   because I am very much in error;
I beg that you   forgive me my error."]

Berceo's representation of the Virgin as specifically interfering in a bishop's performance of an abbess's spiritual oversight may be linked to thirteenth-century ambivalence toward nuns' status. In fact, the Virgin's actions appear deliberately subversive of key medieval practices designed to reinforce nuns' dependence on male supervision (e.g., punishing way-

14. See Kristeva 1985, 133. Note also that the second of the only two miracles to deal with women in the *Milagros* also focuses on the maternal, describing a pregnant (probably unmarried) woman whom the Virgin saves from drowning. In this miracle, too, the woman gives birth painlessly.

ward nuns). In this manner, the miracle provides a fantasy resolution to nuns' quest for autonomy, offering at least imaginary relief from the contradictions of female religious life.

Yet the text does not end with this fantasy of absolute female authority in the medieval monastery. The abbess is ultimately made to acknowledge her subservience and, indeed, is last heard from encouraging the bishop to resume his oversight:

> "Sennor—disso la duenna—   por Dios e la Gloriosa,
> catat vuestra mesura,   non fagades tal cosa.
> Vos sodes omne sancto,   yo peccadriz doliosa.
> si en ál non tornades   seré de vos sannosa."
>
> (stanza 572)

> ["Sir," the lady said,   "for God and the Glorious Virgin,
> Look to your dignity;   don't do such a thing.
> You are a holy man;   I am an unhappy sinner.
> If you don't return to your senses,   I will be angry with you."]

This the bishop willingly does, and the topsy-turvy world that characterizes much of the miracle is brought to a close:

> Metió paz el obispo   enna congregación
> amató la contienda   e la dissensïón,
> quand quiso despedirse,   diólis su bendición
> fo bona pora todos   essa visitación.
>
> (stanza 574)

> [The bishop brought peace   to the congregation;
> he wiped out dispute   and dissent.
> When he decided to leave,   he gave them his blessing;
> for everyone   this visit was good.]

Thus the "humanity" of the feminine, embodied in the images of the Virgin and the abbess, may have offered women an important role. But the balance between the sexes that is ultimately struck affirms "normal" hierarchical relations between men and women. Order, at least in the medieval sense, appears restored.

And yet the abbess's conception, like the Virgin's, results in the birth

of a good man and thus demonstrates women's importance to both religious and secular society. Moreover, the miracle's image of a lasting
friendship (but not, of course, equality) between the abbess and the
bishop, achieved through the abbess's initiative, concedes to women a
limited authority:

> La duenna con el bispo   avié esta entencia,
> mas fináronlo todo   en buena abenencia.
> Jamás ovieron ambos   amor e bienquerencia,
> encerraron su vida   en buena paçïencia
>
> (stanza 573)

> [The lady with the bishop   had this dispute,
> but everything ended   in good will.
> Nevermore did they have anything but   love and mutual admira-
>   tion;
> they enclosed their lives   in good virtue]

The text thus reviews for its audience both the possibilities for feminine
contestations of powerlessness and the limits and constraints to those
challenges.

7

The Widow and the Text: Ambivalent Signs in the *Libro de Buen Amor*

The fourteenth-century *Libro de Buen Amor* (Book of Good Love), composed by Juan Ruiz, Archpriest of Hita,[1] is perhaps the richest of reconquest Castilian literary texts in terms of evidence of both the many possibilities for contestation of feminine powerlessness and the limits and constraints to those challenges. The *Libro de Buen Amor*'s multivalent structure (which includes an autobiographical framestory; didactic contemplations on law, doctrine, music, and literature; and popular tales and lyric poems) and the pluralism of its implied audience[2] indeed project, at nearly every juncture, struggle—on intellectual as well as military planes—between dominant and "other" groups.

One of the book's best-known episodes (stanzas 1067–1224), for example, stages an allegorical Lenten battle for dominion between a male and female Christian—Don Carnal (Sir Carnal) and Doña Cuaresma (Lady Lent). The contest gets underway as Cuaresma steals into Carnal's camp while he and his supporters sleep off a hearty night of feasting. Cuaresma succeeds in routing Carnal's forces, taking Carnal himself as a prisoner. When Carnal eventually manages to escape captivity, he takes

---

1. There is a lengthy bibliography on this work, much of which goes beyond the scope of this study. For a general overview of some important criticism, see Deyermond 1987b and Brownlee 1985. There is also an intense debate regarding establishment of authorship for the text and its manuscript tradition. Concise summaries of some of the problems are found in Zahareas 1989 and Pereira Zazo and Zahareas 1994. A new perspective is found in Dagenais 1994.

2. Brownlee (1985, 12) describes the text's "reader-oriented perspective" and comments: "Juan Ruiz constructs an intentionally polysemous text whereby he repeatedly calls upon his audience to engage in interpretive reading."

Some modern critics have proposed that the work be seen as part of a Hispano-Hebraic literary genre and have argued that the technique of allegorical exegesis used to establish the work's didactic purpose draws on approaches to Scripture common to Christians, Jews, and Muslims alike. See Lida de Malkiel 1961, 30. For a recent study of the text's didactic purpose, see Dagenais 1994.

refuge in the Jewish ghetto, riding to challenge his female rival on a horse furnished by a rabbi. The battle between male and female Christians thus involves "others" centrally. At the close of the episode, Cuaresma, ultimately defeated, takes cowardly flight to Jerusalem.

In another episode (stanzas 1508–12), the *Libro* represents an assertive *mora* (female Muslim) whom the text's author/protagonist fails to snare. Depicted almost exclusively through her refusal of her suitor's attentions, the *mora* pronounces in her own language four increasingly decisive rebuffs: "Iznedrí" [I don't know], "Legualá" [No, by Allah], "Ascut" [Be quiet], and "Amxí" [Go away].

The *Libro* alludes throughout to similarly diverse relations between dominant and "other" groups. Indeed, the text's longest episode—the Doña Endrina episode—depicts a widow, one of reconquest Castile's most powerful women. Though the text specifically proclaims as its literary model the twelfth-century Latin elegiac drama *Pamphilus,* its replacement of that work's virginal and unmarried female protagonist with a widow self-consciously advances the theme of subordinates as neither monolithic nor passive.

The most extensive of some thirteen amorous adventures narrated in the work, the Doña Endrina episode describes an economically secure young woman, Doña Endrina (Lady Sloe), whose husband has recently died. Endrina is pursued by a socially inferior suitor, the book's author/protagonist, Juan Ruiz (also called Don Melón de la Huerta [Sir Mellon of the Garden]).[3] The widow at first resists her suitor's entreaties, but then she softens her stand and eventually agrees to speak with him. Later, she is cajoled by a go-between, Trotaconventos, whom the suitor has engaged as part of his effort to win her favor. Trotaconventos ultimately succeeds in persuading the widow to visit her shop, where the suitor awaits her. The go-between then leaves the couple alone. A lacuna in the text renders ambiguous what transpires in her absence, but when the text resumes, the widow is in tears. Her desperation, the intense anger she directs toward the go-between, whom she accuses of treachery, and the go-between's advice to the widow to marry her suitor (which she does, to the delight of the couple's wedding guests) suggests rather strongly that Endrina has been raped. This conclusion indeed corresponds to a fable, presented allegorically at the close of the episode, in

---

3. For an interesting discussion of the archpriest/Melón character, see Walsh 1979–80.

which a lion violates the body of an ass, ripping it open. The ass, who had been deceived by the lion's messenger, appears as a stand-in for Doña Endrina, who has been tricked by the deceitful cajoling of her suitor's go-between.

The episode's focus on the widow reveals a female voice capable, to a degree, of resisting the dominant discourses of male control. Like the ambivalent attitudes toward widowhood found in much medieval European law, literature, and doctrine, this representation shows the widow to be independent but also needful of supervision. Regarded, on the one hand, as a stage in a woman's life that endowed her with the potential for a special grace (freed from carnal cares, widows could devote themselves to God in a way they could not as married women), widowhood was, on the other hand, seen to free women to act on the wanton, whorish, and unprincipled tendencies ascribed to women in general by medieval misogynist writers. Widows could thus be seen as courageous examples, carrying on the work of husbands, rearing children against odds, and discretely pursuing correct political ends—and, as vulnerable women, needing and deserving the special protection of the church and knights. Yet they were also portrayed as enjoying liberation from male control to a frightening excess, squandering their husbands' fortune and their sons' inheritance when left to their own devices in the marketplace. Literary examples offered graphic depictions of what the widow would do—cut the head, break the teeth, even castrate the body of her dead husband—if she believed she could satisfy in this way her uncontrollable lust.[4] Widows' remarriage, of uncertain status according to law and doctrine, was a pivotal site of ambivalent attitudes toward widowhood during the Middle Ages. Widows were by law generally free to remarry, but they had to wait one year before doing so and might be subject to numerous property restrictions. While the church generally discouraged widows from remarrying—chaste widows could almost approach virgins in holy status—it did not prohibit it. Young and beautiful widows were perceived as a snare for the devil, and for these women remarriage was preferable.[5]

---

4. For detailed discussions of this topic, see Arden 1992 and Vasvari 1992.

5. I have adapted these general remarks on widowhood in medieval Europe from my introduction to *Upon My Husband's Death: Widows in the Literature and Histories of Medieval Europe.* See Mirrer 1992.

In reconquest Castile, widows were, like queens and abbesses, capable of wielding limited power.[6] By law, they were provided with a large number of capacities in which they could act on their own, including the right to assume administrative control over family property and the right to choose their own partner, should they decide to remarry (*Part.* 4, Title 13, Law 3; *Fuero Real* 1.b 3, Title 1, Law 4). As much as the law codes encouraged the widow's independence after the death of her husband, however, they warned against certain behaviors considered inappropriate, punishing them severely. There were laws, for example, governing the establishment of paternity for children born after a first husband's death (*Part.* 4, Title 23, Law 4; *Part.* 6, Title 16, Law 5)[7] and laws requiring a waiting period of one year before a widow's remarriage (*Part.* 4, Title 12, Law 3). When a woman broke these laws, she lost the rights granted her as a widow and faced punitive fines, including the forfeiture of the deceased husband's wedding gift to her (*Part.* 4, Title 12, Law 3). The municipal ordinances of the time also imposed punitive fines when the widow disregarded the one-year restriction on her remarriage (Dillard 1984, 98).

Even when a widow obeyed the laws governing her behavior, there were pitfalls. In Sepúlveda, for example, if a widow went to live with a

---

6. While in medieval Castile, as elsewhere in medieval Europe, widows' access to power, prestige, and authority in the public domain nearly always fell short of direct participation in the workings of politics and the holding of public office, at least two Castilian widows did in fact approach the pinnacle of medieval society's power structures. These were the widowed queens María de Portugal (queen of Castile from 1328 to 1356) and Catalina of Lancaster (queen of Castile from 1390 to 1406). Both of these women enjoyed sanctioned authority in the public sphere for a time, exercising royal power and assuming personae independent from their husbands. Yet neither woman receives much praise from male chroniclers of the period—perhaps as a consequence of these men's unease with women rulers in an essentially patrilineal society.

María de Portugal was the wife of King Alfonso XI. During her husband's lifetime, she wielded little power in her own right. After his death, however, she played a central role in the running of Castilian affairs. Evidence of María's power is found, e.g., in the match she engineered between her son, Pedro I of Castile, and Blanca de Borbón. This match, though problematic on a personal level, achieved an important alliance between Castile and France.

Catalina of Lancaster was the wife of Enrique III of Castile. When Enrique died in 1406, he left a will that stipulated that Catalina and the king's brother, Fernando, share the leadership of the kingdom as coregents. When Catalina later refused to give up custody of her minor child, the future king, Juan II, her right to rule on his behalf—and hence her authority in the kingdom—was firmly established. For discussion, see Estow 1992.

7. The *Siete Partidas* dealt with this concern by outlining a complex series of steps to be taken in the case of a pregnant widow They also put forth a number of laws designed to prevent a widow's mistreatment of her first husband's children—or indeed her consent to their deaths—to please a new husband (Sponsler 1982, 148; *Part.* 6, Title 16, Law 5).

relative or remarried, she immediately lost the independence she had gained through widowhood. She was made to seek the consent of the relative with whom she lived; she lost usufruct of her first husband's *raíz* (family property subject to inheritance by lineage); and, if she remarried, her new husband, while not acquiring any additional property through the marriage, was given the right to manage her property (Dillard 1976, 84).

In remarriage, medieval Castilian widows who chose men of a lower social standing than that of their first husbands had the most to lose; a woman's status followed that of her spouse. Widows of caballeros, for instance, lost their special honors and tax exemptions when they remarried outside the restricted caballero class (Dillard 1984, 124). This ruling perhaps responded to medieval society's abhorrence of misalliance and to medieval legislators' fear that the widow's independence would lead her to the altar with a social inferior. There was in fact, in medieval society, a long-standing tradition of status-conscious interventions in all marriages—an effort to avoid the possible social catastrophe of misalliance.[8] But the widow, whose position of independence was considered to make her especially attractive to suitors, was, above all, a target for such measures.[9]

While the *Libro*'s Doña Endrina episode is not a social document (critics in fact differ widely on the question of whether the episode draws principally on literary and oral traditions depicting widowhood[10] or principally embodies its author's knowledge of actual practices relating to widows in the Middle Ages), there can be no mistaking the influence on it of the socially and legally constructed figure of the widow. A convenient surrogate for the book's underlying theme of ambivalence, the widow's voice and body figure in the text both as part of its more general reflection on the ambiguity of signs and also as part of a strategy—as in Berceo's *Milagros*—for dealing with real women who indeed had a role to play in the text as literary theme and audience.

Touching on some of the finer details of widowhood in fourteenth-century Castile, Endrina speaks, in the text, of the penalties for widows' remarriage before the close of the one-year waiting period. When first approached by the go-between, Endrina offers such penalties as an excuse for eschewing the approaches of all suitors:

---

8. See, for discussion, Pérez de Tudela y Velasco 1983; Ayerbe Iribar 1983, 13–15; Moller 1958, 15; Ferrante 1975, 4.

9. See Brundage 1992 for discussion.

10. See Vasvari 1992.

Non me estarié bien
casar ante del año, que a biuda non convien,
fasta que pase el año de los lutos que tien,
casarse, ca el luto con esta carga vien.
    Si yo ante casase, sería enfamada,
perdería la manda que a mí es mandada.

(lines 759a–760b)[11]

["It would not be
proper for me to marry before a year is up, because it is not
fitting for a widow to marry until the year of her mourning
is over, for mourning carries this obligation with it.
    If I should marry sooner, I would get a bad name;
I would lose the inheritance that has been willed to me.][12]

She mentions, too, her preoccupation with lawsuits by men who seek to take advantage of her:

"Déxame de roído, yo tengo otros coidados
de muchos que me tienen los mis algos forçados.

(lines 742 a–b)

[Spare me your clatter; I have other problems, from a
lot of men who have been looting my property.]

An independent businesswoman managing her affairs on her own, Endrina's discourse is as economical of style as she presumably is of money. Her earthy and scornful rejoinder to her suitor's early entreaties ("Vuestros dichos non los preçio dos piñones" [I don't give two pine kernels for your words], line 664d), much remarked on, is, for example, devoid of the usual time-consuming politeness markers.[13] Endrina's discourse thus suggests the socioeconomic facts of widowhood—the busy woman acting on her own has no time to waste on the linguistic effects of courtesy.

The go-between, Trotaconventos, also refers to issues pertinent to

---

11. All *Libro de Buen Amor* citations in Spanish are from Joset's edition (Ruiz 1974).
12. All *Libro de Buen Amor* citations in English are from Willis's translation (Ruiz 1972).
13. See Brown and Levinson 1978.

widowhood in medieval society. She tries, for instance, to convince Endrina that, as a woman on her own, she needs a man to protect her:

> Éste vos tiraría todos esos pelmazos,
> de pleitos e de afruentas, de vergüenças e de plazos.
>
> (lines 744a–b)

[He would free you of all those annoyances, of lawsuits and looting, of affronts and writs.]

The go-between also addresses, in a long digression, the commonplace at
the root of much medieval legislation that widows are less able to control
their passions than other women and are therefore easy prey for suitors:

> Pues fue casada, creed que s' non arrepienta,
> que non ay mula de alvarda que la troxa non consienta.
> "La çera que es mucho dura e mucho brozna e elada,
> desque ya entre las manos una vez está maznada,
> después con el poco fuego çient vezes será doblada
>
> (lines 710c–711c)

[Since your lady has been married once, you may be
sure that she will not change her views, for there is no pack
mule that will refuse to carry a saddlebag.
Wax that is very hard and stiff and cold, once it is
between one's hands and gets kneaded, can soon, with the slight
warmth be bent a hundred times.

> (lines 711d–710c)][14]

The Doña Endrina episode also takes up medieval society's concern
that the highborn widow might fall victim to a man of lower social status
who wished to advance his own material interests. In casting Melón as a
social inferior and Endrina as a wealthy widow, the episode implicitly
introduces the problem of the social climber—the man whose only hope
for economic and social betterment was hypergamy. As both the go-
between and the text's ending demonstrate, Melón's marital aspirations
with Endrina are legally unencumbered. Moreover, as the text's four-

---

14. The line numbering for this citation in Willis's translation is different from that in
Joset's edition.

teenth-century audience would have known, any social and/or financial ambitions the suitor might have had could have been legitimately satisfied through marriage to a wealthy widow.[15]

The recourse the *Libro* makes in the Doña Endrina episode to contemporary social practices is also part of what distinguishes it from its proclaimed literary model, *Pamphilus,* where the woman violated is a more passive virgin. In the *Libro,* the widow's seduction implies a degree of opposition. As in law and doctrine, the widow is idealized, and yet she is attainable; she is weak and needs special protection, and yet she is able to speak assertively in plain language; she is a member of the "second rank of purity" (which means she is almost like a virgin),[16] and yet her remarriage is publicly celebrated.

The ambivalent legal and social situation of real widows in reconquest Castile also conditions—though more subtly—the episode's complex linguistic scheme. The discourse, marked throughout by inconsistent signs and rapid changes in direction (Lida de Malkiel [1961] used the "zigzag" figure to describe this phenomenon), blends "real" categories of everyday life with speech acts and literary models. The result is a fluid and situational interpretation of gender and power relations—represented in the episode primarily through conversations between the protagonists—and an implicit recognition of, and response to, distinct "masculine" and "feminine" modes of reading.

The episode's initial conversation between Endrina and Melón is a case in point. Language style in this conversation is remarkably suggestive of the rejoinders of spontaneous conversation.[17] Not only is most of the discourse given as syntactically and deictically independent of its frame (classic features of direct discourse), but the rejoinders of the participants are, for the most part, either unintroduced (the lines of the dialogue are presented, as in natural speech, without such lexical introducers as "say," "ask," "reply," "exclaim," etc.) or introduced by the least "literary" of the introducers—"say" in the preterite tense (*dixo,*

---

15. As mentioned earlier, a second husband might be given the right to manage his wife's wealth and property. For discussion of, and some interesing theories on, the role of the audience in the *Libro de Buen Amor,* see Lawrance 1984, Hernández 1987, and Kirby 1986.

16. This is Saint Jerome's description of the widow (*Epistula* 22.15).

17. See, however, Sternberg 1982, 108: "In no form of quotation . . . not even in the direct style, may we identify the representation of the original act of speech or thought with that act itself; to do so would be comparable to equating Balzac's rendering of the Vauquer pension with the pension itself."

"said").[18] Only twice is Melón's discourse presented with lexical introducers ("Yo le dixe" [I said to her], line 666a; "Yo torné en la mi fabla" [I resumed the speech], line 669d); otherwise it is unintroduced (lines 657a, 661a, 682a, 684a). And Endrina's discourse is consistently presented with the word *dixo,* "said" ("Ella dixo" [She said], line 664d; "Esto dixo Doña Endrina" [Then said Lady Sloe], line 679a; "Ella dixo" [She said], line 683d; "Esto dixo Doña Endrina" [Lady Sloe said this], line 685a).

Yet, while the conversation appears "real," the type of behavior exhibited by those who participate in it is quite different from the usual model of naturally ocurring conversation—that is, the collaboration and consensus of participants. Indeed, the conversation's participants largely argue, insult, and assert themselves, behavior typical of dramatic, or "constructed," dialogue—in the sense Tannen (1986) gives it (i.e., part of a well-crafted poetic process that in fact little reflects naturally occuring conversation[19])—but not of natural dialogue.[20]

In the opening conversation between Endrina and Melón, for example, the widow repeatedly "challenges" her suitor's remarks. These "challenging moves"[21] might empower a female audience, asserting a woman's capacity to manage her own affairs and to make her own judgments. For instance, to Melón's request in line 664c, "dezitme vuestro talante, veremos los coraçones" [tell me what your wish is, we shall per-

---

18. See Tannen 1986, 318–24. Tannen argues (323) that presenting dialogue in a literary work with no introducer contributes to its spoken-conversational style, while using lexical introducers in presenting dialogue contributes to its literary style. She further argues (323) that:

the various ways of introducing dialogue fall along a continuum. At one pole is no introducer at all, used in informal conversational narrative because of the great expressive power of the human voice. At the other pole is the use of graphic verbs [e.g., *complain, croon, groan, whisper, cry out,* etc.] as introducers—a form typical of literary narrative.

19. I.e., they are part of a poetic process that functions to make "story into drama," creating interpersonal involvement by reporting talk as if it actually had been spoken (Tannen 1986, 330).
20. Burton (1980, 116) notes this in her analysis of dramatic dialogue and argues that the framework for analyzing conversational behavior should be extended to include drama's typical presentation of conflict.
21. Burton's discussion (1980) of conversational dynamics, including "challenging" and "supporting" moves, helps to identify the types of speech acts involved in Endrina's responses to her suitor's remarks.

ceive each other's hearts], Endrina retorts, "Vuestros dichos non los preçio dos piñones" [I don't give two pine kernels for your words] (line 664d). To his cajoling in lines 683c, "querría fablar, non oso: tengo que vos pesará" [I should like to speak, but I don't dare: I think it might offend you], and in stanza 684a, "Señora, que m' prometades, de lo que de amor queremos, que, si ovier' lugar e tienpo, quando en uno estemos, segund que lo yo deseo, vos e yo nos abraçemos" [Lady, I would have you promise me what we indeed desire from our love, that, if there be opportunity and time when we are together, as I desire it, you and I embrace], she admonishes, "esto yo non vos otorgo, salvo la fabla, de mano" [I will grant you none of this excepting conversation at present] (line 686a).[22]

The conversation between Endrina and Melón in fact puts the social and legal dimensions of widowhood into play on the level of the text itself, working to foreground the widow's capacity to assert herself within the dominant discursive formation of male control. Yet when Melón himself is assertive in his speech, Endrina fails to challenge her suitor's discourse, reaffirming the dominant discourse of male control. To, for example, Melón's command in line 677c, "it e venit a la fabla" [go now, but come back to talk], the widow offers the supporting moves, "Onra es e non desonra en cuerdamente fablar" [There is honor and no disgrace in conversing sensibly] (line 679b); and, "fablarvos he algund día" [I will speak to you some day] (line 681d).

In fact, the distribution of language features denoting gender and power in the conversation interact with a complex web of social and legal meanings, disclosing, among other things, the same instability of relations between more powerful women and men seen throughout this study. Thus, while Endrina's powerful language and "challenging moves" may seem to undermine male strategies to control women's voices,[23] empowering a female audience, her "supporting moves" and her physical description make her subordinate. Powerful features, for example, prevail in Endrina's speech (see table 5), but these features compete with a string of "powerless" corporeal characteristics ascribed to her in the gaze of the episode's male author/protagonist. She is, for instance,

---

22. I have relied here on the work on conversational dynamics by Burton (1980).

23. Burton (1980), who views opening, challenging, and supporting moves as linguistic indicators of the superiority or inferiority of characters, says that in dramatic texts, the character whose conversation is marked by challenging moves dominates over the one whose language is marked by supporting moves. Burton is here building on the model of Sinclair and Coulthard (1975).

endowed with all the delicate characteristics of feminine beauty: a long, slim neck; lovely hair; a small mouth;[24] high color; a graceful walk; and so on:

¡Ay, Dios! Quán fermosa viene Doña Endrina por la plaça!
¡Qué talle, qué donaire, que alto cuello de garça!
¡Qué cabellos, qué boquilla, qué color, que buenandança!

(lines 653a–c)

[O God! how beautiful Lady Sloe is, coming across the town square! What a figure! What grace! What a long, slender throat, like a heron's! What hair! What a darling mouth! What color! What a graceful walk!]

TABLE 5. Strengtheners (powerful language) in the Doña Endrina Episode, by Gender of Principal Speaker

	Principal Speaker	
Strengtheners[a]	Endrina (female)	Melón (male)
Threats	—	—
Imperatives[b]	4	3
Pejorative expressions/insults[c]	2	—
Future tense of assertion[d]	2	2
Total	8	5

[a]The subcategories of strengtheners are not mutually exclusive. I have therefore assigned instances to the category in which they most clearly fall and have specified in the notes to each category which instances have been placed in the category.

[b]ENDRINA:
buscat a quien engañades con vuestras falsas espinas (line 665d)
quanto esto vos otorgo (line 680a)
Pues dezildo (line 683d)
esto yo non vos otorgo (line 686a)
MELÓN:
Id e venit a la fabla (lines 675a, c; 677c)
Otorgatme (line 676a)
vos venid seguramiente (line 676d)

[c]vuestros dichos non os preçio dos piñones (line 664d)
non cuidedes que só loca por oír vuestras parlinas (line 665c)

[d]ENDRINA:
non vos consintré engaño (line 680d)
veré qué tal será (line 683d)
MELÓN:
entendredes mi quexura (line 675d)
yo entenderé de vos algo, e oiredes las mis razones (line 677b)

24. See, for discussion, Zahareas 1965.

She is also young; she goes about in the company of a mother who constantly watches over her ("mas guárdame mi madre, de mi nunca se quita" [my mother watches over me and never leaves my side], line 845b); she worries about her ability to manage her property (lines 742a–b); and she is identified with animals that are sexually passive (see G. Phillips 1983, 88).[25] An implied link between female power and lawless and lascivious behavior, played out in the go-between's discourse and in Endrina's ultimate failure to remain chaste, finally works to reinforce misogynist logic. At the end of the episode, the go-between in fact specifically cites Endrina's agency over her own voice and body as the reason for her violation, supporting the negative stereotype of the independent widow who requires constant reminders of the virtues of continence:

> Cuando yo salí de casa, pues que veyades la redes,
> ¿por qué fincávedes sola, con él, entre estas paredes?"
> A mí non rebtedes, fija, que vos lo meresçedes
>
> (lines 878a–c)

> [When I left the house, since you could see the
> snare, why did you stay with him alone inside these walls?
> Don't blame me, daughter, for you got what you deserve.]

During the course of the episode, a distinctive pattern also emerges in Melón's discourse as he pursues his more aggressive role of conquering

---

25. As in the images of powerful Christian women discussed earlier, Endrina, despite her powerful language, is deliberately made recognizable as a "real" woman; her special capacities as a widow neither erase nor obscure the cultural markers of her gender. As in other images of powerful women as well, Endrina's use of powerful language does not correspond simply to social and economic superiority. While it is clear that Melón seeks her out in the democratic, but otherwise unsatisfactory (because it is so public), setting of the *plaça*, or "town square" (stanzas 654, 656, 668; there is, presumably, no other forum for the casual meeting of these two social unequals), there is no evidence that knowledge of the difference in social status between the pair (described by Melón himself in his early solicitation of Venus's assistence: "[Doña Endrina] es de grand linaje e dueña de buen solar, / es de mejores parientes que yo e de mejor lugar" [(Doña Endrina) is of very high lineage and mistress of a fine family estate, of better family than I, and of a higher status] [lines 598b–c]) is shared by Endrina. Indeed, Endrina and her suitor address each other as equals, using the polite form of address, *vos*. And Melón is described as telling Endrina that his family wishes to marry him off to a wealthy woman. In a later conversation between Endrina and Trotaconventos, Melón is described as hailing from the noblest of lineages (line 727b).

the widow. Melón's discourse is replete with features characteristic of powerless—and, traditionally, women's—language: for example, polite forms, flattery, and self-effacing utterances (see table 6). This type of discourse approximates, to a certain extent, the episode's Latin model, *Pamphilus*, and also *courtoisie*, a more general behavioral pattern characteristic of *Pamphilus* as well as of other "courtly" medieval texts.[26] But it may also correspond to social reality; as Moller suggests (1958), *courtoisie* may not simply be a literary phenomenon. Powerless language, in the context of Melón's speech, may indeed have been conditioned by the actual stresses and strains of the social climber who sought to better his social and economic position through hypergamy—marriage to a high-born woman who could grant him acceptance in privileged society.[27] In

TABLE 6. Weakeners (powerless language) in the Doña Endrina Episode, by Gender of Principal Speaker

	Principal Speaker	
Weakeners[a]	Endrina (female)	Melón (male)
Polite expressions/flattery[b]	—	7
Meek/self-effacing utterances[c]	—	4
Naive utterances	—	—
Hedges[d]	1	—
Utterances of hopelessness	—	—
Total	1	11

[a]The subcategories of weakeners are not mutually exclusive. I have therefore assigned instances to the category in which they most clearly fall and have specified in the notes to each category which instances have been placed in the category.

[b]En el mundo non es cosa que yo ame a par de vos (line 661a)
que por vuestro amor me pena: ámovos más que a Dios (line 661c)
vuestro amor e deseo, que me afinca e me aquexa, / no s'me tira, no s'me parte, non me suelta, non me dexa; / tanto [más] me da la muerte quanto más se me alexa (lines 662b-d)
que vos diga la muerte mía (line 670b)
non sé graçias que lo valan quantas vos mereçedes: / a la merçed, que agora de palabra me fazedes, / egualar non se podrían ningunas otras merçedes (lines 682b-d)
Señora; la vuestra cortesía (line 670a)
[c]non oso poner persona que lo fable entre nos (line 661d)
Reçelo he que non me oídes esto que vos he fablado (line 663a)
Señora, yo non me atrevo de dezirvos más razones (line 664a)
querría fablar, non oso (line 683c)
[d]Onra es e non deshonra en cuerdamiente fablar: / las dueñas e [las] mugeres deven su repuesta dar / a qualquier que las fablare o con ellas razonar (lines 679b-d)

26. See, for interesting discussion, Seidenspinner de Nuñez 1981.
27. See, for discussion, Moller 1958, esp. 159.

recasting the female protagonist of *Pamphilus* as a widow, the text explicitly introduces this possibility, for, as the episode eventually concludes, Melón's marital aspirations are legally unencumbered.[28]

The peculiar conversational structure of the opening dialogue between Endrina and Melón is reinforced by the introduction of a male speaking "I" who represents the exchange between Endrina and Melón. While this speaking "I" might be expected to interpret the dialogue it represents, it instead elaborates its own, quite different representation, producing beyond the conversation's limits a number of signifiers relating to its own desire and listening place in the work—a metaphor, not a mirror, of the protagonists' speech.[29]

In most cases, the discourse of the speaking "I" either ultimately suppresses the speech it reports or overturns it. For example, a conversation with Endrina that ends optimistically with the widow's affirmation of willingness to speak with her suitor again ("tienpo verná qu podremos fablarnos este verano" [the time will come when you and I can talk this spring], line 686d) is transformed into new material by the speaking "I," who follows up on the widow's words with his own discourse on the fickleness of women ("Si la non sigo, non uso, el amor se perderá; / si veye que la olvido, ella otro amará" [But if I do not keep after her nor spend time with / her, my love will go to waste; / if she sees that I am neglecting her, she will give her love to someone else], lines 689a–b). In effect, the speaking "I" poses its own speech on female changeability as a substitute for the widow's declarations. Asserting that women are fickle, the speaking "I" of the episode renders insignificant the promises made by Endrina in the preceding text. So effective is the substitution of the speaking "I"'s discourse for that of Endrina that Endrina herself seems to take note of it. When we next hear her speak, she has completely revised her opinion about future meetings with Melón. She tells the go-between,

---

28. Another well-known medieval Castilian story that details hypergamy rests similarly on the subjection and submission of a wealthy and powerful "manly" woman. As Sandoval (1989, 71) comments, in Juan Manuel's thirty-fifth exemplum of his *Libro de Patronio y Lucanor* (Book of Patronio and Lucanor), "the young man must dis-articulate [the woman's] 'manly' attributes and take over the property he lacks—money, household and social power." See also my discussion of this exemplum in chap. 3 of this book.

29. I borrow some of these terms from Montrelay's description (1987, esp. 243) of the discourse of analyst and analysand—relevant here because the two discourses in the Doña Endrina episode appear to function in a similar fashion. The voice of the speaking "I" in the episode does not interpret but rather, as Montrelay says of the analyst's voice, structures.

"Callad ese pedricar,
que ya ese parlero me coidara engañar.

(lines 740a–b)

"Hush your preaching, for that smooth
talker has already had designs to deceive me.]

But, while the speaking "I"'s discourse may suppress women's speech, by failing to "go with" the conversations it reports, it also leads to an opening up of the episode's meaning, particularly for the text's female audience. Calling into question the utterances made by the protagonists, the discourse of the speaking "I" jeopardizes the authority of its own point of view. This lack of neat correspondence between represented and representing voices—what Sternberg (1982, 109) calls a "perspectival montage"—indeed results in the impression that the speaking "I" sometimes misapprehends the very voices it creates, widening the spectrum of possible interpretations and raising the possibility that the discourse or "system" it represents may be challenged.

Resistance, however, is limited in the episode. The widow's voice and also her body are ultimately restrained. Though, as table 6 shows, conventional male and female roles appear reversed as Melón embraces such stereotypically female behaviors as lying, begging, and cajoling,[30] they are periodically reasserted as he strays in his conversation with Endrina from the customary linguistic behaviors of a courtly lover[31] to the much less reserved language maneuvers of the imperative and future verb forms. Endrina, as table 5 shows, also hedges in her address to her suitor, periodically reestablishing traditional hierarchical relations. Endrina's rape and subsequent remarriage confirm the limits of female resistance that were suggested as early as the protagonists' initial conversation. Resolving the very ambiguities of social, sexual, and marital status that at the outset conditioned the widow's linguistic strategies, her violation by Melón guarantees her an unambiguous female status. On the level of lan-

---

30. See E. J. Burns 1993, 127, in which the author speaks of men's "feminization" when cast in the role of the Ovidian-conditioned medieval lover.

31. Courtly language, moreover, can be so highly stylized that it works to remove the men and women it implicates from reality, making characters "exceptions to the rule" of femaleness and maleness, their speech distant from the "natural" speech of real people. In fact, *courtoisie* may form part of a linguistic strategy for creating "ideal" or "literary," rather than real, images of courtly women and men. See Lacarra 1988a for discussion.

guage, this change is reflected in a shift in the discourse, which increasingly restricts Endrina in her ability and opportunity for verbal reaction. The gap in the manuscript suppresses the widow's initial response to her betrayal (following stanza 877). Powerless features (e.g., subjunctive/conditional clauses and negatives) pervade her subsequent lament: "Si las aves lo podiesen bien saber e entender / quántos laços les paran, non las podrían prender" [If the birds could only know and understand / how many snares are set for them, they could not be caught'] (lines 883a, b); "non" (883b, d; 884d; 885a, b, d); "nin" (884d). She verbally throws in the towel: "pues otro cobro non tiene" [for she has no other recourse] (line 885b); "pues yo non he otro cobro" [since I have no other recourse] (line 885d). And, finally, she offers the response of the powerless—that is, silence—when the go-between, Trotaconventos, recommends a marriage that will make her legally subordinate once more.[32]

Melón is no longer in the powerless role of the courtly lover, for by sexually possessing Endrina he is restored to "masculine" status and social identity. Even the social distance between the pair is leveled when "en uno" [in one] they are wed (line 891a).[33] Perhaps this is why the guests rejoice so when the protagonists marry (line 891b); they are relieved to see traditional hierarchical relations between men and women restored.

Juan Ruiz concludes his remake of the *Pamphilus* with a warning to women about the dangers of false men and *viejas* (old women) and the duplicity of words (line 907a). Widows, this conclusion suggests, have a role to play within the dominant culture, but the spaces within which they can assert themselves are limited and specifically exclude the domain of passionate love. To reiterate this point, the text's author recounts a fable, presented as a cautionary tale for women. The fable tells of an ass whose loud merrymaking so angers a lion that he attempts to claw him. The ass manages to escape, but later, the lion sends a messenger to him, promising safe-conduct and inviting him back to continue his revelry. The lion's words of flattery completely deceive the ass. He presents himself before the lion, who promptly rips him down to the flanks. The lion then commands a wolf to keep watch over the ass's body until he is ready to feast on the carcass. Immediately, the wolf begins eating the ass, con-

---

32. For an interesting discussion of silence in another episode of the *Libro,* see Clarke 1984.

33. For discussion of marriage and the phrase *en uno* in the *Libro,* see Rivarola 1973 and Burke 1986.

suming first the ears and the heart. When the lion returns, he furiously denounces the wolf. But the wolf protests that in fact he has eaten nothing:

Dixo al león el lobo que' el asno tal nasçiera,
que si él coraçón e orejas toviera,
entendiera sus mañas e sus nuevas oyera,
mas que non los tenía e por ende veniera.

(lines 903a–d)

(The wolf told the lion that the ass had been born
that way, for if he had had a heart and ears, he would
have sensed the lion's trickery and would have heard of his
reputation, but he had no heart and ears and therefore he had
    returned.)

The analogy between the ass, who is deceived by the lion's messenger, and Endrina, who is tricked by the deceitful cajoling of her suitor's go-between, is rather explicit. Thus the text not only cautions women against false words but also reiterates for their benefit the chilling implications of trespassing the boundaries within which the system allows them to act. For even in death the ass continues to suffer violence and humiliation, his missing ears and heart guaranteeing his appropriateness as a symbol, for posterity, of foolish and corporally punishable behavior.

Part 4
Women's Language,
Women's Power: Castile's Earliest
Women Writers

8

Leonor López de Córdoba and the Poetics of Women's Autobiography

I have argued to this point that the fragments of female discourse presented as "reported" speech in texts portraying medieval Castile's more powerful women frequently collaborated with the doctrinal and legal sources that tried to forcibly exclude women from holding power in medieval Castile. While these male-authored texts often reveal ambivalence and instability—often in indecisive or ambiguous resolutions—they nevertheless reason that allowing women access to the discourses of power threatens the dominant discursive formation of male control.

It is easy to understand, in this context, why writing, a major source of power in the Middle Ages, seemed wholly unsuitable for women, and why almost no women writers emerged in Castile during the period. It is also easy to see why those very few women who did write tended to do so defensively, often avoiding the topics usually dealt with by male writers, and focusing on the particular circumstances of their own lives that led them to write in the first place. While modern critics have frequently condemned such "women's" writing as self-absorbed and cliché,[1] this narrow focus on the personal and private may have been a strategy for ensuring women a place in the domains heretofore defined—intellectually as well as politically—as excluding them.

Indeed, one of the most interesting aspects of early women's writing is its innovative response to the culture that marginalized women. Creating new literary forms and adapting old ones, early Castilian women writers, such as Leonor López de Córdoba, Florencia Pinar, and Teresa de Cartagena, brought a different perspective on literary production that responded both to women's exceptional position as writers and to their traditional role as subordinates. Leonor's *Memorias,* for example, says

---

1. De Beauvoir (1970, 665–66), e.g., criticizes such women's works as "adornment" and says they lack "audacity."

nothing about her years at court as chief advisor to Queen Catalina of Lancaster,[2] yet they dwell at length on her personal quest for honor and the value of her example as an unfortunate woman. This focus, frequently described by modern critics as little more than a means for exhibiting the author in public,[3] may in fact have been a consequence of Leonor's frustration as subject and her marginalization and lack of recognition in the dominant masculine culture of her period. Florencia Pinar, about whom much less is known, presents herself as "a woman speaking to other women."[4] The three poems attributed to her in fifteenth-century *cancionero* collections stress, as in Leonor's work, the personal and private spheres, specifically avoiding discussion of public events written about by men. Florencia writes, for example, of the private areas of love and sex, using the exemplum of the suffering female to warn women against victimization. Her recourse to multiple perspectives in her poetry takes specific account of women's dual role in female-authored lyric as both the traditional love object of male-authored love poetry and speaking subject.[5] Teresa de Cartagena, a nun who suffered from deafness, similarly stresses in her work the personal and private over the public and official. Cartagena draws on her own afflictions and everyday experiences as a female religious for the themes and imagery of her two texts, the *Arboleda de los enfermos* [Grove of the sick] and the *Admiraçion operum dei* [Wonder at the works of God].[6] The *Arboleda*, which proposes the spiritual benefits of illness, speaks of "those of us who have made our profession in the *convent of afflictions*" (emphasis mine)."[7] The *Admiraçion* reflects on the author's own creative processes and offers an apology for "the lowliness and crudity of my woman's intellect" (Cartagena 1967, 38).[8] As Surtz (1995, 68–84) points out, other less well known nuns who wrote during the period, such as María de Ajofrín, used mystical experiences to authorize their writing.

That these early women writers all share a similar emphasis in their

---

2. I am assuming here that Leonor wrote her *Memorias* toward the end of her life.

3. See, e.g., Curry 1988, 158.

4. See Fulks 1989–90: 42. Another woman writer of the period, Constanza de Castilla, presented herself similarly as a woman writing to other women. A nun, Constanza specifically replaces masculine, with feminine, nouns to address a female audience. See Surtz 1995, 41–67.

5. See Nichols 1988, in which the author discusses a similar phenomenon with respect to early French women writers.

6. I have used Deyermond's translations (1983, 38 and 41) of these two titles.

7. Here I have used Deyermond's translation (1983, 39).

8. Here I have used Deyermond's translation (1983, 41).

works suggests a point of entry into understanding the peculiar hallmarks of early "women's" writing. The focus on the personal and private rather than on broad questions of spirituality or politics may have been a mode of resistance to cultural domination in medieval Castile—a response to male authors' traditional appropriation of the female voice and body and to their repeated attempts in the domains of law, literature, and religion to bring female expression under control.[9]

Leonor López de Córdoba recorded her life story in the early part of the fifteenth century.[10] Her project was remarkable both for its genre and because of her gender: the *Memorias* is Castile's first autobiography;[11] Leonor López de Córdoba is among Castile's earliest women writers.

   Leonor was a noblewoman from southern Spain born around 1362/3. She witnessed some of the most astonishing and horrific events in Castilian history: the violent overthrow of a legitimate ruler by his bastard brother, the Black Death, and the first organized and publicly sanctioned destruction of Jewish lives and property in Spain. She herself made history as chief advisor and confidante to Queen Catalina of Lancaster, who

---

   9. This may also account for the work of other, non-Castilian early women writers, such as Margery Kempe in medieval England, who focuses on personal experience, not broad questions of spirituality; or Madame de Gournay in early modern France, who presents herself as an example of an unfortunate woman whose experience in the private arena should be studied by others to prevent them from making the same mistakes.

   10. The precise date of the text is unknown, and critics disagree even about whether it was written in the first or second decade of the fifteenth century. For important discussions of the *Memorias* and of Leonor, see Ayerbe-Chaux 1977 and 1992, Curry 1988, Deyermond 1983, Ellis 1982, Estow 1982, Firpo 1980, Ghassemi 1989, Kaminsky and Johnson 1984, Lauzardo 1993, Llorca 1990, Pope 1974, Rivera Garretas 1990, and Suelzer 1993. All quotations from the *Memorias* in this chapter are from Ayerbe-Chaux 1977; translations are mine.

   11. It is noteworthy that the first efforts at autobiography in Castile were carried out by a woman. Indeed, the coincidence of women's autobiographical writing with the earliest manifestations of the genre all over Europe and in the New World has been noted in a number of critical studies. S. Smith (1987), e.g., comments on the yield of early examples of Continental, English, and American autobiography in the life stories of Saint Teresa of Avila, Madame Guyon, Margery Kempe, Margaret Cavendish, and Anne Bradstreet. She remarks (42) that "the very fact that women began writing autobiographies contemporary with the genre's emergence . . . is startling, disconcerting, and infinitely interesting." Stanton (1984, 8–9) suggests that autobiography in fact may have originated with women. Atkinson (1983, 194) relates early examples of autobiography to the "new creation of the late Middle Ages": women saints who traveled widely and spoke out publicly. And Franco (1989) discusses the early autobiographies of the New World—life stories of women mystics in New Spain.

was coregent with her brother-in-law, Fernando de Antequera, for her son, the *infante,* Juan II.

Because of Leonor's prominence in the royal court and her own autobiographical text, we have more information about her than about most other medieval Castilian women. We know from her description in Pérez de Guzmán's *Generaciones y semblanzas* (Genealogies and portraits) that she was a powerful figure in fifteenth-century Castilian politics—although Pérez de Guzmán makes it clear he did not like her, calling her "frivolous and wretched" (liviana y pobre).[12] We also know of her position of authority from the *Crónica del rey don Juan II* (Chronicle of King Juan II), which comments that Queen Catalina "trusted [Leonor] so much, and loved her in such a manner, that nothing was ever done without her counsel."[13] Letters exchanged between Leonor and Queen Catalina further confirm the extent of Leonor's political clout—so extraordinary that a modern historian has been led to remark that Leonor was the "real arbiter of Castile's internal policies for some time."[14]

Leonor's own life story tells us that she was a member of a family whose fortunes largely equaled those of the king they supported. This king was Pedro I of Castile, who died at the hands of his illegitimate half brother, Enrique, in 1369. As a young girl, Leonor lived under siege in the fortified town of Carmona, near Seville. In 1371, her family surrendered to Enrique, who had become king of Castile after his brother's death. Despite his promises to protect Leonor's family, Enrique immediately executed Leonor's father. He then imprisoned Leonor and her husband—to whom she had been married at the age of seven—as well as other members of her family. Leonor describes in her *Memorias* the horrors of prison life—in particular, the deaths of her thirteen-year-old brother and all the other members of her household, except for her husband.

Leonor writes in her *Memorias* that she was admitted to the "Orden de Guadalajara" after her release from prison. This "orden" may well have been the Order of Santa Clara, whose famous convent in Guadalajara was intimately connected with Leonor's family.[15] Since we know

---

12. See Pérez de Guzmán 1965, 34.
13. *Crónica del rey don Juan II* 1875, 287.
14. Torres Fontes 1964.
15. I am indebted to Heath Dillard for suggesting this connection to me. I have consulted, among other documents, Layna Serrano's study (1943) of the ancient convents of Guadalajara. Layna Serrano mentions several names related to Leonor's family. *Carillo,* e.g., the surname of Leonor's mother, figures prominently.

that medieval monasteries and convents were centers not only of piety but of erudition and learning,[16] we can suppose that, with the Clarisas, Leonor might have received some formal instruction.

We know from historical records that Leonor was the mother of at least three sons and one daughter.[17] We know from her *Memorias* that one of these sons died tragically of the plague after tending an infected adoptive son—a Jewish boy orphaned, presumably, in the notorious Córdoba pogrom of 1392. Leonor's support of this Jewish boy in a climate of intense anti-Semitism, to the startling extent that she allowed one of her own, biological sons, to die tending him, suggests sympathy with the plight of the Jews and may account for some of the hostility contemporaries felt toward her.

The *Memorias*'s initial phrases suggest that the text was some kind of a public document:

En el nombre de Dios Padre, y del hijo, y del Espiritu Santo tres Personas, y un solo Dios verdadero en trinidad, al qual sea dada gloria á el Padre, y al hijo, y al Espiritu Santo, asi como era en el comienzo, asi es agora, y por el Siglo delos Siglos amen. En el nombre del qual Sobredicho Señor y dela Virgen Santa Maria su Madre, y Señora y Abogada delos Pecadores, y á honrra, y ensalsamiento de todos los Angeles, é Santos y Santas dela Corte del Cielo amen.

Por ende, Sepan quantos esta Esscriptura vieren, como yo Doña Leonor Lopez de Cordoba, fija de mi Señor el Maestre Don Martin Lopez de Cordoba, e de Doña Sancha Carrillo, á quien dé Dios gloria y Parayso. Juro por esta significancia de + en que Yo adoro, como todo esto que aqui es escrito, es verdad que yo lo vi, y pasó por mi, y escribolo á honrra, y alabanza de mi Señor Jesu Christo, é dela Virgen Santa Maria su Madre que lo parió. (16)

[In the name of God the Father, and of the Son, and of the Holy Spirit, three persons, and one true God in the Trinity, to which be given glory to the Father, and to the Son, and to the Holy Spirit, thus as it was in the beginning, it is now, and forever, amen. In the name of this abovementioned Lord and of the Virgin Holy Mary, his mother, and lady and lawyer of sinners, and to the honor and exaltation of all the angels and [male and female] saints in the court of heaven, amen.

---

16. See Lucas 1983, 137–56.
17. See Márquez de Castro 1981, 204–5.

Know those who see this written work how I, Doña Leonor López de Córdoba, daughter of my lord the master, Don Martín López de Córdoba, and of Doña Sancha Carrillo, to whom may God give glory and Paradise. I swear by the significance of the + that I adore that everything that is here written, it is true that I wrote it, and that it happened to me, and I write it for the honor and praise of my Lord Jesus Christ, and for the Virgen Saint Mary, his mother, who gave birth to him.]

Indeed, this part of the text is saturated with wording found commonly in fifteenth-century Spanish legal documents. For this reason, the *Memorias* has been considered a work written with the help of a male notary.[18] Yet a comparison of the *Memorias*'s opening lines with fifteenth-century legal documents in fact makes the initial phrases of the *Memorias* look like a caricature of legal, or notarial, style—or, at best, like the work of an amateur. Leonor's amalgam of formulas goes well beyond what was both customary and appropriate in the formulistic diction of fifteenth-century papers.[19]

A more plausible explanation of the "notarial" style in the *Memorias*'s opening lines is that Leonor herself tried to imitate official language as a means of validating her intervention in the larger, public arena of men's writing. Leonor's employment of notarial formulas, like the use of scribal metaphors by other early women writers across Europe,[20] may have at once signaled her sense of authority and her recognition of the social constraints placed on it.[21] As a woman writer, she was, after all, a transgres-

---

18. See, e.g., Deyermond 1983.

19. Ayerbe-Chaux (1977, 25) calls it "amplification."

20. E.g., in the works of Hildegard of Bingen and Christine de Pizan. Moreover, as L. Johnson has argued (1991, 820), medieval writers often "elaborated upon the figurative language associated with the book as a symbol and incorporated scribes into their texts as tropes."

21. In any case, a resemblance between the initial phrases of Leonor's text and fifteenth-century Spanish legal documents could not alone establish male notarial intervention. Medievalists often find filiations between literary or epistolary writing and dictaminal or notarial models, for writers came into direct contact with such models in their personal legal dealings and letter writing and may have copied model letters or documents when composing their own works. They also may simply have used, or been influenced by, commonly accepted notions of format and style. What's more, Leonor's opening phrases not only are suggestive of the language of law but also manifest common topoi of fifteenth-century male literary and historical writing. E.g., the guarantee Leonor makes in the first four lines that the experiences and events recounted in the text are factual is very much like that made by her male contemporary Pero López de Ayala, in his prologue to the *Crónica del rey don Pedro*.

sor in the universe of male discourse. By incorporating the range of linguistic codes suggestive of officialdom in the initial lines of her text, she may have attempted to locate herself and her *Memorias* within the parameters of writing developed and privileged by (male) political, ecclesiastical, and literary authorities. Moreover, by relying on legal discourse early on in the text, she de-emphasizes the role of her subjective, female self and draws attention instead to the "objective" truths contained in her work.

In this manner, Leonor may have attempted to secure the legitimacy of her (female) claim to authority. Hence the legal formulas may be seen as part of a coherent strategy designed to ensure her work's place in the public domain and in history. The autobiographer may have looked to the language of law—what Foucault calls the "juridico-discursive" representation of power[22]—to insist on the authority of her text and to establish its validity. Indeed, the juridico-discursive authority that empowered her to tell her story also endowed her text with the seeds of longevity: the *Memorias* is in fact framed as a public record destined for wide and long-lived dissemination. This much is evident from the way in which the *Memorias* anticipates its textual community, assimilating in its locutions the two medieval traditions of audienceship—that is, readers and listeners.[23] Leonor expressly says (16) that she writes both for those who are nonliterate ("y por que quien lo oyere sepan la relacion de todos mis echos é milagros que la Virgen Santa Maria, me mostró" [so that those who *hear* (the work) shall know the story of all my deeds and the miracles that the Virgin Saint Mary showed me]; emphasis mine) and for those who are literate ("Sepan quantos esta Esscriptura vieren, como yo Doña Leonor López de Cordoba . . ." [Know those who see this written work how I, Doña Leonor López de Córdoba . . .]; "mandelo escrevir asi como vedes" [I recorded it (the text)/ordered it (the text) to be written just as you *see* it][24]).

---

22. Foucault writes (1980, 87), "In Western societies since the Middle Ages, the exercise of power has always been formulated in terms of law."

23. See Stock 1990, esp. chap. 2.

24. The syntagm *mandélo escrevir,* commonly understood to mean "I ordered it written," may have in fact been borrowed from forensic discourse. The Latin expression *mandare scriptis* describes the act of recording in writing the allegations of all parties in a law case so that a judge might make a determination. See *Diccionario de Autoridades* 1976, 3: "Escribir. En lo forense es reducir a escrito las causas, formar alegatos y papeles en derecho, para que constando por lo escrito los motivos y fundamentos de las partes y de su dependencias y litigios, los Jueces puedan hacer justicia, y determinar según derecho. Lat. *Scribere. Scriptis mandare* [to commit in writing]."

Indeed Leonor's self-conscious acknowledgment of the importance and effectiveness of written documents—even in nonliterate domains where texts can be *read* aloud—is underscored by the number of times she uses words etymologically related to writing when tracing the events of her life. Apart from the fact that the extant manuscript versions of the text begin with the term *escriptura* (written work),[25] which may or may not have been present in the original version,[26] there are the words *esscriptura, escrito* (written), and *escribolo* (I write it) and the phrase *mandélo escrevir* (I recorded it/ordered it written)—all in the early lines of the text. Later on in the work, Leonor makes even clearer her self-conscious relationship to the merits of the written word by noting that the contents of her dowry, of which she is so proud, were so vast that "they could not be *written* on two sheets of paper" [no las pudieran escrevir en dos pliegos de papel] (17), and by complaining that she suffered such a quantity of bitter experiences that they could not all be written down ("pase tantas amarguras, que no se podian escrivir," 23).

Leonor is of course not alone in the medieval world in her consciousness of the power of writing. Over and again medieval Castilian writers focus in their works on the special properties associated with written texts.[27] But as a woman writer of the Castilian Middle Ages, Leonor's attentiveness to writing is remarkable. Moreover, she is attentive to her own agency in the writing of her work. Just a few lines earlier she uses the first-person singular form of the verb "to write" to describe her relationship to her work—"everything that is here written . . . I write it" [todo esto que aqui es escrito, . . . escribolo] (16).

Those who have argued that Leonor's work was composed with the help of a male notary have had to explain the fact that the text quickly shifts from the language of law (i.e., official, notarial phrases that conventionally open legal documents) to topics and styles associated with female authorship (e.g., mystical visions, communings with saints, and

---

25. According to the *Enciclopedia del Idioma* 1947, 2:1822, the use of *escriptura* in the sense of "legal instrument" dates only from the sixteenth century. We thus understand the word as it was used in earlier centuries. E.g., Juan Ruiz, in the mid–fourteenth century, appears to use it in the sense of "book" in the *Libro de Buen Amor:* "En general a todos fabla la escriptura [In general the book speaks to everyone]" (line 67a).

26. Later editors of the text clearly saw it as a legal document and perhaps placed the word at the head of the text to make this clear. There is certainly evidence that other materials may have been added to the top of the text. See Curry 1988.

27. See Clanchy's argument (1983, 17–22) that printing emerged from a complex culture that gave "extraordinary prestige to the written word."

the "feminine" discourse of self-effacement). One solution to this problem has been to suggest that Leonor's notary was overwhelmed by her verbal outpouring.[28] But this type of reasoning becomes unnecessary if the mixture of official, legal language and "feminine" discourse is seen in the context of a single, female author appealing to two domains. These domains are the public, masculine arena, suffused with legal discourse, and the private, feminine arena, characterized by self-effacement. Indeed, this mixed discourse, deriving from a female author's attempt to situate her writings in the public domain, is characteristic of other early women's autobiographies, such as those of her English near contemporaries Margery Kempe (b. around 1373) and Julian of Norwich (b. 1343)—as well as, in America, the *Reply to Sor Philotea* of Sor Juana Inés de la Cruz (1648–95). These works, too, bear the peculiar hallmarks of two distinct universes of discourse—the public, male, legal discourse, and the private, female, discursive spaces of the self-effacing woman. Leonor, like these other early women autobiographers, must have sought, in the mixing of male, official language with feminine discourse, a strategy that would authorize her public, female voice in a culture that encouraged women's silence.

That Leonor was conscious of herself as a woman writing seems plain from the materials she chose to include in her text. The *Memorias* largely depicts a world of men's absence.[29] Although Leonor is careful to establish herself at the start of the work as her father's daughter and her husband's wife, she thereafter dwells on the deaths of the men closest to her—her father, her young brother, and her son—and on the absence of her husband during his seven years of wandering in search of the fortune he lost as a result of his imprisonment. Her description of life on her own is structured around women's spaces: a convent founded by her maternal grandparents and resided in by her mother, and the household of a wealthy aunt. And though Leonor reports in the *Memorias* that her husband eventually did return home (after he had heard of her material triumph), he is never, after this report, mentioned again.

A comparison between Leonor's work and that of other early women autobiographers also suggests that she was conscious of herself as a female *author*. She goes to great lengths in her work to establish her authorial prerogative. Leonor, like Margery Kempe in England, who claims a special relationship with Saint Anne and the Virgin Mary,

---

28. See Deyermond 1983, 33.
29. This important point was first made by Kaminsky and Johnson 1984.

among other females,[30] carefully situates herself among other powerful women, tracing her story through a series of powerful foremothers.

The particular "powerful [female] life script"[31] Leonor chooses as a pretext for her work belongs to the Virgin Mary. Like Leonor, the Virgin is a mother. Also like Leonor, the Virgin is, in Leonor's characterization, a legal advisor—she calls her "lawyer of the sinners" [Abogada delos Pecadores] (16). This gives Leonor—a woman whose counsel was indispensible to decision making in the Castilian court—a double filiation with the Holy Mother—a woman whose life story had already been sanctified by male officials.

Significantly, Leonor grounds herself in other celestially empowered foremothers as well. She writes her text specifically in the name of female, in addition to male, saints ("Santos y Santas," 16). And once again she uses a legal term to characterize those honored in her work, noting that the male and female saints in whose name she writes inhabit the court of heaven ("Santos y Santas dela Corte del Cielo," 16). Thus women, in the *Memorias,* are firmly established as bona fide members, along with men, of both heavenly and legal precincts.

Despite her use of hagiographical and devotional models in the *Memorias,* Leonor is, of course, not a saint, and her *Memorias* is not a spiritual autobiography. Yet by implicating her text in the discourse of hagiography, she is able to further her own struggle for interpretive authority within the public sphere. Hagiographical discourse, which had already successfully immortalized other women, might also immortalize her.

The influence of at least two important elements found in women's spiritual autobiography is plain in Leonor's text. These are, first, the establishment of celestial authorization for the life stories told in the works, and second, the autobiographer's self-representation as an "ideal" woman, obedient and self-effacing despite her bold speech. These elements are made manifest in the life story of Margery Kempe, who, for example, insisted that it was God who commanded her to tell her story and that she thus made no departure, outspoken as she was, from the accepted feminine discourse of obeisance. They are present in the life story of Saint Birgitta of Sweden (c. 1303), who also declared that she was commanded by God to tell her story. And although Birgitta abandoned her children to travel and to speak publicly, she entered the public

---

30. See Kempe 1936.
31. I borrow this phrase from S. Smith (1987, 55).

arena with specific and repeated reassurances from the Virgin Mary that her work was more important. They are seen in the writing of Sor Juana Inés de la Cruz, who also reassured readers that she was an ordinary woman, for her public "reasonings" were legitimized by the feminine figure of the Virgin, who gave birth to the Word and was therefore the matrix of Christian reason.[32] And they are evident in the life story of Julian of Norwich, whose *Revelations* has recently been seen to make patent the unusual learning of its author,[33] but who relied to such an extent on the "ideal" feminine discourse of self-denigration that until recently she, like Leonor, was assumed to have had male notarial intervention in her text.[34]

Leonor's projection in the *Memorias* into the "female" universe of hagiographical discourse as well as into the public, male discourse of letters and learning is what testifies to the text's roots in a woman-centered and woman-identified epistemology.[35] While she may indeed have authentically felt a special relationship with God, the Virgin, and the saints—she was, after all, the survivor of a horrible imprisonment that killed most of the members of her family—she needed primarily a strategy to authorize the telling of her life story, which was otherwise a "non-story"[36] in terms of medieval Castilian letters.

While Leonor's *Memorias* shares many features with the early autobiographies of women written during the medieval period in Europe and in colonial New Spain, it is in one respect quite different. Leonor was not, like Angela of Foligno (1248?–1309), Saint Birgitta of Sweden, or María de San José (1656–1736), a female religious. Her text tells chiefly of material, not spiritual, achievement—the prestige of her lineage, the contents of her dowry, and her attainment of such worldly possessions as a home of her own. She does write of answered prayers to the Virgin and of miracles—for example, the Virgin's miraculous intervention leads to her acquisition of the much-coveted private house—but the thrust of her story is always her personal and material situation. Leonor is clearly no mystic. Her intimacy with the Virgin and her visions lead neither to prophecy nor to pilgrimage. She does not seek to eschew sexual intimacy with her husband in favor of chastity, as does Margery Kempe; nor does

---

32. See Franco 1989, xv.
33. See Colledge and Walsh 1976.
34. See Colledge and Walsh 1976.
35. See Donovan 1987, 99.
36. See S. Smith 1987, 50.

she enter the reclusive spaces of a convent cell, as does Julian of Norwich. And Leonor's life story is not, like the women autobiographers of seventeenth-century New Spain, a confession dictated to, or elicited by, a priest.[37]

But precisely because Leonor is a secular woman autobiographer, her life story is of great significance to the genre. For the *Memorias* gives important testimony to women's quest for autobiographical authority even within the framework of their secular and private identities as wives, mothers, and daughters.

Indeed, Leonor's choice of the autobiographical mode should be understood as part of a program of resistance—a form developed out of her struggle, as a secular woman, for the interpretive power otherwise denied her by the types of male-constructed female images discussed throughout this book. As we have seen, these images, which exaggerated and condemned the authority of medieval Castile's more powerful women, overrode women's historical reality and usurped their right to speak for themselves. Leonor's strange mix of discourse and personal focus recouped, perhaps as well as possible, women's signifying and representing functions in reconquest Castilian culture.

---

37. Ayerbe-Chaux (1992, 18) argues that the text in fact is a confession: "Las *Memorias,* más que un documento más o menos público de defensa de su honor humillado, es posible que sean una confesión y un examen privado de su vida que entrega Leonor al convento de San Pablo" [It is possible that the *Memorias* is not a more or less public document defending (Leonor's) wounded honor, but rather a confession and private examination of her life that she handed over to the convent of San Pablo]. I believe, however, that Leonor's concern for her audience and for her own posterity strongly indicate that the text was in fact meant for wider consumption.

9

Gender, Power, and Language in the
Poems of Florencia Pinar

The innovative, and linguistically anomalous, writing style of the poet Florencia Pinar (late fifteenth century), may also have been a mode of resistance to domination in a culture where men routinely assumed women's signifying and representing functions. Pinar's poems suggest a link between women's more passive role as poetic theme and patron,[1] women's more active role as writers and readers,[2] and the development of a peculiar "women's" language to give women's voice authority in the official world of writing. Distinguished by the use of marked terms, the register of the lament, and the manipulation of multiple perspectives— including the reluctant incorporation of a speaking, or poetic, "I"—the poems draw particular attention to the issue of women's social, political, and doctrinal identities during the late medieval period.

Destas aves su nación (The nature of these birds)[3] is one of three poems attributed to Pinar in the *cancionero* collections of the fifteenth and early sixteenth centuries. The text begins:

Destas aves su nación
es cantar con alegría,
y de vellas en prisión

I have significantly modified here my observations in Mirrer 1995c.

1. Barbara Weissberger, in her work on *Cárcel de amor* (1992), demonstrates just how central women could be to the production and consumption of love literature in fifteenth-century Spain. Written by a man, *Cárcel* explores female desire for an audience into which women figured prominently—Queen Isabel owned a copy of the text, and a sixteenth-century anecdote about a woman's reception of the work shows how popular it was among a female readership.

2. See, for discussion of early women writers' paradoxical "double identity," Nichols 1988.

3. For relevant discussions of this and other poems attributed to Pinar in the *cancioneros,* see Broad 1990, Deyermond 1983 and 1978, Flores and Flores 1986, Fulks 1989–90, Recio 1992, Snow 1984, and Wilkins 1990.

siento yo grave passión,
sin sentir nadie la mía.[4]

[The nature of these birds
is to sing with happiness,
and seeing them in prison
I feel deep suffering,
without anybody's feeling mine.]

From the start, the poem appears aggressively feminine, incorporating, in the first strophe, a rhyme scheme that depends exclusively on feminine grammatical gender—each verse ends in a feminine noun or pronoun. There appears to be also in these early lines a specifically female articulation of the relationship between the personal and the institutional. *Nación*, translated above as "nature," refers, more literally, to the political concept of "nation"; it is a term squarely located in the masculine domain of official power.[5] But in Pinar's text, *nación* seems specifically to strain against this masculine domain, projecting instead a nonmaterial image of the world and an imaginative, rather than official, power. It is not legally enforced, political formations that bind the birds together but instead the private and personal language of happy song.

Nación may also refer to "lineage."[6] Here, too, antagonisms between the term's common appearance within the discourses surrounding public institutions of government and its use in Pinar's text are apparent. In the medieval public sphere, *nación*'s reference to lineage marked a difference between dominant and subordinate groups—that is, between Christian groups and groups of Jews and Muslims. In the poem, the term also seems to mark a difference between dominant and subordinate groups, here men and women.

Indeed, the use of the term *nación* in the context of the *aves* (birds)—identified with the female through the feminine pronoun *ellas* (feminine "they") in the third line of the text—may have been an innovative way of signifying female power and subjectivity while recognizing the political

---

    4. This text is from *Cancionero general recopilado por Hernando del Castillo* [1511] 1958. Translations into English are mine.

    5. The first definition for the word in volume 1 of Martín Alonso's *Diccionario medieval español* (1986) is "conjunto de los habitantes de un país regido por el mismo gobierno" [group of inhabitants of a country ruled by the same government].

    6. "Linaje" is Alonso's final definition of the term for the fifteenth century (Alonso 1986, 1424).

and social constraints placed on it. This interpretation is supported by the particular syntactical arrangement of the verse, which places its grammatical object (*aves*) first, and its subject (*nación*) last. In Spanish, the suppression of a grammatical subject until the end of a sentence functions to allow it a special emphasis. However, since *aves*, the line's grammatical object, appears in what is potentially the subject position, it also becomes a special focus of attention, although it is of course grammatically barred from the subject function.[7]

Just as the discourse syntactically manages to shift emphasis from *nación* as subject to the *aves* with their happy song, Pinar's feminized reading of *nación* shifts emphasis from the public, masculine world of institution to the more personal, private, and feminine world of emotion (song, e.g.). But Pinar explicitly refuses, in the first strophe, to make birds the true subject of the discourse. Women's assumption of the right to "sing"—or speak or write—in a culture that made silence a feminine convention could not guarantee their subjectivity in love poems. The limited effect of women's discourse is borne out by the large body of *cancionero* poetry in which women often appear as poetic themes within the love situation but not as speaking subjects.[8]

It comes as no surprise, in this context, to find that Pinar only reluctantly asserts her own subjectivity in the poem, proffering the expression of her personal sentiment, "siento yo grave passión" [I feel deep suffering], rather late in the strophe. (Moreover, of the three poem's written by Pinar and preserved in the *cancioneros*, this is the only one to introduce a speaking "I" into the text.) Even when Pinar asserts her subjectivity within the text's discourse, her speaking "I" seems to speak more from women's traditional, marginalized position in love poetry as object than from the active, speaking position of agent in the love situation. Her voice, she declares, is heard (*sentir* refers also to the sense of "hearing") by no one ("siento yo grave passión, / sin sentir nadie la mía"). She is thus effectively speechless—as silent as the tree in the much-cited philosophical question of whether a tree that falls in the forest when no one is present to witness it makes a sound. Yet here, too, is an example of women's multiple identity within the medieval world of literary production. While Pinar's subjectivity in the poem may be obscured by its silencing in a society that refused to authorize the female voice, her writing of the text and

7. For discussion of syntax in the poem, see Wilkins 1990.
8. For a discussion of early *cancionero* texts that incorporate a female speaking subject, see Whetnall 1984.

its preservation in the *cancionero* collections do show that women could, and did, resist the historical reality that denied them access to the modes of public discourse.

As in the case of Leonor López de Córdoba, Pinar makes of her text a gendered mirror that focuses on sexual division. The tension between men and women reflected through her feminized reading, in the first strophe, of a term conventionally marked for the masculine domain (i.e., *nación*) is reinforced in the second strophe through her exposure of male aggression against women in the text's sole reference to men:

Ellas lloran, que se vieron
sin temor de ser cativas,
y a quien eran más esquivas,
essos mismos las prendieron.

[They weep, because they had no
fear of being captives,
and by those very ones whom they most disdained,
they were caught.]

The theme of the birds held in captivity by those who caught them has been linked by Deyermond (1983) to the use of hunt imagery in many other medieval texts. Referring to the work's heading, which reads, "Otra canción de la misma señora a unas perdizes que le embiaron bivas" [Another song by the same lady who was sent some live partridges], he stresses a connection between the poem's imagery and the section relating to partridges (*perdices*) in the medieval bestiary. Deyermond argues that Pinar's choice of the partridge as the central symbol in her poem functions to identify the poet's instincts with those described by the bestiary and most graphically expressed in the bestiary's declaration that "[d]esire torments the females so much that even if a wind blows toward them from the males they become pregnant by the smell."[9] Deyermond's interpretation suggests that the poem is about female sexual desire. Yet uncertainty about the text's heading—that is, whether it was authored by Pinar or simply added by an editor—recognized by Deyermond in a footnote and discussed in turn by Wilkins,[10] tends to decenter the partridge as the poem's main image, particularly as Pinar speaks only

---

9. Deyermond 1983, 47. Deyermond cites White 1954, 137.
10. Deyermond 1983, 47 n. 34; Wilkins 1990, 127.

of *aves,* and not of *perdices,* in the body of her work. If the poem is indeed about female sexual desire, as Deyermond's interpretation suggests, it is decidedly not the same concept of female desire held in love literature authored by men and embodied in the bestiary's rather transparently masculinist illustration of the means by which female partridges achieve sexual satisfaction. (Such a concept has been aptly described by Irigaray [1985] as women's longing to be not only, in the Freudian sense, *the* object of desire, but the object of *men*'s desire.)[11] Women, in this text, long to be desiring subjects—not the objects of men's fantasies about them. This explains their former disdain for those who now hold them captive and their sadness at finding themselves love objects rather than agents in the love situation. (Here I understand the word *esquivas* to mean "disdain," a reading in line with the term's repeated use in another of Pinar's poems, *¡Ay!, que ay quien más no bive* [A sigh! For there are some who languish][12].)

The question of taking sexual initiative or pursuing erotic fantasy, proposed in both the symbolism of the birds' happy song and the description of the birds' disdain for those who hold them captive, is quickly overtaken by the symbolic expression of women's privation, as love object, of even the means to actively seek sexual satisfaction. Thus when the birds finally find their way to self-assertion in the poem's second strophe—they are here the grammatical subject of the discourse—the focus is squarely on their oppression: "Ellas lloran, que se vieron / sin temor de ser cativas" [They weep, because they had no fear of being captives]. Here, again, is the paradox of woman's condition. As in the case of many other early women writers, including Leonor López de Córdoba, Pinar's frustration as subject and her marginalization in the dominant masculine culture of her period led her to seek authorization by presenting herself as an example of an unfortunate, suffering woman—a warning to other women against victimization, as Fulks (1989–90) has put it. The theme of the suffering woman is of course affirmed, and reaffirmed, in the poem's refrain, "y de vellas en prisión / siento yo grave passión" [and seeing them in prison / I feel deep suffering].

Pinar's lament, "Sus nombres mi vida son / que va perdiendo alegría" [Their names are my life, which is losing its happiness] provides further evidence of the poem's focus on sexual division and its enactment of women's struggle for subjectivity. Although Pinar explicitly links the

---

11. See Irigaray 1985, 32.
12. I have used Snow's translation (1984, 329).

birds' names to her own life, she fails to actually name the birds. As discussed in chapter 1 of this study, namelessness, in regard to women, is
frequently a metaphor for speechlessness.[13] Pinar's poetic expression of
her life—"Sus nombres mi vida son"—thus reestablishes the theme of
women's silence as well as their predicament within a historical reality
that insisted on it. The verse also reverts back to the paradox of woman's
subjectivity in the strophe's opening phrase, "Ellas lloran." Crying is, par
excellence, the sound—and here I believe the double meaning of the word
son (i.e., a verb form meaning "they are" and a noun meaning "sound")
is paramount—of early women writers' response to the dialogue of
unequals that characterized their culture. Indeed, crying is a hallmark of
early women writers' intervention in the public domain. The tears of the
medieval English woman writer Margery Kempe (b. around 1373), for
example, flow copiously in the public spaces of church and town, where
her voice was often forcibly suppressed.[14]

Both the word *aves* (birds), linked with women in the body of the text,
and the word *perdices* (partridges), mentioned in the poem's heading, are
sexually and, in the case of *perdices,* textually ambiguous symbols. From
neither term can biological sex be deduced, yet both words are coded
grammatically for the female gender. But regardless of whether or not the
partridge is an animal central to the poem's interpretation,[15] the text's
use of either, or both, terms does in fact motivate an interpretation (even
if only in the mind of an editor in the case of *perdices*) based on the possibility of including a masculine presence in a feminine space. Thus,
within the linguistic economy of the text, sexual difference is explored
both in the light of historical reality, where the dominant male culture
prevails, and according to the peculiar imaginative power of language,
where alterity is preserved via grammatically feminine, but sexually biva-
lent, terms. Nichols, who has examined early women writers of love literature in France, finds a related phenomenon. In such twelfth-century
writers as Héloise, the Comtessa de Dia, and the presumably female

13. Bal (1988) notes this in her study of the Book of Judges.
14. See Kempe 1936.
15. Recio (1992, 333) declares the bird's importance in emphasizing the theme of the
poeta cautivo (poet-as-captive). Broad (1990, 31) sees the symbolic world of the poem,
inflected with the traditional symbolism of the partridge, as a means of relating the less private emotion of compassion to the deep, personal feeling of the poet. Wilkins (1990) sees
the poem as expressive of the female experience of oppression during the late Middle Ages
and believes that the poem's heading, which contains the text's only mention of partridges,
was probably added by an editor. For Wilkins (129), the *aves,* not the partridges, are the
text's central symbol.

authors of the *chansons de toile* (spinning songs), there is, Nichols argues (1988, 93), a recognition of a "fundamental truth about love and its relationship to the feminine." This recognition anticipates what the twentieth-century philosopher Emmanuel Levinas has termed "le pathétique de l'amour"—love's pathos that "lies in the insurmountable duality of beings."[16] Florencia Pinar, too, may have sought to speak of love not simply from the position of love object or poetic subject but also from a position "beyond the divide."[17]

---

16. Levinas 1985, 78. See also Nichols 1988, 93–94.
17. I quote here from Nichols 1988, 94.

Conclusion

In a recent collection of lectures on race in American literature, Toni Morrison observes that the Africanist presence in American literary texts does not signify the Africanist character but instead plays a crucial role in (white) writers' sense of Americanness:

> Africanism is the vehicle by which the American self knows itself as not enslaved, but free; not repulsive, but desirable; not helpless, but licensed and powerful; not history-less, but historical; not damned, but innocent; not a blind accident of evolution, but a progressive fulfillment of destiny. (Morrison 1992, 52)

As we have seen throughout this study, women, Jews, and Muslims could play a remarkably similar role in the texts of reconquest Castile, shoring up male Christian Castilian identity through images that displaced their reality and established difference within the dominant cultural body. Images of "others," marked by an "economy of stereotype"[1] that allowed singers and writers to make their point without fully developing their characters, provided a shortcut to affirming Christian Castilian men's authority. For example, certain names assigned to Jews and Muslims in epic and frontier ballad displaced, rather than signified, these groups. *Mora* (Muslim woman, black, [black] cow), and its diminutive forms, *morica* and *morilla*, coded for color and relating to animals, size, and gender, summoned up Christian manliness and muscle by collapsing Muslim character with race, bestiality, and powerlessness in such texts as *Pártese el moro Alicante* and *La morilla burlada*. *Rachel* and *Vidas* (the latter from the Hebrew *Hawwā*, "Eve"), assigned to Jewish men in the *Cantar de mio Cid*, added sexual deviance to the constellation, qualifying Christian men alone for power in medieval Castile. *Chiquillo*, or *chiquito*

---

1. This is Morrison's term (1992).

(tiny), used to designate Emir Muhammad b. 'Ali, the last Muslim king in Spain, did the same, devaluing and effectively usurping the Muslim point of view.

Images of Christian women, if not their names, could also be of service in establishing male Christian Castilian identity. We have seen here how society's more powerful women, frequently characterized in the literature as reckless, lascivious, or criminal, played out men's fears and desires; how a fabricated female presence reinforced men's sense of themselves as powerful, manly, and superior. While it is also possible for us to "listen" or "read" for the feminine in these male-authored depictions and to recognize in the often ambiguous and unstable resolutions of men's texts possibilities for female contestation of powerlessness, it is difficult for us to know, beyond a limited number of examples of early women writers in Castile, to what extent these voices offered real options to female readers and listeners.

And yet we read, in much of the critical literature, of male Christian Castilians' extraordinary ability to represent the realities of women and "others," particularly in the texts of the frontier. We hear of these men's unusual capacity to see the "Moorish point of view," even in the midst of heated battle. We read, too, that Christian writers depicted Jewish women, in portayals without a trace of anti-Semitism, as beautiful. We find Jimena, the Cid's dutiful wife, hailed by contemporary critics as an extraordinary model of womanhood, as well as an important sign of male Christian Castilians' respect for their women. And we learn that Berceo's depiction of three mothers—but no other women—in his work is to be valued for underscoring the "maternal" aspect of the female nature. Nearly everywhere, moreover, the term *convivencia* (coexistence) is used to describe Christian writers' and singers' profound consciousness of, and empathy for, the "others" that inhabited their domain.

It is far from obvious in such evaluations as these that the images under discussion were mediated by male Christian Castilians during an age of increasing social intolerance;[2] that the subject of the texts, like the subject of the dream, were the singers and writers themselves, or the dreamers.[3] Thus, while real women and "others" clearly strained against the boundaries that delineated their participation in the dominant culture, literary images of women, Jews, and Muslims rarely tell us wha

2. Greenblatt (1991) notes a similar phenomenon in the case of cultural encounters in the New World.

3. I paraphrase Morrison (1992) here.

subordinate groups—at times powerful players in the newly dominant Christian states—were "really" like. The voices of "others," represented in the literature as alien and estranged, are more frequently fabrications designed to assert the privilege and power of a masculine, Christian Castilian culture.

It is, of course, certain that male Christian Castilians' belief in the absolute and exclusive truth of their religion helped to formulate their textual representations.[4] Yet the fabricated presence of "others" in the texts was surely central in elaborating this religious belief, overlaying, as it did in epic and ballad literature of the frontier, Christianity with masculine attributes. It is certain, too, that during the centuries spanned by the texts discussed in this study, there were many changes in medieval Castile. These changes could not fail to have had an impact on images of women and "others" in medieval Castilian literature. The nature and scale of frontier warfare in the 1200s, for example, differed significantly from that in the 1400s, and colonists in newly reconquered towns radically altered the political, economic, and cultural life of the south. Intellectual and artistic structures in the fourteenth and fifteenth centuries also changed from those of previous centuries. Writers increasingly traveled outside of Spain, and women, virtually absent from the earlier literary corpus, brought a new perspective and, indeed, a new genre to fifteenth-century letters and learning. Civil and religious institutions were also altered during the later period, and new laws, conceived as the reconquest progressed to establish order in the towns of the frontier, significantly modified the legal relationship between men and women, from rape to concubinage. While we have argued throughout this study that Jewish and Muslim exclusion was already formulated in the literature of thirteenth-century Castile, the Inquisition, which officially closed off the possibility of peaceful coexistence, was not established until 1478.

I have tried to show the impact of some of these changes on the images described in this study. I proposed, for example, a relationship between the particulars of thirteenth-century monastic life and Berceo's focus on an encounter between an abbess and her supervising bishop. I tried to highlight, too, the peculiar dynamics of Christian-Muslim encounters in the waning years of reconquest and their influence on the texts' representations. I considered how the widow Endrina served as a marker and a vehicle for late medieval society's ambivalence about independent

---

4. Greenblatt (1991, 7) notes the same for Christian Europeans' encounters with "others" in the New World.

women, even when their independence was legally and doctrinally sanctioned. And I explored the difficulties of women's entry into the world of learning and letters through a discussion of Leonor López de Córdoba's *Memorias* and Florencia Pinar's poetry.

But in an important sense, images of women and "others" remained static during the period discussed here, deliberately reflecting an "essential" female, Jew, and Muslim. Indeed, it appears that singers and writers preferred to draw on a well-stocked library of misogynist and anti-Semitic conventions in their representations of these groups, purposely avoiding reference to, or interaction with, any particular moments in history. If, in my analyses, Jewish men are always avaricious, Jewish—and also Muslim—women are always sexually available, and powerful Christian matrons eternally pose danger to men and society, it is because such images as these were persistently employed to establish difference in the texts. Relying on stereotypes to withhold specificity, these images enabled male Christian Castilians to gather identity unto themselves.

In attempting to redirect attention in this study from the represented in medieval Castilian literature to the representers, instead, I could not help but notice a striking similarity between the representational practices that characterized later reconquest Castile and those of the New World. It has frequently been remarked that years of warfare to establish dominion in Muslim territories provided the conquistadores with a blueprint for military maneuvers against the native Americans[5] and a model for the administration of newly conquered territories. W. Phillips and C. Phillips (1992), for example, have described in detail the practices borrowed from reconquest Spain and the Canary Islands, including grants of land and local self-government managed by town councils. It has less often been observed that the experience of an "other" culture in Spain, particularly as recorded and popularized in epic and frontier ballad, gave Spanish Christians a template for describing their cultural encounters in the New World. *Romances,* sung with fervor by Spaniards as they fought for dominion in America, lent a semblance of continuity from reconquest to conquest in their color and caste implications. Christian victories against Muslim aristocrats, as well as their sexual conquest and conversion of beautiful Jewesses and young Muslim princesses, provided a ready-made formula for evoking Christian privilege and power in New

---

5. MacKay (1977, 5) describes the later medieval period in Spain as "a laboratory for testing and developing some of the governmental, social and economic institutions and forces which were to be prevalent in early modern Spain and parts of its Empire."

World images, from the defeated Indians of *La Araucana* to *La Mal-inche*, the aristocratic young woman given as a gift to Cortés by a Tabas-can tribe. It is no wonder that the deeds of the conquistadores echoed those of the frontier warriors; taking possession in the New World involved not only the assimilation of native American effects, through language, to the culture of the already defeated Muslims (e.g., native American scarves were called *almaizares,* the name given to veils worn by Muslims in Spain;[6] Cortés compared Aztec architecture to "Moorish" styles) but also a recycling of the metaphorical uses of gender and race that had so successfully reinforced the "otherness" of the now van-quished Old World infidels.

In light of the many recent studies of Spain in the age of Columbus that deconstruct the familiar notions of "culture" and "conquest,"[7] it has become increasingly difficult (although many critics continue to attempt it) to sustain the argument that *convivencia*—the living together of Chris-tians, Jews, and Muslims in medieval Spain—meant a happy and suc-cessful appropriation of "others'" discourse. Uncritical readings of the texts' pervasive image of, for example, defeated Muslims so in awe of their captors that they heap praise on them now compete with more nuanced analyses of the "docile Moor" and the *casta triunfante* (tri-umphant caste).[8] One striking demonstration of the extent to which uncritical readings are on the wane is in fact the catalog for the recent exhibition on *convivencia* at the Jewish Museum in New York. While validating the term's use, the catalog, declaring that *convivencia* does not mean total harmony, suggests major revisions in the concept's under-standing.[9] Now that women writers are studied as never before, it has also become difficult to ignore the deformation of women's discourse in the almost exclusively male-authored texts of the period.[10] But critics still strain to speak for and about "real" women, Jews, and Muslims based on

---

6. Greenblatt (1991, 86) notes the use of this name.

7. See, for an excellent overview of this issue, the Introduction to Jara, et al. 1989.

8. I have noted throughout this book the contributions of (most notably) Aizenberg, Burshatin, and Goldberg in the United States, and Lacarra in Spain. Díaz-Quiñones' semi-nal work on the *romancero fronterizo* (1973) has also contributed greatly to the rethinking of stereotypes.

9. This catalog *Convivencia: Jews, Muslims, and Christians in Medieval Spain* was published in 1992. For another recent discussion and critique of *convivencia,* see C. Smith 1992.

10. Most notable are María Eugenia Lacarra and the group at the Universidad Autónoma, which has been publishing a series of essays on women in medieval Spain.

their representations in medieval Castilian texts.[11] And the implications of the images discussed here—that the same masculinist ideologies may have been responsible for both women's and others' discourse in medieval Castilian literature—have yet to be fully explored.

11. That critics have to make a conscious effort not to engage in such exercises is illustrated by Greenblatt (1991, 7), who, in discussing a similar issue in the New World context, describes himself as specifically resisting such a temptation.

Bibliography

Abbreviations used in the bibliography are as follows:

BHS	*Bulletin of Hispanic Studies*
ComM	*Communication Monographs*
ELH	*Journal of English Literary History*
HR	*Hispanic Review*
JHP	*Journal of Hispanic Philology*
KRQ	*Kentucky Romance Quarterly*
LR	*Les Lettres Romanes*
MLR	*Modern Language Review*
NRFH	*Nueva Revista de Filología Hispana*
PMLA	*Publications of the Modern Language Association*
QJS	*Quarterly Journal of Speech*
RCEH	*Revista Canadiense de Estudios Hispánicos*
REH	*Revista de Estudios Hispánicos*
RF	*Romanische Forschungen*
RFE	*Revista de Filología Española*
RPh	*Romance Philology*
YFS	*Yale French Studies*

Ackerman, Jane E. 1983. "The Theme of Mary's Power in the *Milagros de Nuestra Señora.*" *JHP* 8.1: 17–31.

Aguirre, J. M. 1972. "Moraima y el Prisionero: Ensayo de interpretación." In *Studies of the Spanish and Portuguese Ballad*, ed. N. D. Shergold, 53–72. London: Tamesis.

Ahmed, Leila. 1992. *Women and Gender in Islam: Historical Roots of a Modern Debate.* New Haven: Yale University Press.

Aizenberg, Edna. 1980. "Raquel y Vidas: Myth, Stereotype, Humor." *Hispania* 63: 478–86.

———. 1984. "'Una judía muy fermosa': The Jewess as Sex Object in Medieval Spanish Literature and Lore." *La Corónica* 12.2 (spring): 187–94.

Alfonso X el Sabio. 1972. *Siete Partidas.* 3 vols. Madrid: Atlas.

165

————. 1955. *Primera Crónica General de España que mandó componer Alfonso el Sabio y se continúa bajo Sancho IV en 1289.* Ed. Ramón Menéndez Pidal. Madrid: Gredos.

————. 1981. *Cantigas de Santa Maria.* Ed. Walter Mettmann. 2 vols. Vigo: Xerais de Galicia.

al-Ibadi, .Hunayn ibn Ishaq, 809?–873. 1970. *The Libro de los buenos proverbios,* ed. Harlan Sturm. Lexington: University Press of Kentucky.

Alloula, Malek. 1986. *The Colonial Harem.* Trans. Myrna Godzich and Wlad Godzich. Minneapolis: University of Minnesota Press.

Alonso, Martín. 1986. *Diccionario medieval español.* Vol. 1. Salamanca: Universidad Pontífica de Salamanca.

Alvar, Manuel. 1955. "Granada y el Romancero." *Clavileño* 32 (March–April): 7–18.

Anahory-Librowicz, Oro. 1989. "Las mujeres no-castas en el romancero: Un caso de honra." In *Actas del IX Congreso de la Asociación Internacional de Hispanistas,* ed. Sebastian Neumeister, 1:321–31. Frankfurt am Main: Vervuert Verlag.

Arden, Heather. 1992. "Grief, Widowhood, and Women's Sexuality in Medieval French Literature." In *Upon My Husband's Death: Widows in the Literature and Histories of Medieval Europe,* ed. Louise Mirrer, 305–19. Ann Arbor: University of Michigan Press.

Armistead, Samuel G. 1978. "Existió un Romancero de tradición oral entre los moriscos?" In *Actas del Coloquio Internacional sobre Literatura Aljamiada y Morisca,* 211–36. Madrid: Gredos.

Armistead, Samuel G. and James T. Monroe. 1984. "A New Version of *La Morica de Antequera.*" *La Corónica* 12.2 (spring): 228–40.

Armistead, Samuel G. and Joseph Silverman. 1965. "Christian Elements and De-Christianization in the Sephardic *Romancero.*" In *Collected Studies in Honour of Américo Castro's Eightieth Year,* ed. M. P. Hornik, 21–38. Oxford: Lincombe Lodge Research Center.

————. 1979. *Tres calas en el romancero sefardí (Rodas, Jerusalén, Estados Unidos).* Madrid: Castalia.

Armistead, Samuel G., et. al. 1971. *The Judeo-Spanish Ballad Chapbooks of Yacob Abraham Yoná.* Berkeley: University of California Press.

————. 1978. *El romancero judeo-español en el Archivo Menéndez Pidal: Catálogo-índice de romances y canciones.* 3 vols. Madrid: Cátedra and Seminario Menéndez Pidal.

Atkinson, Clarissa W. 1983. *Mystic and Pilgrim: The Book and the World of Margery Kempe.* Ithaca, N.Y.: Cornell University Press.

Augier, Michelle. 1975 "A propos de quelque conversions féminines dans l'epopée française." *Mosaic* 8.4: 97–105.

Ayerbe-Chaux, Reinaldo. 1977. "Las memorias de Doña Leonor López de Córdoba." *JHP* 2.2: 11–33.

———. 1992. "Leonor López de Córdoba y sus ficciones históricas." In *Historias y ficciones: Coloquio sobre la literatura del siglo XV,* ed. R. Beltrán, J. L. Canet, J. L. Sierra, and Evangelina Rodríguez, 17–23. Valencia: Departamento de Filología Española, Universidad de Valencia.

Ayerbe Iribar, María Rosa. 1983. "La mujer y su proyección familiar en la sociedad visigoda a través de los concilios." In *Las mujeres medievales y su ámbito jurídico, Actas de las II jornadas de investigación interdisciplinaria,* 11–31. Madrid: Seminario de estudios de la mujer-Universidad Autónoma de Madrid.

Azam, Gilbert. 1984. "Mythe ou réalité de la femme chez Berceo." In *La femme dans la pensée espagnole: Ouvrage collectif,* 3–21. Paris: Centre National de Recherches Scientifiques.

Azcona, T. de. 1964. *Isabel la Católica.* Madrid: Biblioteca de Autores Castellanos.

Bagby, Albert I., Jr. 1971. "The Jew in the *Cantigas* of Alfonso X, el Sabio." *Speculum* 46: 670–88.

———. 1987. "The Figure of the Jew in the *Cantigas* of Alfonso X." In *Studies on the Cantigas de Santa Maria: Art, Music, and Poetry,* ed. Israel Katz, John E. Keller, Samuel G. Armistead, and Joseph T. Snow, 235–45. Madison, Wisc.: Seminary of Medieval Studies.

Bakhtin, M. M. 1986. "The Problem of Speech Genres." In *Speech Genres and Other Late Essays,* trans. Vern W. McGee, ed. Caryl Emerson and Michael Holquist, 60–102. Austin: University of Texas Press.

Bal, Mieke. 1988. *Death and Dissymmetry: The Politics of Coherence in the Book of Judges.* Chicago: University of Chicago Press.

Bancourt, Paul. 1982. *Les Musulmans dans les chansons de geste du Cycle du Roi.* 2 vols. Aix-en-Provence: Univérsité de Provence.

Banī Naṣr, Akhbār mūlūk. 1940. *Fragmento de la época sobre Noticias de los reyes nazaritas; o, Capitulación de Granada y emigración de los andaluces a Marruecos,* ed. Alfredo Bustani; trans. Carlos Quirós. Larache (Morocco): Artes gráficas Bosca.

Barkai, Ron. 1984. *Cristianos y musulmanes en la España medieval: El enemigo en el espejo.* Madrid: Ediciones Rialp.

Baron, Salo. 1952. *A Social and Religious History of the Jews.* 2d ed. Philadelphia: Jewish Publication Society of America.

Barthes, Roland. 1977. *Roland Barthes.* Trans. Richard Howard. New York: Hill and Wang.

Barugel, Alberto. 1990. *The Sacrifice of Isaac in Spanish and Sephardic Balladry.* New York: Peter Lang.

Bauschatz, Cathleen. 1990. " 'L'horreur de mon exemple' in Marie de Gournay's

Proumenoir de Monsieur de Montaigne (1594)." L'Esprit Créateur 30.4 (winter): 97–105.

Bell, Katherine Marie. 1984. "The Relationship of Gender and Sex Role Identity to Politeness in Speech Behavior." Ph.D. diss., University of North Carolina at Chapel Hill.

Bello, Andrés. 1881. "Notas a la *Gesta de Mio Cid*." In *Obras completas de Andrés Bello,* 2:210–11. Santiago: P. G. Ramírez.

Bénichou, Paul. 1968. *Romancero judeo-español de Marruecos.* Madrid: Castalia.

Benmayor, Rina. 1979. *Romances judeo-españoles de Oriente: Nueva recolección.* Madrid: Gredos.

Berceo, Gonzalo de. 1967. *Los Milagros de Nuestra Señora.* Vol. 2 of *Obras Completas.* Ed. Brian Dutton. London: Tamesis.

Berko-Gleason, J. 1975. "Fathers and Other Strangers: Men's Speech to Young Children." In *Developmental Psycholinguistics: Theory and Applications,* ed. D. P. Dato, 287–97. Washington, D.C.: Georgetown University Press.

Bernáldez, Andrés. 1962. *Memorias del reinado de los Reyes Católicos.* Ed. Manuel Gómez-Moreno and Juan de Mata Carriazo. Madrid: Real Academia de la Historia.

Black, Peter W. 1985. "Ghosts, Gossip, and Suicide: Meaning and Action in Tobian Folk Psychology." In *Person, Self, and Experience: Exploring Pacific Ethnopsychologies,* ed. Geoffrey M. White and John Kirkpatrick, 245–300. Berkeley: University of California Press.

Boreland, Helen. 1983. "Typology in Berceo's *Milagros:* The *Judïezno* and the *Abadesa preñada.*" BHS 60.1: 15–29.

Bornstein, Diane. 1983. *The Lady in the Tower: Medieval Courtesy Literature for Women.* Hamden, Conn.: Archon.

Boswell, John. 1980. *Christianity, Social Tolerance, and Homosexuality. Gay People in Western Europe from the Beginning of the Christian Era to the Fourteenth Century.* Chicago: University of Chicago Press.

Bradac, James J., and Anthony Mulac. 1984. "Attributional Consequences of Powerful and Powerless Speech Styles in a Crisis-Intervention Context." *Journal of Language and Social Psychology* 3.1: 1–19.

Brandes, Stanley. 1980. *Metaphors of Masculinity: Sex and Status in Andalusian Folklore.* Philadelphia: University of Pennsylvania Press.

Brenneis, Donald. 1984. "Grog and Gossip in Bhatgaon: Style and Substance in Fiji Indian Conversation." *American Ethnologist* 11.3 (August): 487–506.

Broad, Peter. 1990. "Florencia Pinar y la poética del cancionero." In *La Escritora Hispánica,* ed. Nora Erro-Orthmann and Juan Cruz Mendizabal, 26–36. Miami: Ediciones Universal.

Brotherton, P. L., and R. A. Penman. 1977. "A Comparison of Some Characteristics of Male and Female Speech." *Journal of Social Psychology* 103: 161–62.

Brouwer, Dédé. 1982. "The Influence of the Addressee's Sex on Politeness in Language Use." *Linguistics* 20.8: 697–711.

Brown, Penelope. 1980. "How and Why Are Women More Polite: Some Evidence from a Mayan Community." In *Women and Language in Literature and Society,* ed. Sally McConnell-Ginet, Ruth Borker, and Nelly Furman, 111–36. New York: Praeger.

Brown, Penelope, and Stephen Levinson. 1978. "Universals in Language Usage: Politeness Phenomena." In *Questions and Politeness: Strategies in Social Interaction,* ed. Esther Goody, 56–289. Cambridge Papers in Social Anthropology 8. Cambridge: Cambridge University Press.

Brownlee, Marina Scordilis. 1985. *The Status of the Reading Subject in the "Libro de Buen Amor."* Chapel Hill: University of North Carolina Department of Romance Languages.

Brundage, James A. 1987. *Law, Sex, and Christian Society in Medieval Europe.* Chicago: University of Chicago Press.

———. 1992. "Widows as Disadvantaged Persons in Medieval Canon Law." In *Upon My Husband's Death: Widows in the Literature and Histories of Medieval Europe,* ed. Louise Mirrer, 193–206. Ann Arbor: University of Michigan Press.

Buetler, Gisela. 1986. "Some Remarks on the Moorish Ballads in Spain and Elsewhere." In *Ballad Research: The Stranger in Ballad Narrative and Other Topics,* ed. Hugh Shields, 171–82. Dublin: Folk Music Society of Ireland.

Burke, James F. 1986. "La cuestión del matrimonio en el *LBA.*" In *Actas del VIII Congreso de la Asociación Internacional de Hispanistas,* ed. A. David Kossoff, et al., 1:285–91. Madrid: Ediciones Istmo.

Burns, E. Jane. 1993. *Bodytalk. When Women Speak in Old French Literature.* Philadelphia: University of Pennsylvania Press.

Burns, Robert I., S.J., ed. 1990. *Emperor of Culture: Alfonso X the Learned of Castile and His Thirteenth-Century Renaissance.* Philadelphia: University of Pennsylvania Press.

Burshatin, Israel. 1984. "The Docile Image: The Moor as a Figure of Force, Subservience, and Nobility in the *Poema de mio Cid. KRQ* 31.3: 269–80.

———. 1985. "The Moor in the Text: Metaphor, Emblem, and Silence." *Critical Inquiry* 12.1: 98–118.

———. 1992. "Playing the Moor: Parody and Performance in Lope de Vega's *El primer Fajardo.*" *PMLA* 107 (May): 566–81.

Burton, Deirdre. 1980. *Dialogue and Discourse: A Sociolinguistic Approach to Modern Drama, Dialogue, and Naturally Occurring Conversation.* London: Routledge and Kegan Paul.

Bynum, Caroline Walker. 1982. *Jesus as Mother: Studies in the Spirituality of the High Middle Ages.* Berkeley: University of California Press.

Cancionero de Romances [1550] 1967. Ed. Antonio Rodríguez Moñino. Madrid: Castalia.

Cancionero general recopilado por Hernando del Castillo [1511] 1958. Ed. Antonio Rodríguez-Moñino. Madrid: Real Academia Española.

Cantera, Francisco. 1958. "Raquel e Vidas." *Sefarad* 18: 99–108.

Carpenter, Dwayne E. 1986. "Minorities in Medieval Spain: The Legal Status of Jews and Muslims in the *Siete Partidas.*" Romance Quarterly 33.3: 275–87.

Carrasco Urgoiti, María. 1956. *El moro de Granada en la literatura (del siglo XV al XX).* Madrid: Revista de Occidente.

Cartagena, Teresa de. 1967. *Arboleda de los enfermos: Admiraçion operum Dey.* Ed. Lewis J. Hutton. Boletín de la Real Academia Española, supp. 16. Madrid: Real Academia Española.

Castillo, David, and Nicholas Spadaccini. 1995. "'Lazarillo de Tormes' and the Picaresque in Light of Current Political Culture." Department of Spanish and Portuguese, University of Minnesota. Photocopy.

Castro, Américo. 1914. "Disputa entre un cristiano y un judío." *RFE* 1: 173–80.

———. 1954. *The Structure of Spanish History.* Trans. Edmund L. King. Princeton: Princeton University Press.

Catarella, Teresa. 1990. "Feminine Historicizing in the *romancero novelesco.*" *BHS* 67.4 (October): 331–43.

Cerquiglini, Bernard. 1986. "The Syntax of Discursive Authority: The Example of Feminine Discourse." *YFS* 70: 183–98.

Chambers, Ross. 1986. "Gossip and the Novel: Knowing Narrative and Narrative Knowing in Balzac, Mme. de Lafayette, and Proust." *Australian Journal of French Studies* 23.2: 212–33.

Cirot, Georges. 1938. "La Maurophilie littéraire en Espagne au XVIe siècle." *Bulletin Hispanique* 40: 281–96.

Clanchy, Michael T. 1983. "Looking Back from the Invention of Printing." In *Literacy in Historical Perspective,* ed. Daniel P. Resnick, 7–22. Washington, D.C.: Library of Congress.

Clarke, Dorothy Clotelle. 1978. "*Libro de Buen Amor:* Line 1034e, *SYN,* and Speech Mimicry." *La Corónica* 7.1 (fall): 17–20.

———. 1984. "Juan Ruiz: A Romance Viejo in the *Libro de Buen Amor* (la mora)? *KRQ* 31.4: 391–402.

Colledge, Edmund O.S.A., and James Walsh. 1976. "Editing Julian of Norwich's *Revelations:* A Progress Report." *Medieval Studies* 38: 404–27.

Combet, Louis. 1971. *Recherches sur le "Refranero" Castillan.* Paris: Société d'Edition "Les Belles Lettres."

Convivencia: Jews, Muslims, and Christians in Medieval Spain. 1992. Ed. Vivian B. Mann, Thomas F. Glick, and Jerrilynn D. Dodds. New York: George Braziller.

Copenhagen, Carol A. 1984. "Salutations in Fifteenth-Century Spanish Vernacular Letters." *La Corónica* 12.2 (spring): 254–64.

———. 1986. "The *Conclusio* in Fifteenth-Century Spanish Letters." *La Corónica* 14.2 (spring): 213–19.

Corominas, Joan, and José A. Pascual. 1987–91. *Diccionario crítico etimológico castellano e hispánico.* 6 vols. Madrid: Gredos.

Crónica del rey don Juan II. 1875. In *Biblioteca de autores españoles: Crónicas de los reyes de Castilla,* ed. Cayetano Rosell. 68:173–392. Madrid: M. Rivadeneyra.

Cruz, Anne J. 1992. "The Politics of Illicit Love in the 'Pedro el cruel' Ballad Cycle." *Scandinavian Yearbook of Folklore* 48: 1–16.

Curry, Kathleen Amanda. 1988. "Las 'Memorias' de Leonor López de Córdoba." Ph.D. diss., Georgetown University.

Dagenais, John. 1994. *The Ethics of Reading in Manuscript Culture: Glossing the "Libro de Buen Amor."* Princeton: Princeton University Press.

Danby, Herbert, ed. and trans. 1933. *The Mishnah.* London: Oxford University Press.

Daniel, Norman. 1983. *Heroes and Saracens: An Interpretation of the Chansons de Geste.* Edinburgh: Edinburgh University Press.

Davis, Natalie Zemon. 1975. *Society and Culture in Early Modern France: Eight essays.* Stanford: Stanford University Press.

Débax, Michelle. 1982. *Romancero.* Madrid: Alhambra.

de Beauvoir, Simone. 1970. *The Second Sex.* Trans. H. M. Parshley. New York: Bantam.

de Combarieu, Micheline. 1979. "Un personnage épique: La jeune musulmane." In *Mélanges de langue et littérature françaises du Moyen-âge offerts à Pierre Jonin,* 181–96. Aix-en-Provence: Cuerma.

Denich, Bette. "Sex and Power in the Balkans." In *Women, Culture, and Society,* ed. Michelle Zimbalist Rosaldo and Louise Lamphere, 243–62. Stanford: Stanford University Press.

de Nogent, Guibert. 1970. *Memoirs. Self and Society in Medieval France. The Memoirs of Abbot Guibert of Nogent.* Ed. John Benton. New York: Harper.

Departamento de Arabe e Islam. Universidad Autónoma de Madrid. 1983. "La mujer andalusí, elementos para su historia." In *Las mujeres medievales y su ámbito jurídico, Actas de las II jornadas de investigación interdisciplinaria,* 183–89. Madrid: Universidad Autónoma de Madrid.

Deyermond, Alan. 1973. "Structural and Stylistic Patterns in the *Cantar de Mio Cid.*" In *Medieval Studies in Honor of Robert White Linker,* 55–71. Madrid: Castalia.

———, ed. 1977. *"Mio Cid" Studies.* London: Tamesis.

———. 1978. "The Worm and the Partridge: Reflections on the Poetry of Florencia Pinar." *Mester* 7: 3–8.

————. 1983. "Spain's First Women Writers." In *Women in Hispanic Literature: Icons and Fallen Idols,* ed. Beth Miller, 27–52. Berkeley: University of California Press.

————. 1987a. *El "Cantar de Mio Cid" y la épica medieval española.* Barcelona: Sirmio.

————. 1987b. "El *Libro de Buen Amor* a la luz de las recientes tendencias críticas." *Insula: Revista de Letras y Ciencias Humanas* 42.488–9 (July-August): 39–40.

————. 1988. "La sexualidad en la épica medieval española." *NRFH* 36.2: 767–86.

————. 1992. "Álora la bien cercada: Structure, Image, and Point of View in a Frontier Ballad." In *Hispanic Medieval Studies in Honor of Samuel G. Armistead,* ed. E. Michael Gerli and Harvey L. Sharrer, 97–109. Madison, Wisc.: Hispanic Seminary of Medieval Studies.

Díaz-Plaja, Fernando. 1984. *Historia de España en sus documentos: Siglo XV.* Madrid: Cátedra.

Díaz Quiñones, Arcadio. 1973. "Literatura y casta triunfante: El romancero fronterizo." *Sin Nombre* 3.3: 8–25.

Diccionario de Autoridades. 1969. 6 vols. Edición Facsímil. Madrid: Gredos.

Diccionario de la lengua española. 1992. Madrid: Real Academia Española.

Diego de Valera, Mosén. 1941. *Memorial de diversas hazañas, crónica de Enrique IV.* Ed. Juan de Mata Carriazo. Colección de Crónicas Españolas 4. Madrid: Espasa-Calpe.

Dillard, Heath. 1976. "Women in Reconquest Castile: The *Fueros* of Sepúlveda and Cuenca." In *Women in Medieval Society,* ed. Brenda M. Bolton, et al., 71–94. Philadelphia: University of Pennsylvania Press.

————. 1984. *Daughters of the Reconquest. Women in Castilian Town Society, 1100–1300.* Cambridge: Cambridge University Press.

Diz, Marta Ana. 1988. "Raquel y Vidas: La guerra en la paz o el 'art' del desterrado." *Romance Quarterly* 35.4: 449–55.

Domínguez Rey, Antonio. 1981. *Antología de la poesía medieval española.* Vol. 2. Madrid: Narcea.

Donovan, Josephine. 1987. "Towards a Women's Poetics." In *Feminist Issues in Literary Scholarship,* ed. Shari Benstock, 98–109. Bloomington: Indiana University Press.

Duggan, Joseph J. 1989. *The "Cantar de Mio Cid": Poetic Creation in Its Economic and Social Contexts.* Cambridge: Cambridge University Press.

Durán, Agustín, ed. 1945. *Romancero General.* Vol. 2. Biblioteca de Autores Españoles 16. Madrid: Atlas.

Eagleton, Terry. 1983. *Literary Theory: An Introduction.* Minneapolis: University of Minnesota Press.

Ellis, Deborah Sue. 1982. "The Image of the Home in Early English and Spanish Literature." Ph.D. diss., University of California, Berkeley.

Enciclopedia del Idioma. 1947. Ed. Martín Alonso. 3 vols. Madrid: Aguilar.

England, John. 1980. "The Second Appearance of Rachel and Vidas in the *Poema de Mio Cid.*" In *Hispanic Studies in Honour of Frank Pierce Presented by Former and Present Members of the Department of Hispanic Studies in the University of Sheffield,* ed. John England, 51–58. Sheffield: Department of Hispanic Studies, University of Sheffield.

Entwistle, William J. 1930. "The Romancero del Rey Don Pedro in Ayala and the Cuarta Crónica General." *MLR* 25: 306–26.

Erler, Mary, and Maryanne Kowaleski. 1988. "Introduction." In *Women and Power in the Middle Ages,* ed. Mary Erler and Maryanne Kowaleski, 1–18. Athens: University of Georgia Press.

Estow, Clara. 1982. "Leonor López de Córdoba: Portrait of a Medieval Courtier." *Fifteenth-Century Studies* 5: 23–46.

———. 1992. "Widows in the Historical Literature of Medieval Castile." In *Upon My Husband's Death: Widows in the Literature and Histories of Medieval Europe,* ed. Louise Mirrer, 153–67. Ann Arbor: University of Michigan Press.

Fenster, Thelma S. 1987. "The Son's Mother: Aalais and Marsent in Raoul de Cambrai." *Oliphant* 12.2 (summer): 77–93.

Fernández Jiménez, Juan. 1982. "Cowardice in Two Romance Epic Poems: *La Chançun de Willame* and *Poema de Mio Cid.*" In Literary and Historical Perspectives of the Middle Ages, ed. Patricia W. Cummins, Patrick W. Connor, and Charles W. Connell, 38–51. Morgantown, W. V.: West Virginia University Press.

Ferrante, Joan M. 1975. *In Pursuit of Perfection: Courtly Love in Medieval Literature.* Port Washington, N.Y.: Kennikat.

Finke, Wayne. 1978. "Women in *Los Milagros* of Gonzalo de Berceo." Paper presented at Onondaga Community College, Syracuse, N.Y., October 28.

Firpo, Arturo Roberto. 1980. "Un ejemplo de autobiografía medieval: Las 'Memorias de Leonor López de Córdoba (1400).'" *Zagadnienia Rodzajów Literackich* 23, no. 1: 19–31.

Fita, Fidel. 1886. "La judería de Segovia: Documentos inéditos." Boletín de la Real Academia de la Historia 9: 344–89.

Fletcher, Richard. 1992. *Moorish Spain.* London: Weidenfeld and Nicolson.

Flores, Angel, and Kate Flores. 1986. *The Defiant Muse: Hispanic Feminist Poems from the Middle Ages to the Present.* New York: Feminist.

Foucault, Michel. 1980. *The History of Sexuality.* Trans. Robert Hurley. Vol. 1. New York: Vintage.

———. 1983. "The Subject and Power." Trans. Leslie Sawyer. In *Michel Fou-*

cault, Beyond Structuralism and Hermeneutics, ed. Hubert L. Dreyfus and Paul Rabinow, 2d ed., 208–26. Chicago: University of Chicago Press.

Franco, Jean. 1973. *Spanish American Literature since Independence.* London: Ernest Benn Ltd.

———. 1989. *Plotting Women: Gender and Representation in Mexico.* New York: Columbia University Press.

Franklin, Peter. 1986. "Peasant Widows' 'Liberation' and Remarriage Before the Black Death." *Economic History Review* 39 (May): 186–204.

Freud, Sigmund. 1973. "The Taboo of Virginity." In *The Standard Edition of the Complete Psychological Works of Sigmund Freud,* ed. and trans. James Strachey, 11:191–208. London: Hogarth.

Fuero Juzgo. 1872. Vol. 1 of *Los Códigos españoles concordados y anotados.* Madrid: Antonio de San Martín.

Fuero de Usagre. 1907. In Biblioteca Jurídica Española anterior al siglo XIX. Vol. 1. Ed. R. de Ureña y Smenjaud and A. Bonilla y San Martín. Madrid: Hijos de Reus.

Fulks, Barbara. 1989–90. "The Poet Named Florencia Pinar." *La Corónica* 18.1: 33–44.

Gampel, Benjamin. 1992. "Jews, Christians, and Muslims in Medieval Iberia: *Convivencia* through the Eyes of Sephardic Jews." In *Convivencia: Jews, Muslims, and Christians in Medieval Spain,* ed. Vivian B. Mann, Thomas F. Glick, and Jerrilyn D. Dodds, 11–37. New York: George Braziller.

Garci-Gómez, Miguel. 1975. "*Mío Cid*": *Estudios de endocrítica.* Barcelona: Planeta.

———. 1993. *Dos autores en el Cantar de mio Cid: Aplicación de la Informática.* Cáceres: Universidad de Extremadura.

Gaylord, Mary M. 1992. "Spain's Renaissance Conquests and the Retroping of Identity." *JHP* 16: 125–36.

Gerli, E. Michael. 1992. "Poet and Pilgrim: Discourse, Language, Imagery, and Audience in Berceo's *Milagros de Nuestra Señora.*" In *Hispanic Medieval Studies in Honor of Samuel G. Armistead,* ed. E. Michael Gerli and Harvey L. Sharrer, 139–51. Madison, Wisc.: Hispanic Seminary of Medieval Studies.

Gerli, E. Michael, and Harvey L. Sharrer, eds. 1992. *Hispanic Medieval Studies in Honor of Samuel G. Armistead.* Madison, Wisc.: Hispanic Seminary of Medieval Studies.

Ghassemi, Ruth Lubenow. 1989. "La 'crueldad' de los vencidos: Un estudio interpretativo de *Memorias de doña Leonor López de Córdoba.*" *La Corónica* 18.1: 19–32.

Gilman, Sander. 1991. *The Jew's Body.* New York: Routledge.

Gilmore, David D. 1987. *Aggression and Community: Paradoxes of Andalusian Culture.* New Haven: Yale University Press.

———. 1990. *Manhood in the Making: Cultural Concepts of Masculinity.* New Haven: Yale University Press.

Girard, René. 1972. *La violence et le sacré.* Paris: Grasset.

———. 1978. *To Double Business Bound: Essays on Literature, Mimesis, and Anthropology.* Baltimore: Johns Hopkins University Press.

———. 1982. *Le Bouc émissaire.* Paris: Grasset.

Glick, Thomas F. 1992a. "*Convivencia:* An Introductory Note. In *Convivencia: Jews, Muslims, and Christians in Medieval Spain,* ed. Vivian B. Mann, Thomas F. Glick, and Jerrilyn D. Dodds, 1–9. New York: George Braziller.

———. 1992b. "Science in Medieval Spain: The Jewish Contribution in the Context of *Convivencia.* In *Convivencia: Jews, Muslims, and Christians in Medieval Spain,* ed. Vivian B. Mann, Thomas F. Glick, and Jerrilyn D. Dodds, 83–111. New York: George Braziller.

Gluckman, Max. 1963. "Gossip and Scandal." *Current Anthropology* 4: 307–16.

Godwin, Marjorie Harness. 1980. "He-said-she-said: Formal Cultural Procedures for the Construction of a Gossip Dispute Activity." *American Ethnologist* 7.1 (February): 674–94.

Godzich, Wlad. 1986. "The Further Possibility of Knowledge." Foreword to *Heterologies: Discourse on the Other,* by Michel de Certeau, trans. Brian Massumi. Minneapolis: University of Minnesota Press.

Gold, Penny Schine. 1987. *The Lady and the Virgin: Image, Attitude, and Experience in Twelfth-Century France.* Chicago: University of Chicago Press.

Goldberg, Harriet. 1979. "Two Parallel Medieval Commonplaces: Antifeminism and Antisemitism in the Hispanic Literary Tradition." In *Aspects of Jewish Culture in the Middle Ages: Papers of the Eighth Annual Conference of the Center for Medieval and Early Renaissance Studies, SUNY-Binghampton,* ed. Paul Szarmach, 85–119. Albany: State University of New York Press.

———. 1983. "Sexual Humor in Misogynist Medieval Exempla." In *Women in Hispanic Literature: Icons and Fallen Idols,* ed. Beth Miller, 67–83. Berkeley: University of California Press.

Gómez Sierra, Esther. 1992. "La experiencia femenina de la amargura como sustento de un discurso histórico alternativo: Leonor López de Córdoba y sus *Memorias.*" In *La voz del silencio, I: Fuentes directas para la historia de las mujeres, siglos VIII–XVIII,* ed. Cristina Graiño Segura, 111–29. Madrid: Asociación Cultural Al-Mudayna.

González, Aurelio. 1984. *Formas y funciones de los principios en el Romancero viejo.* Mexico City: Universidad Autónoma Metropolitana-Iztapalapa.

González Vázquez, Marta. 1984. *Las mujeres de la Edad Media y el Camino de Santiago.* Santiago de Compostela: Xunta de Galicia.

Gordon, Jan B. 1985. "Affiliation as (Dis)semination: Gossip and Family in

George Eliot's European Novel." *Journal of European Studies* 15.59 (September): part 3, 155–89.

———. 1984. "Gossip, Diary, Letter, Text: Anne Brontë's Narrative *Tenant* and the Problematic of the Gothic Sequel." *ELH* 51.4 (winter): 719–45.

Greenblatt, Stephen. 1991. *Marvelous Possessions: The Wonder of the New World.* Chicago: University of Chicago Press.

Haas, Adelaide. 1979. "Male and Female Spoken Language Differences: Stereotypes and Evidence." *Psychological Bulletin* 86.3: 616–26.

Hanawalt, Barbara, ed. 1986. *Women and Work in Preindustrial Europe.* Bloomington: Indiana University Press.

Harvey, L.P. 1990. *Islamic Spain, 1250–1500.* Chicago: University of Chicago Press.

Hatton, Vikki, and Angus Mackay. 1983. "Anti-Semitism in the *Cantigas de Santa Maria.*" *BHS* 60.3: 189–99.

Herlihy, David. 1962. "Land, Family, and Women in Continental Europe, 701–1200." *Traditio* 18: 89–120.

Hernández, Francisco Javier. 1987. "Juan Ruiz en su mundo." *Insula* 42 (July-August): 488–89.

Hillgarth, J. N. 1976–78. *The Spanish Kingdoms, 1250–1516.* 2 vols. Oxford: Clarendon.

Irigaray, Luce. 1983. *Speculum of the Other Woman.* Trans. Gillian C. Gill. Ithaca, N.Y.: Cornell University Press.

———. 1985. "Sexual Difference." In *French Feminist Thought: A Reader,* ed. Toril Moi, 118–130. Oxford: Basil Blackwell.

Irizarry, Estelle. 1987. "Echoes of the Amazon Myth in Medieval Spanish Literature." In *Women in Hispanic Literature: Icons and Fallen Idols,* ed. Beth Miller, 53–66. Berkeley: University of California Press.

Jara, René, Nicholas Spadaccini, Mario Gómez-Moriana, Lawrence Mantini, and Luis A. Ramos-García, eds. 1989. *1492–1992: Re/Discovering Colonial Writing.* Minneapolis: Prisma Institute.

Johnson, Fern L. 1986. "Coming to Terms With Women's Language." *QJS* 72: 318–30.

Johnson, Lynn Staley. 1991. "The Trope of the Scribe and the Question of Literary Authority in the Works of Julian of Norwich and Margery Kempe." *Speculum* 66.4 (October): 820–38.

Jones, Dorothy. 1986. "Digging Deep: Olga Masters, Storyteller." *Kunapipi* 8.3: 28–35.

Joset, Jacques. 1988. *Nuevas investigaciones sobre el "Libro de Buen Amor."* Madrid: Cátedra.

Kagay, Donald J. 1993. "Columbus as Standardbearer and Mirror of the Spanish Reconquest." *American Neptune* 53 (fall): 254–59.

Kaminsky, Amy Katz, and Elaine Dorough Johnson. 1984. "To Restore Honor and Fortune: 'The Autobiography of Leonor López de Córdoba.'" In *The Female Autograph*, ed. Domna C. Stanton and Jeanine Parisier Plottel, vol. 12–13, 77–88. New York: New York Literary Forum.

Kaye, Jacqueline. 1985. "Islamic Imperialism and the Creation of Some Ideas of 'Europe.'" In *Europe and Its Others: Proceedings of the Essex Conference on the Sociology of Literature*, July, 1984, ed. Frances Barker, Peter Hulme, Margaret Iverson, and Diana Loxley, 59–71. Colchester: University of Essex Press.

Keller, John Esten. 1982. "*Miracle of the Jewess Thrown from a High Cliff*: Miracle 107 of the *Cantigas de Santa Maria*." *Xavier Review* 2.1–2: 63–67.

———. 1987. "The Threefold Impact of the Cantigas de Santa Maria: Visual, Verbal, and Musical." In *Studies on the Cantigas de Santa Maria*, ed. Israel J. Katz and John E. Keller, 6–33. Madison, Wisc.: Hispanic Seminary of Medieval Studies.

Keller, John Esten, and Richard P. Kinkade. 1984. *Iconography in Medieval Spanish Literature*. Lexington: University Press of Kentucky.

Kempe, Margery. 1936. *The Book of Margery Kempe*. Trans. W. Butler-Bowdon. London: Jonathan Cape.

Kirby, Steven D. 1986. Juan Ruiz's *Serranas:* The Archpriest–Pilgrim and Medieval Wild Women." In *Hispanic Studies in Honor of Alan D. Deyermond: A North American Tribute*, ed. John S. Miletich, 151–69. Madison, Wisc.: Hispanic Seminary of Medieval Studies.

Knudson, Charles A. 1969. "Le thème de la princesse sarrasine dans *La Prise d'Orange*." *RPh* 22.4: 449–62.

Kodish, Deborah G. 1980. "Moving Towards the Everyday: Some Thoughts on Gossip and Visiting as Secular Procession." *Folklore Papers of the University Folklore Association* 9: 93–104.

Kraeling, Emil Gottlieb Heinrich. 1924–25. "The Names 'Rachel' and 'Reu.'" *American Journal of Semitic Languages and Literatures* 41: 193–94.

Kramer, Cheris. 1975. "Sex-Related Differences in Address Systems." *Anthropological Linguistics* 17: 198–210.

Kristeva, Julia. 1985. "*Stabat Mater*." Trans. Arthur Goldhammer. *Poetics Today* 6.1–2: 133–52.

———. 1991. *Strangers to Ourselves*. Trans. Leon Roudiez. New York: Columbia University Press.

Labov, William. 1972a. *Language in the Inner City: Studies in the Black English Vernacular*. Philadelphia: University of Pennsylvania Press.

———. 1972b. *Sociolinguistic Patterns*. Philadelphia: University of Pennsylvania Press.

Lacarra, María Eugenia. 1980. *El poema de Mío Cid: Realidad histórica e ideológica*. Madrid: J. Porrúa Turanzas.

———. 1988a. "'L'amour discourtois': Del miedo a la castración a la prepotencia del discurso." *Insula* 498: 5–6.

———. 1988b. "Notes on Feminist Analysis of Medieval Spanish Literature and History." *La Corónica* 17.1: 14–22.

Lakoff, Robin. 1975. *Language and Woman's Place.* New York: Harper and Row.

Larsen, Anne R. 1990. 'Un honnest passetems': Strategies of Legitimation in French Renaissance Women's Prefaces." *L'esprit créateur* 30.4 (winter): 11–23.

Las mujeres medievales y su ámbito jurídico. 1983. Actas de las II jornadas de investigación interdisciplinaria. Madrid: Universidad Autónoma de Madrid.

Lasry, Anita Benaim de. 1987. "Marisaltos: Artifical Purification in Alfonso el Sabio's *Cantiga* 107." In *Studies on the Cantigas de Santa Maria: Art, Music, and Poetry,* ed. Israel J. Katz and John E. Keller, 299–311. Madison, Wisc.: Hispanic Seminary of Medieval Studies.

Lauzardo, Aurora. 1993. "El derecho a la escrita: Las *Memorias* de Leonor López de Córdoba." *Medievalia* 15 (diciembre): 1–13.

Lawrance, Jeremy. 1984. "The Audience of the Libro de Buen Amor." *Comparative Literature* 36.3: 220–37.

Layna Serrano, Francisco. 1943. *Los conventos antiguos de Guadalajara.* Madrid: Consejo Superior de Investigaciones Científicas.

Lejeune, Philippe. 1982. "The Autobiographical Contract." In *French Literary Theory Today,* ed. Tzvetan Todorov. Cambridge: Cambridge University Press.

Lemaire, Ria. 1986. "Explaining Away the Female Subject: The Case of Medieval Lyric." *Poetics Today* 7: 729–43.

Lerner, Gerda. 1986. *The Creation of Patriarchy.* New York: Oxford University Press.

Levinas, Emmanuel. 1985. *Le Temps et l'autre.* 2d ed. Paris: Quadrige/Presses Universitaires de France.

Lida de Malkiel, María Rosa. 1961. *Two Spanish Masterpieces: "The Book of Good Love" and "The Celestina".* Urbana: University of Illinois Press.

Llorca, Carmen Marimón. 1990. *Prosistas castellanas medievales.* Alicante: Caja de Ahorros Provincial.

López de Ayala, Pero. 1875–77. *Crónica del rey don Pedro: Crónicas de los reyes de Castilla.* Ed. Cayetano Rosell. Biblioteca de Autores Españoles 66. Madrid: Rivadeneyra.

López Martínez, Nicolás. 1954. *Los judaizantes castellanos y la inquisición en tiempo de Isabel la Católica.* Burgos: Luciano.

Lucas, Angela. 1983. *Women in the Middle Ages: Religion, Marriage, and Letters.* Brighton, Sussex: Harvester.

MacKay, Angus. 1976. "The Ballad and the Frontier in Late Medieval Spain." *BHS* 53: 15–33.

————. 1977. *Spain in the Middle Ages: From Frontier to Empire, 1000–1500.* London: Macmillan.

————. "The Virgin's Vassals." 1989. In *God and Man in Medieval Spain: Essays in Honour of J. R. L. Highfield,* ed. Derek W. Lomax and David Mackenzie, 49–58. Warminster, England: Aris and Phillips.

Manuel, Juan. 1987. *El Conde Lucanor: A Collection of Medieval Spanish Stories.* Ed. John England. Warminster, England: Aris and Phillips.

Márquez de Castro, Tomás. 1981. *Compendio histórico y genealógico de los títulos de Castilla y señoríos antiguos y modernos de la ciudad de Córdoba y su reyno (1779).* Ed. José Manuel de Bernardo Ares. Córdoba: Diputación Provincial de Córdoba.

Mauss, Marcel. 1967. *The Gift: Forms and Functions Exchange in Archaic Societies.* Trans. Ian Cunnison. New York: W. W. Norton.

McGrady, Donald. 1985. "Did the Cid Repay the Jews? A Reconsideration." *Romania* 106.3–4: 518–27.

Memorias de don Enrique IV de Castilla. 1835–1913. Vol. 2, *Colección diplomática.* Madrid: Real Academia Española.

Menéndez Pidal, Ramón. 1934. *La leyenda de los Infantes de Lara.* Madrid: Centro de Estudios Históricos.

————. 1953. *Romancero hispánico (hispano-portugués, americano y sefardí): Teoría e historia.* 2 vols. Madrid: Espasa-Calpe.

————, ed. 1913. *Poema de Mío Cid.* Madrid: Ediciones de "La Lectura."

Menéndez y Pelayo, Marcelino. 1916–24. *Antología de poetas líricos castellanos desde la formación del idioma hasta nuestros días.* 14 vols. Madrid: Sucesores de Hernando.

————. *Tratado de los romances viejos.* Vols. 11–12 of *Antología de poetas líricos castellanos.*

Menocal, María Rosa. 1987. *The Arabic Role in Medieval Literary History: A Forgotten Heritage.* Philadelphia: University of Pennsylvania Press.

Mirrer, Louise. 1991. "Adultery, Intermarriage, and the Theme of Group Destruction in the Eastern Judeo-Spanish Ballad Tradition." *Shofar* 9.2. (winter): 2–15.

————. 1992. *Upon My Husband's Death. Widows in the Literature and Histories of Medieval Europe.* Ann Arbor: University of Michigan Press.

————. 1994a. "The Jew's Body in Medieval Iberian Literary Portraits and Miniatures." *Shofar* 12, no. 3: 17–30.

————. 1994b. "Representing 'Other' Men: Muslims, Jews, and Masculine Ideals in Medieval Castilian Epic and Ballad." In *Medieval Masculinities,* ed. Clare Lees, 169–86. Minneapolis: University of Minnesota Press.

————. 1995a. "*Entre la gente se dice*: Gossip and Indirection as Modes of Representation in the *Romances noticieros.*" In *Studies on Medieval Spanish Literature in Honor of Charles F. Fraker,* ed. Mercedes Vaquero and Alan Deyermond, 219–27. Madison, Wisc.: The Hispanic Seminary of Medieval Studies.

———. 1995b. "Men's Language, Women's Power: Female Voices in the *Romancero Viejo.*" In *Oral Tradition and Hispanic Literature. Studies in Honor of Samuel G. Armistead,* ed. Mishael M. Caspi., 523–47. New York: Garland.

———. 1995c. "Género, Poder et Lenguaje en los poemas de Florencia Pinar." *Medievalia* 19:9–15.

Mitchell, Stephen A. 1988. *Relational Concepts in Psychoanalysis: An Integration.* Cambridge: Harvard University Press.

Mitchell, Timothy J. 1988. *Violence and Piety in Spanish Folklore.* Philadelphia: University of Pennsylvania Press.

Moller, Herbert. 1958. "The Social Causation of the Courtly Love Complex." *Comparative Studies in Society and History* 1: 137–63.

Montrelay, Michèle. 1987. "Inquiry into Femininity." In *French Feminist Thought: A Reader,* ed. Toril Moi, 227–49. Oxford: Basil Blackwell.

Morreale, Margherita. 1983 and 1984. "Los 'Gozos' de la Virgen en el *Libro* de Juan Ruiz." Parts 1 and 2. *Revista de Filología Española* 63: 223–90; 64: 1–69.

Morrison, Toni. 1992. *Playing in the Dark: Whiteness and the Literary Imagination.* Cambridge: Harvard University Press.

Mulac, Anthony, Torborg Louisa Lundell, and James J. Bradac. 1986. "Male/Female Language Differences and Attributional Consequences in a Public Speaking Situation: Toward an Explanation of the Gender-Linked Language Effect." *ComM* 53.2: 115–29.

Nader, Helen. 1979. *The Mendoza Family in the Spanish Renaissance 1350–1550.* New Brunswick, N. J.: Rutgers University Press.

Nichols, Stephen G. 1988. "Medieval Women Writers: *Aisthesis* and the Powers of Marginality." *YFS* 75: 77–94.

O'Barr, William M., and Bowman K. Atkins. 1980. "'Women's Language' or 'Powerless Language'?" In *Women and Language in Literature and Society,* ed. Sally McConell-Ginet, Ruth Borker, and Nelly Furman, 93–110. New York: Praeger.

O'Callaghan, Joseph F. 1975. *History of Medieval Spain.* Ithaca, N. Y.: Cornell University Press.

Odd, Frank L. 1983. "Women of the Romancero: A Voice of Reconciliation." *Hispania* 66.3: 360–68.

Orduña, Germán. 1989. "La sección de romances en el *Cancionero general* (Valencia, 1511): Recepción cortesana del romancero tradicional." In *The Age of the Catholic Monarchs, 1474–1516. Literary Studies in Memory of Keith Whinnom,* ed. Alan Deyermond and Ian Macpherson, *BHS* special issue, 113–22. Liverpool University Press.

Ornstein, Jacob. 1942. "Misogyny and Pro-feminism in Early Castilian Literature." *Modern Language Quarterly* 3: 221–34.

Pereira Zazo, Óscar, and Tony Zahareas, eds. 1994. *Libro de Buen Amor.* By Juan Ruiz, Arcipreste de Hita. Madrid: Espasa-Calpe.

Pérez de Guzmán, Fernán. 1965. *Generaciones y semblanzas.* Ed. R. B. Tate. London: Tamesis.

Pérez de Tudela y Velasco, María Isabel. "La mujer castellano-leonesa del pleno medievo: Perfiles literarios, estatuto jurídico y situación económica." In *Las mujeres medievales y su ámbito jurídico,* 59–77. Madrid: Universidad Autónoma de Madrid.

Peristiany, Jean G. 1966. Introduction to *Honour and Shame: The Values of Mediterranean Society.* Ed. J. G. Peristiany. Chicago: University of Chicago Press.

Phillips, Gail. 1983. *The Imagery of the "Libro de Buen Amor."* Spanish Series 9. Madison, Wisc.: Hispanic Seminary of Medieval Studies.

Phillips, William D., Jr. 1978. *Enrique IV and the Crisis of Fifteenth-Century Castile 1425–1480.* Cambridge, Mass.: Medieval Academy of America.

Phillips, William D., Jr., and Carla Rahn Phillips. 1992. *The Worlds of Columbus.* Cambridge: Cambridge University Press.

Pita, Isabel Beceiro. 1986. "La mujer noble en la baja Edad Media castellana." In *La condición de la mujer en la edad media,* Actas del coloquio celebrado en la Casa de Velázquez del 5 al 7 de noviembre de 1984, 289–313. Madrid: Casa de Velázquez, Universidad Complutense.

Pitt-Rivers, Julian. 1977. *The Fate of Sechem; Or, the Politics of Sex: Essays in the Anthropology of the Mediterranean.* Cambridge: Cambridge University Press.

Pleck, Joseph H. 1987. "The Theory of Male Sex-Role Identity: Its Rise and Fall, 1936–Present." In *The Making of Masculinities: The New Men's Studies,* ed. Harry Brod, 21–38. Boston: Allen and Unwin.

Pliegos poéticos españoles en la Universidad de Praga. 1960. 2 vols. Madrid: Colección Joyas Bibliográficas.

Poema de Fernán González. 1946. Ed. Alonso Zamora Vicente. 2d ed. Madrid: Espasa-Calpe.

Pope, Randolph. 1974. *La autobiografía española hasta Torres Villarroel.* Frankfurt: P. Lang; Bern: H. Lang.

Powers, James F. 1988. *A Society Organized for War: The Iberian Municipal Militias in the Central Middle Ages, 1000–1284.* Berkeley: University of California Press.

Pulgar, Hernando del. 1943. *Crónica de los Reyes Católicos.* Ed. Juan de Mata Carriazo. 2 vols. Madrid: Espasa-Calpe.

Rakow, Lana F. 1986. "Rethinking Gender Research in Communication." *Journal of Communications* 36.4: 11–26.

Ratcliffe, Marjorie. 1984. "Adulteresses, Mistresses, and Prostitutes: Extramarital Relationships in Medieval Castile." *Hispania* 67: 346–50.

Recio, Roxana. 1992. "Otra dama que desaparece: La abstracción retórica en tres modelos de canción de Florencia Pinar." *RCEH* 16.2: 329–39.

Reilly, Bernard. 1982. *The Kingdom of León-Castilla Under Queen Urraca, 1109–1126*. Princeton: Princeton University Press.

Reiss, Edmund. 1989. "Ambiguous Signs and Authorial Deceptions in Fourteenth-Century Fictions." In *Sign, Sentence, Discourse: Language in Medieval Thought and Literature,* ed. Julian Wasserman and Lois Roney, 113–37. Syracuse: Syracuse University Press.

Rigolot, Françoise. 1990. "Ecrire au féminin à la Renaissance: Problèmes et perspectives." *L'esprit créateur* 30.4 (winter): 3–10.

Rivarola, José Luis. 1973. "Doña Endrina e don Melón en uno casados son: Sobre el desenlace del episodio de Melón y Endrina en el Libro de Buen Amor." *RF* 85: 341–47.

Rivera Garretas, María-Milagros. 1990. "Leonor López de Córdoba: La autorepresentación," In *Textos y espacios de mujeres (Europa, siglos IV-XV),* ed. María-Milagros Rivera Garretas, 159–78. Barcelona: Icaria.

Roman, Camille, Susan Juhasz, and Christanne Miller, eds. 1994. *The Women and Language Debate: A Sourcebook.* New Brunswick: Rutgers University Press.

Rosaldo, Michelle Zimbalist, and Louise Lamphere, eds. 1974. *Women, Culture, and Society.* Stanford: Stanford University Press.

Rosenthal, Joel. 1987. "Other Victims: Peeresses as War Widows, 1450–1500." *History* 6: 213–30.

Roth, Norman. 1990. "Jewish Collaborators in Alfonso's Scientific Work." In *Emperor of Culture: Alfonso X the Learned of Castile and His Thirteenth-Century Renaissance,* ed. Robert I. Burns, S.J., 59–71. Philadelphia: University of Pennsylvania Press.

Ruiz, Juan, Archpriest of Hita. 1972. *Libro de Buen Amor.* Ed. Raymond S. Willis with an introduction and English paraphrase. Princeton: Princeton University Press.

———. 1974. *Libro de Buen Amor.* Ed. Jacques Joset. Madrid: Espasa-Calpe.

Said, Edward. 1978. *Orientalism.* New York: Pantheon.

———. 1985. "Orientalism Reconsidered." In *Europe and Its Others: Proceedings of the Essex Conference on the Sociology of Literature,* ed. Francis Barker, et al., 14–27. Colchester: University of Essex.

———. 1993. *Culture and Imperialism.* New York: Knopf.

Salomonski, Eva. 1956. "Raquel e Vidas." *Vox Romanica* 15.2: 215–30.

Sánchez Albornoz. 1986. *La españa musulmana.* 2 vols. Buenos Aires: "El Ateneo."

Sandoval, Alberto. 1989. "De-Centering Misogyny in Spanish Medieval Texts:

The Case of Don Juan Manuel's XXV Exemplum." *Ideologies and Literatures* 4.1 (spring): 65–94.

Sartre, Jean Paul. 1948. *Anti-Semite and Jew.* Trans. George J. Becker. New York: Schoken.

Saugnieux, Joël. 1977. "Tradition mariale et les *Milagros de Berceo.*" *LR* 31: 32–65.

Schneider, Jane. 1971. "Of Vigilance and Virgins: Honor, Shame, and Access to Resources in Mediterranean Societies." *Ethnology* 10.1 (January): 1–24.

Schneider, Peter. 1969. "Honor and Conflict in a Sicilian Town." *Anthropological Quarterly* 42: 130–55.

Schwartz Lerner, Lía. 1988. "The Categories *Male/Female* in Seventeenth Century Narrative." Paper presented at the MLA Convention, San Francisco, 28 December.

Seidenspinner de Nuñez, Dayle. 1981. *The Allegory of Good Love: Parodic Perspectivism in the "Libro de Buen Amor."* Berkeley: University of California Press.

———. 1993. "'El solo me leyó': Gendered Hermeneutics and Subversive Poetics in *Admiraçion operum Dey* of Teresa de Cartagena." *Medievalia* 15: 14–23.

Selke, Angela. 1986. *The Conversos of 17th-Century Majorca: Life and Death in a Crypto-Jewish Community in XVII-Century Spain.* Jerusalem: Magnes Press.

Silva-Corvalán, Carmen. 1986. "The Social Profile of a Syntactico-Semantic Variable: Three Verb Forms in Old Castile." In *Diversity and Diachrony,* ed. David Sankoff, 279–92. Amsterdam: John Benjamins.

Silva de Romances [1550–1551]. 1970. Ed. Antonio Rodríguez-Moñino. Zaragoza: Publicaciones de la Cátedra Zaragoza.

Silva de varios romances. [1561] 1957. Barcelona: Castalla.

Sinclair, J. McH., and R. M. Coulthard. 1975. *Towards an Analysis of Discourse: The English Used by Teachers and Pupils.* London: Oxford University Press.

Smith, C. Colin. 1965. "Did the Cid Repay the Jews?" *Romania* 86: 520–38.

———, ed. 1971. *Spanish Ballads.* Oxford, New York: Pergamon.

———, ed. 1972. *Poema de mío Cid.* Oxford: Clarendon.

———. 1972. "On the Ethos of the 'Romancero Viejo.'" *Studies of the Spanish and Portuguese Ballad,* ed. N. D. Shergold, 5–24. London: Tamesis.

———. 1992. "*Convivencia* in the *Estoria de España* of Alfonso X." In *Hispanic Studies in Honor of Samuel G. Armistead,* ed. E. Michael Gerli and Harvey L. Sharrer, 291–301. Madison, Wisc.: Hispanic Seminary of Medieval Studies.

Smith, C. Colin, and J. Morris. 1967. "On 'Physical' Phrases in Old Spanish Epic and Other Texts." *Leeds Philosophical and Literary Society Proceedings* 12.5: 129–90.

Smith, Paul Julian. 1988. *Writing in the Margin: Spanish Literature of the Golden Age.* Oxford: Clarendon Press.

———. 1989. *The Body Hispanic.* Oxford: Clarendon.

———. 1992. *Representing the Other: 'Race,' Text, and Gender in Spanish and Spanish-American Narrative.* Oxford: Oxford University Press.

Smith, Sidonie. 1987. *A Poetics of Women's Autobiography: Marginality and the Fictions of Self-Representation.* Bloomington: Indiana University Press.

Snow, Joseph T. 1977. *The Poetry of Alfonso X, el Sabio: A Critical Bibliography.* London: Grant and Cutler.

———. 1984. "The Spanish Love Poet: Florencia Pinar." In *Medieval Women Writers,* ed. Katharina M. Wilson, 320–32. Athens: University of Georgia Press.

Sola-Solé, Josep. M. 1965. "En torno al Romance de la morilla burlada." *HR* 33: 136–46.

———. 1976. "De nuevo sobre las arcas del Cid." *KRQ* 23: 3–15.

Sponsler, Lucy A. 1982. "The Status of Married Women Under the Legal System of Spain." *Journal of Legal History* 3.2: 125–52.

Stanton, Domna C. 1984. "Autogynography: Is the Subject Different?" In *The Female Autograph,* ed. Domna C. Stanton and Jeanine Parisier Plottel, vol. 12–13, 5–22. New York: New York Literary Forum.

Sternberg, Meir. 1982. "Proteus in Quotation-Land: Mimesis and the Forms of Reported Discourse." *Poetics Today* 3.2: 107–56.

Stock, Brian. 1990. *Listening for the Text: On the Uses of the Past.* Baltimore: Johns Hopkins University Press.

Strack, Herman L. 1909. *The Jews and Human Sacrifice.* London: Cope and Fenwick.

Suelzer, Amy. 1993. "The Intersection of Public and Private Life in Leonor López de Córdoba's Autobiography." *Revista Monográfica* 9: 36–46.

Surtz, Ronald E. 1995. *Writing Women in Late Medieval and Early Modern Spain: The Mothers of Saint Teresa of Avila.* Philadelphia: University of Pennsylvania Press.

Swietlicki, Catherine. 1988. "Lope's Dialogic Imagination: Writing Other Voices of Monolithic Spain." *Bulletin of the Comediantes* 40.2: 205–26.

Synan, Edward A. 1967. *The Popes and the Jews in the Middle Ages.* New York: Macmillan.

Tannen, Deborah. 1986. "Introducing Constructed Dialogue in Greek and American Conversational and Literary Narrative." In *Direct and Indirect Speech,* ed. Florian Coulmas, 311–32. Berlin: Mouton de Gruyter.

Tate, Robert B. 1961. "An Apology for Monarchy." *RPh* 15: 111–23.

Thompson, Billy Bussell. 1987. "Jews in Hispanic Proverbs." *Yiddish* 6.4: 13–21.

Tinnell, Roger D. 1988–89. "Marisaltos and the 'Salt de la Bella Dona.'" *Cantigueiros* 2 (fall-spring): 69–77.

Torres Fontes, Juan. 1964. "La regencia de don Fernando de Antequera." *Anuario de Estudios Medievales* 1: 375–429.

Trachtenberg, Joshua. 1961. *The Devil and the Jews: The Medieval Conception of the Jew and Its Relation to Modern Antisemitism.* Cleveland: World Publishing Company.

Trieste, Marina Sbisa'. 1986 "Some Remarks on Women's Language." In *Pragmatics and Linguistics,* 173–78. Odense: Odense University Press.

Trivison, Mary Louise, S.N.D. 1988. "Prayer and Prejudice in the *Cantigas de Santa Maria.*" *Cantigueiros* 1.2 (spring): 119– 27.

Uriarte Rebaudi, Lía Noemí. [1972] 1973 "Un motivo folklórico en el Poema del Cid." *Filología* 16: 215–30.

Valera, Diego de. 1927. *Crónica de los Reyes Católicos.* Ed. Juan de Mata Carriazo. Madrid: J. Molina.

———. 1978. *Epístolas de Mosén Diego de Valera, embiadas en diversos tiempos e a diversas personas.* Ed. José A. de Balenchana. Madrid: Imprenta de M. Ginesta.

Vasvari, Louise O. 1992. "Why is Doña Endrina a Widow? Traditional Culture and Textuality in the *Libro de Buen Amor.*" In *Upon My Husband's Death: Widows in the Literature and Histories of Medieval Europe,* 259–87. Ann Arbor: University of Michigan Press.

Viera, David J. 1985. "The Treatment of the Jew and the Moor in the Catalan Works of Francesc Eiximenis." *RCEH* 9.2 (winter): 203–13.

Walsh, John. 1979–80. "Juan Ruiz and the *mester de clerezía:* Lost Context and Lost Parody in the *LBA. RPH* 33.1: 62–86.

———. 1990. "Performance in the *Poema de Mío Cid.*" *RPh* 44.1 (August): 1–25.

Warner, Marina. 1983. *Alone of All Her Sex: the Myth and Cult of the Virgin Mary.* New York: Vintage.

Weissberger, Barbara. 1988. "Role Reversal and Festivity in the Romances of Juan de Flores." Paper presented at the MLA Convention, San Francisco, 28 December.

———. 1989. "Role Reversal and Festivity in the Romances of Juan de Flores." *JHP* 13.3 (spring): 197–213.

———. 1992. "The Politics of Cárcel de Amor." *REH* 26 no. 3: 307–26.

White, T. H. 1954. *The Book of Beasts, Being a Translation from a Latin Bestiary of the Twelfth Century.* London: Jonathan Cape.

Westphal-Wihl, Sara. 1989. "The Ladies' Tournament: Marriage, Sex, and Honor in Thirteenth-Century Germany." *Signs:* 14.2: 371–98.

Whetnall, Jane. 1984. "Lírica femenina in the Early Manuscript Cancioneros." In *What's Past is Prologue: A Collection of Essays in Honour of L. J. Woodward,* ed. Salvador Bacarisse, Bernard Bentley, Mercedes Claraso, and Douglas Gifford, 138–50. Edinburgh: Scottish Academic Press.

———. 1992. "Isabel González of the *Cancionero de Baena* and Other Lost Voices." *La Corónica* 21.1: 59–83.

Wilkins, Constance L. 1990. "Las voces de Florencia Pinar." In *Studia Hispanica Medievalia*, vol. 2, ed. Rosa E. Penna and María A. Rosarossa, 124–30. Buenos Aires: Universidad Católica Argentina.

Wilkins, Heanon. 1986. "Dramatic Design in Berceo's *Milagros de Nuestra Señora*." In *Hispanic Studies in Honor of Alan D. Deyermond: A North American Tribute*, ed. John Miletich, 309–24. Madison, Wisc.: Hispanic Seminary of Medieval Studies.

Willis, Raymond S. 1983. "An Archpriest and an Abbess?" In *Essays on Hispanic Literature in Honor of Edmund L. King*, ed. Sylvia Molloy and Luis Fernández Cifuentes, 245–54. London: Tamesis.

Wright, Roger, ed. and trans. 1987. *Spanish Ballads*. Warminster, England: Aris and Phillips.

Zahareas, Anthony N. 1965. *The Art of Juan Ruiz, Archpriest of Hita*. Madrid: Estudios de Literatura Española.

———. 1989. *Juan Ruiz, Libro del Arcipreste*. With Thomas McCallum. Edición Sinóptica. Madison, Wisc.: Hispanic Seminary of Medieval Studies.

Zaid, Rhona. 1988–89. "Some Adverse Criticism of Women in the *CSM*." *Cantigueiros* 2: 79–88.

Zizek, Slavoj. 1989. *The Sublime Object of Ideology*. London: Verso.

Index

Plates

Fig. 1. Marisaltos, the Jewess saved from death by Holy Mary

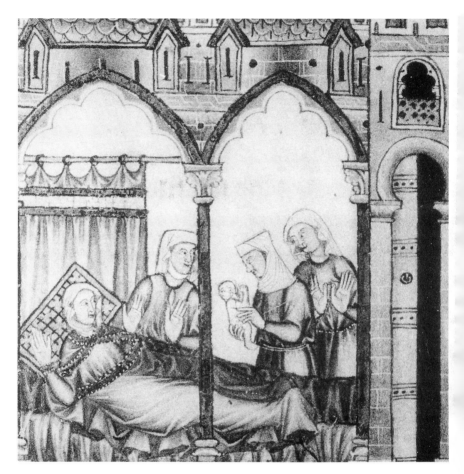

Fig. 2. Jewish baby born with his head on backward

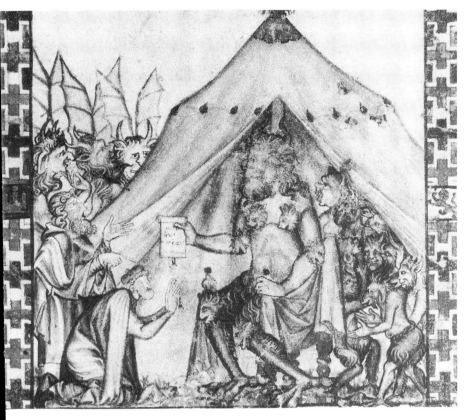

Fig. 3. "Jewish" devil

Fig. 4. Christian and Muslim (with sword) playing chess

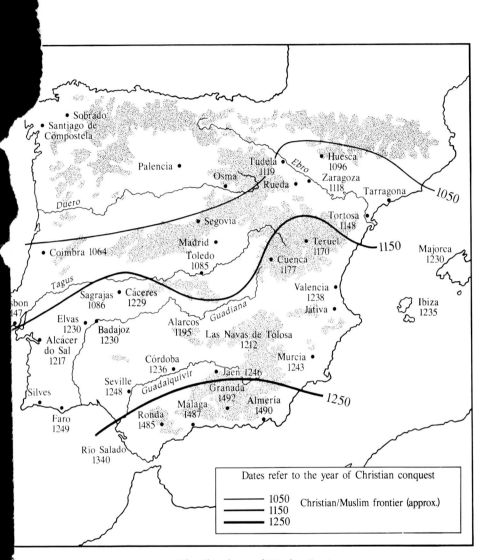

Map 1. The Shrinking of Muslim Spain

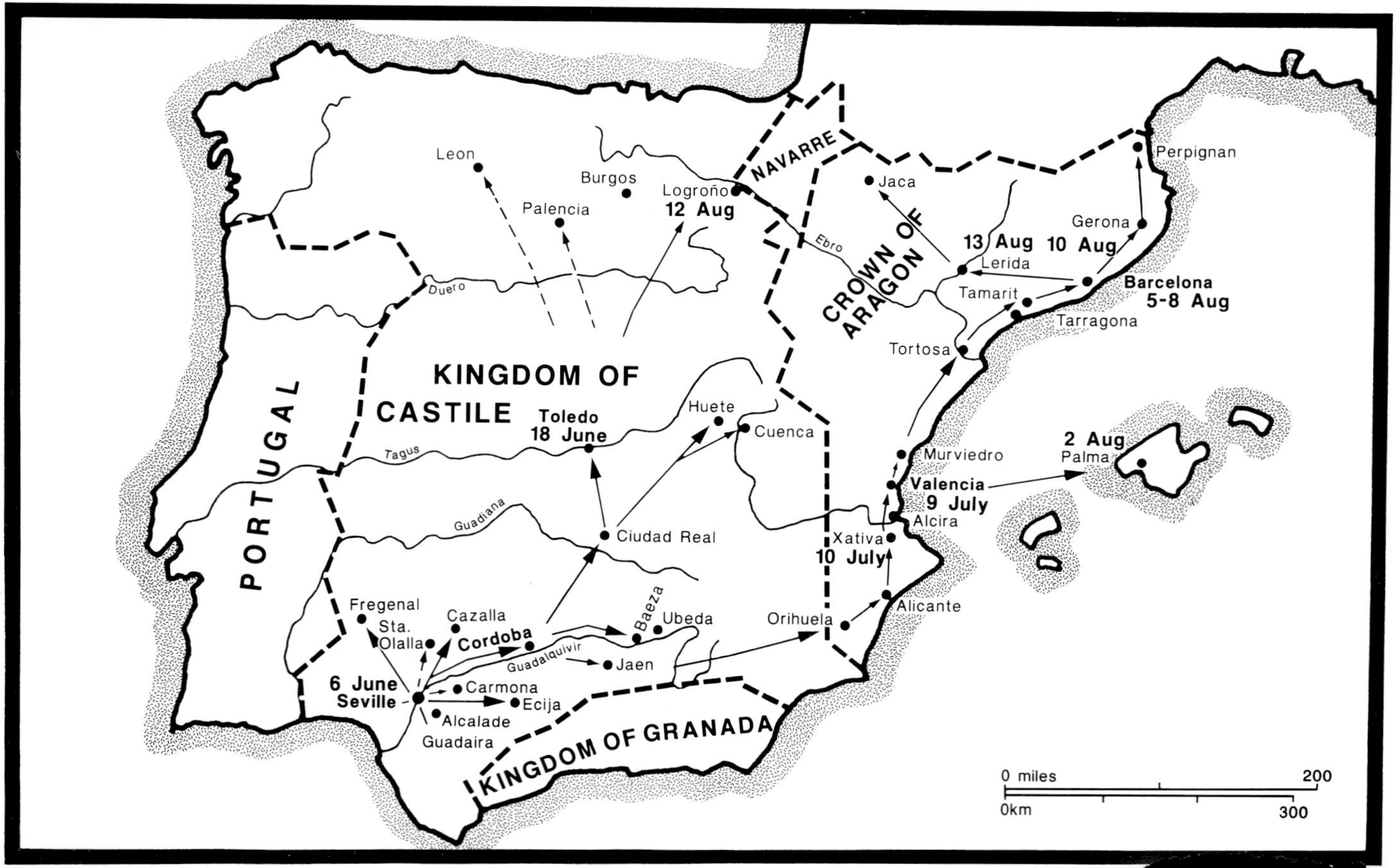

Map 2. The rapid spread of pogroms in Spain